The true history of the angels

Many cultures throughout the world hold the belief that angels can take human form and manifest themselves to human beings on Earth. *Return of the Angels* guides you through the wealth of information contained in classic texts such as the the Bible, the Apocrypha, and the Kabbalah. It illuminates the wonderful history of these inhabitants of Heaven who choose to play a role in mortals' lives.

Author Migene González-Wippler has done the research for you—and you can reap the benefits of her research and tap into the power of angelic energy. Scholarly yet readable, this important resource reintroduces the angel knowledge, power, and magic that the ancients knew so well:

- angel names
- angels' assignments and guardian angels
- angels and the zodiac
- prayers & invocations
- the Ritual of the Pentagram, and other rituals of angel magic

There are other books that tell the stories of the Creation and the Fall of Satan. But only in *Return of the Angels* can you read an account by an angel called Megadriel, who relates the story of Creation and the awesome battle among the angels for the Throne of God.

As the world moves forward, the special magic of the angels will continue to be of vital importance in human history. Based upon messages received from angels, González-Wippler offers insight into events taking place in the beginning of the new millennium and the steps we can take to protect our planet from cataclysmic disasters.

This unique book is both an introduction to the true history of angels and a guide to your empowerment through celestial guidance and intervention.

About the Author

Migene González-Wippler was born in Puerto Rico and has degrees in psychology and anthropology from the University of Puerto Rico and from Columbia University. She has worked as a science editor for the Interscience Division of John Wiley, the American Institute of Physics, and the American Museum of Natural History, and as an English editor for the United Nations in Vienna, where she lived for many years. She is a cultural anthropologist and lectures frequently at universities and other educational institutions. She is the noted author of many books on religion and mysticism, including the widely acclaimed *Santería: African Magic in Latin America*; *The Complete Book of Spells, Ceremonies & Magic*; *Dreams and What They Mean to You*; *What Happens After Death*; and more.

To Write to the Author

If you wish to contact the author or would like more information about this book, please write to the author in care of Llewellyn Worldwide and we will forward your request. Both the author and publisher appreciate hearing from you and learning of your enjoyment of this book and how it has helped you. Llewellyn Worldwide cannot guarantee that every letter written to the author can be answered, but all will be forwarded. Please write to:

Migene González-Wippler
℅ Llewellyn Worldwide
P.O. Box 64383, Dept. K293-3
St. Paul, MN 55164-0383, U.S.A.

Please enclose a self-addressed stamped envelope for reply, or $1.00 to cover costs. If outside U.S.A., enclose international postal reply coupon.

Return
of the
Angels

MIGENE
GONZÁLEZ-
WIPPLER

1999
Llewellyn Publications
St. Paul, Minnesota 55164-0383, U.S.A.

FIRST EDITION
First Printing, 1999

First published in Spanish as *Angelorum: El libro de los ángeles* (Llewellyn, 1999)

Book design by Pam Keesey and Rebecca Zins
Cover design by Anne Marie Garrison
Editing and typesetting by Rebecca Zins

Library of Congress Cataloging-in-Publication Data
González-Wippler, Migene.
   [Angelorum. English]
   Return of the Angels / Migene González-Wippler.—1st ed.
      p.   cm.
   Includes bibliographical references and index.
   ISBN 1-56718-293-3
   1. Angels—Miscellanea.   2. Magic.   I. Title.
BF1623.A53 G6513 1999
291.2'15—dc21
                                                                99-045108

Llewellyn Worldwide does not participate in, endorse, or have any authority or responsibility concerning private business transactions between our authors and the public.
   All mail addressed to the author is forwarded but the publisher cannot, unless specifically instructed by the author, give out an address or phone number.

Llewellyn Publications
A Division of Llewellyn Worldwide, Ltd.
P.O. Box 64383, Dept. K293-3
St. Paul, MN 55164-0383, U.S.A.
www.llewellyn.com

♲ Printed in the United States of America on recycled paper

This book is dedicated to YHVH, Lord of Hosts,
and to his Regent Princes,
Raphael, Michael, Gabriel, and Uriel,
and all the Heavenly Hosts

~つ

Contents

Illustrations

Introduction

The last decade has seen the publication of dozens of books about angels. It seems that the closer we get to the end of the century, the greater the fascination with these celestial beings. Films, television shows, magazine articles, jewelry, music, perfumes, writing paper, dinnerware, clothing, and even bed linen have been created around this ethereal theme. This renaissance of the angel cult is linked to the new millennium because many people consider this event both cataclysmic and apotheosic in nature. Angels have always been a part of the apocalyptic visions of the saints and the prophets. Therefore it is not surprising that they should make a new appearance now that we find ourselves at the threshold of a new century, a new millennium, and a new age, with all their biblical implications.

The concept of this book came to me ten years ago, and I have been wrestling with it mentally and spiritually ever since then. My first intention was to write a book about the War in Heaven related by an angel. But every time I tried to work on the book, something would happen that would stop me from continuing my labor. Now it seems clear to me that the reason the book was not written sooner was that the time for its publication had not yet arrived. The book was to appear in print near the end of the century.

Every book is important to its author, but this one is specially significant to me because my life has been strongly involved with the angels since a very early age. In the most important moments of my life, there has always been a presence around me that is not of this world. Even my birth was marked by this ethereal touch. My mother always told me that the Archangel Gabriel had a special connection with me because he had announced the moment of my birth and had marked me with the sign of the moon, which he rules, according to ancient traditions. I was born at home at 5:35 in the morning. According to my mother, at that precise moment reveille was being played at a nearby soldier camp. The midwife told my mother that Gabriel was heralding my entry into the world and that I had something special to do with the angels. Gabriel's instrument is the trumpet and he is one of the angels of life and death.

While she was carrying me, my mother went out one night on the balcony of our house to gaze at the full moon. Inadvertently, she placed her hand on her abdomen, and one of her aunts, who was with her, told her to remove her hand because otherwise the moon was going to mark the child.

My mother took her hand away immediately but it was too late. When I was born, I had the exact markings of the moon on my left leg, extending toward the hip. As I grew older this mark took less space, but I still have it on my left thigh.

The title of this book also has a story. I always choose the title of all my books before I begin to write. But the title of this book was not chosen consciously by me but rather came to my mind spontaneously. When I thought of the title, *Angelorum* (*note:* this is the title of the Spanish edition of this work), I was not sure of its meaning because my knowledge of Latin is rudimentary. To find out what it meant, I called Fordham University, which is Catholic and has an excellent Latin department. The priest who spoke to me told me that Angelorum means "of the angels" and everything that has to do with the angels. That is the source of the title and subtitle of the book (*note:* the Spanish subtitle is "El libro de los ángeles," or "the book of the angels").

This book was written from the Judeo-Christian viewpoint and is an intensely religious work. And even though in this, as in all my other books on mysticism, I have tried to present my theme in a logical and rational manner, this does not represent an apology on my part about my faith or my religious convictions. It is rather a reflection of my continuous effort to find a solid basis for what we know in the depths of our souls to be an absolute reality. And in spite of its obvious spirituality, this book is not only for those who believe in angels, but for anyone who may be interested in this fascinating subject.

A book about angels has perforce to be "a course in miracles" because miracles are the principal domain of the angelic realm. For that reason we will discuss many miraculous events throughout the book, most of which have no apparent logical or reasonable explanation. The reader must accept or reject their supernatural origin based on the events themselves.

The book places special emphasis on the Kabbalah because this esoteric doctrine of the Jews is a very rich source of magnificent angelic lore. Both Christianity and Islam have profound kabbalistic roots in their liturgic and angelic traditions.

A book about angels has to be based largely on extensive research on the part of the author, and this book is no exception. Among the hundreds of texts I consulted are the Bible, especially Genesis, the Prophets, and Revelation; and the Apocryphal books, especially the *Pseudepigrapha*, with a special emphasis on the three *Books of Enoch*. The *Pseudepigrapha* is a collection of ancient writings that date from the same time as the Bible and some even earlier. These documents are apocryphal in nature, that is, they are considered sacred, but were not chosen to be part of the biblical books, either in the Old or New Testaments. Some are Jewish and others are Christian, but they all serve to illuminate the Scriptures and help us understand them better. Also of great importance on the subject of angels are Saint Thomas Aquinas' *Summa Theologica*; Saint Augustine's *The City of God*; the Encyclopaedia Britannica, which is a treasure trove of angelic information; and, in modern times, *A Dictionary of Angels* by Gustav

Davidson, who is undoubtedly the principal source of inspiration behind many of today's most popular books on angels. The bibliography at the end of this book provides an extensive list of works related directly or indirectly with the subject.

Return of the Angels is divided into four parts. The first part, God and His Angels, discusses the historical and spiritual origin of angels and gives detailed information about the angelic orders, the seven heavens, the great archangels, and paradise.

The second part, War in Heaven (an excerpt from the *Book of Megadriel*, a work still in progress), is especially fascinating because it is the account of Creation and the struggle between the angels of light and the fallen angels as written by an archangel named Megadriel. This celestial being describes in detail the struggle of the dark angels for the throne of God, the reason for the temptation of Eve, and the day of Final Judgment.

The third part, Angel Messages, is also written by Megadriel, who gives a series of inspiring messages to humankind about events that will take place shortly after the turn of the century, and angelic suggestions about what humanity can do to help the planet and themselves during the changes that will be forthcoming.

The fourth part, Angel Biographies, is a list of the most important and best-known angels, both the faithful and the fallen.

Many personal accounts of experiences with angels, including my own, will be found throughout the book, especially in chapter 1, Angel Encounters.

The magical aspects of the angels and how they may be contacted is also part of the book and can be found especially in chapter 10, Invoking the Angels. This chapter gives detailed instructions for simple rituals that can be performed by anyone to receive the help of the angels and to propitiate their intercession on our behalf for the solution of our human problems.

Many of the books written in recent years about angels describe the experiences of hundreds of people who claim to have had personal encounters with angelic beings. Unfortunately, the vast majority of these experiences are never reported. Statistical research done on angels in the United States and abroad indicate that more than eighty percent of the world population believes in angels and that most of these people have had at least one experience of a supernatural nature with an angel. This indicates that the existence of angels is a reality to millions of people.

It is my hope that this book will substantiate the faith of those who believe in angels and give food for thought to those who do not. Maybe one day we will discover that the angel is not a separate reality, but a very real part of the innermost depth of our soul.

Part I

God and His Angels

1

Angel Encounters

In recent years an increasing number of people have related their experiences with angels and how they have affected and, in some instances, transformed their lives. Statistics show that two out of every three people around the world have had some type of supernatural experience. Many of these experiences involved an encounter with an angel.

According to ancient traditions, an angel is a divine messenger whose mission on earth is to serve and guide humanity. This mission is largely carried out by each individual's guardian angel. Both the Old and the New Testaments are rich in angelic lore. But the biblical angels are not pacific, ethereal beings or dainty cherubs with dimpled cheeks and wispy wings.

Instead, they are mighty warriors, strong and aggressive, armed to the teeth with swords, spears, and shining armors. They must be combative because they are continuously battling the forces of evil, who are the enemies of God and humanity. These angels are organized in a divine hierarchy known as the Heavenly Host or the Armies of God. And the Creator himself is known as the Lord of Hosts, a warrior God who sends his armies to do battle against the enemies of Heaven.

The books of Zechariah and Revelation tell us that the angels ride on white horses and that their numbers are counted in the "milliards of milliards," presumably billions of billions. The Bible mentions angels 294 times, which means that these celestial beings are of great importance to the spiritual destinies of humanity. In Genesis, an angel removes Adam and Eve from Eden, an angel does battle with Jacob during an entire night, an angel holds back Abraham's hand when he is about to sacrifice his son Isaac to God, an angel saves Hagar and her son Ishmael in the desert, and three angels visit Abraham and Lot before the destruction of Sodom and Gomorrah. It is also an angel who saves Daniel's companions from the fiery furnace, an angel who reveals to Joseph that Mary has conceived through the grace of the Holy Spirit, and an angel who reveals to Mary her immaculate conception. The prophets Elijah, Isaiah, Zechariah, Ezekiel, and Daniel tell us of their experiences with angels, and Moses, David, and Solomon had deals with them. Jesus tells us in the New Testament that angels rejoice in Heaven when a sinner repents, and John describes them in great detail in Revelation.

But the Bible is not the only source of information on angels. The Koran also speaks of the angels' constant struggle to save humanity, and many of the apocryphal books, especially the *Pseudepigrapha*, describe the incessant battles between the angels of light and the dark angels.

The concept of the angel can be traced to the greatest antiquity. The Assyrians, the Persians, and the Babylonians all believed in these winged beings. The eons of Gnosticism and the bhodisattvas of Hinduism are remarkably similar to the angels, and their

mission is also that of protecting, guiding, and illuminating human beings in their spiritual evolution.

Perhaps the most disturbing question that haunts humanity is why a loving God allows so much pain and suffering on Earth, and why he permits tragedy, crime, and misery to take its ever-increasing toll on a suffering world. Why do the innocent have to suffer, why do so many children die of starvation, cruelty, neglect, and terribly destructive illnesses? Why do good people, who never hurt anyone or break any law, often suffer the most devastating tragedies? And why do others, who despoil the helpless and break every human and divine law, appear to go unpunished and often live long and prosperous lives? Where are the angels then?

The answer to these questions is dual. In the first place, God created humanity with free will and this precludes his intervention in human affairs. Human tragedy is the result of our own actions or inactions, and only we can bring it under control. If God were to intervene, he would be depriving us of the gift of free will, and we would be like marionettes in his hands. And God wants us to return to him through our own choice, not through his divine power. We must be in control of our own destinies, we must make our own choices and live with the consequences. We are the ones who must stop our moral decline. We must be the protectors of the innocent and the deterrers of injustice. We must find the solutions to our human dilemmas and rescue the future of our world.

Secondly, human suffering is the result of the presence of evil forces on the Earth. The incurable diseases, the injustices, the tragedies all result from the imbalance that exists in nature and from the destructive vibrations that surround us continually. This imbalance is created by the negative cosmic energies that we equate with evil forces or fallen angels.

There is a continuous, pervasive struggle on Earth between negative forces, which we identify with the satanic hordes, and positive forces, which we personify as angels of light. Unfortunately, the angels do not always win the battle. When a person's guardian angel loses in this perennial conflict with evil forces, the inevitable result is tragedy and sorrow. And very often, the ones who suffer most acutely the angel's defeat are the weakest among us because they do not have sufficient positive energy at their disposal to counteract the onslaught of evil.

Every human act or thought, whether positive or negative, affects the delicate balance of the energies that surround the Earth. Everything that exists is based on the interaction of these cosmic energies. The planet itself is deeply influenced by this cosmic interplay. When these forces are not in harmony, the result may be atmospheric disturbances and natural disasters.

We have learned in recent years that collective meditations, where large numbers of people pool their mental energies to help heal the planet, can be tremendously effective. For example, it is possible, through these group meditations, to bring much-needed water to areas devastated by prolonged droughts. Conversely, it is also possible to stop torrential rains or fires that are raging out of control. Several years ago, one of my seminar groups in New York was asked to meditate to help relieve a severe drought that had been affecting Colombia for several months. We conducted the meditation with only twenty people, all concentrating on a map of Colombia and visualizing it covered with water. This was done on a Sunday at approximately two in the afternoon. Within two hours of the meditation, it began to rain in Colombia. Meteorologists in the region were astounded because they had predicted that the drought would last for many weeks and maybe for many months more. So heavy was the rain that it soon threatened to flood the region. We were then asked to conduct a second meditation to reverse the effects of the first.

The reason why group meditations are so successful is that all living things are surrounded by an electromagnetic field that can be altered and deeply influenced by concentrated mental energies. We can all affect in a positive manner the Earth's energy field by sending harmonious and healing thoughts to the planet and everything that inhabits it. We can identify the positive cosmic energies around the Earth with angels of light. These energies are sentient, conscious, and intelligent, and they function through the cosmic laws that rule the universe. By uniting our own mental and spiritual energies with these cosmic forces, we can help stabilize the planet and bring under control the negative energies that threaten to destroy it.

The concept of a cosmic force personified as a sentient, intelligent entity such as an angel is known as anthropomorphism—that is, to give a human form to something that is not human. This has happened with angels because throughout many centuries we have created telesmatic images of these celestial beings. A telesmatic image is the visualization of any given entity, real or imagined, with a specific form and detailed characteristics. With the passing of time, this image becomes part of the collective unconscious of the human race and it becomes as real to the unconscious as a physical image.

The telesmatic image of the angel, with its wings and halo, flowing white robes, and surrounding light, comes to us perfectly delineated through the biblical stories and the powerfully conceived thought forms of very ancient cultures. To the human unconscious, the angel is real; it exists because it was integrated into its depths over five thousand years ago. This lets us give a visible form to a cosmic force and give voice and action to the

soul of the universe. The angel is as real to us as our concept of its essence and exists for us because it is an integral part of our inner self. It is simply an archetype of the collective unconscious and as such it is part of our mental and spiritual makeup.

The stronger our belief in angels, the more powerful is their influence on our lives. This happens because each archetype within the unconscious is formed of psychic energies, known as libido in Jungian psychology. Belief in angels allows the psychic energies that form the angelic archetype to rush outward into the conscious awareness of the individual, who then perceives the angel as a visible entity. This would explain the origin of the visions of angels and angelic encounters. Because the angel is a concentration of very powerful psychic energies, it possesses not only the ability to manifest physically, but also the total knowledge of the collective unconscious accumulated since the creation of the universe. The angel knows things and has powers that are not part of our conscious awareness but which are our cosmic inheritance because all knowledge and power, from the beginning of time, is locked in our genetic code, to which we have no conscious access.

This does not mean that angels are a human invention and that they do not have a spiritual identity. Everything we can imagine and that we believe in exists in our deep unconscious. It has a reality of its own and can be projected outward under certain circumstances. The angel exists on a superior mental level. We did not create the angel. Its existence was revealed to us through a process of cosmic osmosis. This phenomenon may be compared to human intuition, when we know with complete certainty that something has happened or is about to happen without receiving this knowledge from an outside source. This is true universal knowledge, which is not based on human concepts but rather on divine revelation.

My first experience with an angel happened when my oldest son was born. My obstetrician was Dr. Landrum Shettles, who was the first physician to photograph the human ovum at the moment of fertilization. Dr. Shettles had told us that the baby was due on or around July 4, but this date came and went and the baby was not born. Toward the end of July, Dr. Shettles, now seriously concerned, decided to do a caesarean section. I was brought to the operating room at eleven in the morning, and several minutes later my son was born without any complications. But immediately after the birth I began to bleed internally. In spite of the efforts of the excellent medical team that was with me at the time, the hemorrhage could not be contained. I sank rapidly into deep shock and the doctors around me began to lose hope of saving my life. Finally, in desperation, Dr. Shettles decided to call one of his colleagues, the obstetrician who

had delivered Elizabeth Taylor's daughter, Liza Todd, also through a caesarean. This doctor, Dr. Anthony de Sopo, lived in New Jersey and, because of the gravity of the situation, there was no time for him to travel to New York, where I was, to join Dr. Shettles and the other doctors in the operating room. Therefore he was forced to give detailed instructions to Dr. Shettles over the telephone on the procedure he was to follow to try and stop the bleeding. This treatment had not been used in obstetrics for many years but it was the only hope the doctors had to save my life. Dr. Shettles followed the recommendations of this great doctor and was able to stop the hemorrhage. Thanks to them I am still alive, for which I will always be grateful.

Around six in the evening I regained consciousness. I struggled through a great, black void from a place very far away. When I opened my eyes I was still in the operating room, and directly above my head was the face of an angel, who smiled tenderly at me. His hair was the palest gold and surrounded his head like a radiant halo. The impression I received was so powerful that I began to sob uncontrollably. The image disappeared at once, and I found myself once more on the operating table, surrounded by many doctors and nurses, all of them happy and relieved because they had been able to save my life. Where did I go while I was unconscious? Was I in Heaven but brought back by the angel to care for my newborn child? I will never know, but I will never forget that beautiful face and its tender, loving smile.

This was the first of many experiences with angels. Eight months after my son was born, my mother came to our house to spend several weeks with us. One afternoon, while my husband was at work, I lay down for a nap with the baby by my side. Some time later my mother entered the room to awaken me, as we had made plans to go shopping. The vision that she saw nearly made her faint in terror. For standing by the side of the bed was the immense figure of an angel, with widespread wings that nearly reached the ceiling. He was dressed in white armor and Roman sandals and his tunic was short and of a dazzling white. The angel had a large shimmering sword in his hands that he extended protectively over me and the child. Overcome with awe, but unable to take her eyes away from the vision, my mother walked slowly backward out of the room and closed the door. When she reached her own bedroom, she collapsed on a chair, trembling uncontrollably. Shortly afterward I woke up, and she told me her extraordinary experience. In her opinion, the angel she had seen was the Archangel Michael.

From that moment onward, and throughout my life, not only I, but several members of my family, have had profound experiences with Michael. Later on in this book, I will describe a ritual that is done to contact the archangel on the date of your birthday. My father, who was a very religious and mystical man, gave me the ritual more than twenty years ago, which he said came to him during meditation. Psalm 85, which, according to tradition, was written by Michael, is also said to be a powerful aid in contacting the archangel if it is read at night before going to sleep.

Many years after my mother's vision of Michael, I had a terrifying experience with the archangel. It happened around six in the morning, as the sun was beginning to rise on the horizon. Something awakened me from a deep slumber. I sat in bed, in the grip of a strange foreboding. I looked through the window at the apartment complex across the way and saw, rising above the building, a gigantic figure that covered all the sky. I saw the white wings and the face of an angel, so bright it was almost impossible to define its features. The figure seemed to be rising with the sun. Somehow I knew it was Michael. Stunned by the sight, I dove under the covers and lay there for a few minutes, trembling with fear. I don't know why I was filled with such dread, but I felt totally overcome with a deep anguish, as if something calamitous was about to happen. After what seemed like an interminable time, I was able to gather enough courage to raise my head from under the sheets and look again at the window. But all I saw was a serene blue sky, gently tinged with the amber rays of the rising sun. The building across my window was as steadfast and normal as ever, and there was no angel in sight.

I did not tell my experience to any member of my family. Later that day, my younger son returned from school with a strange story. He said that as he left the school building, he saw a great angel in the sky with a silver sword in one hand and a balance in the other. He ran all the way home to tell me his vision. As I comforted the child, assuring him that angels are heavenly messengers that can only help and protect us from harm, I had a strong feeling that Michael was trying to tell me that something terrible was about to happen and that I should prepare myself for that moment. I prayed constantly during the next few weeks, asking for help and protection for myself and my family. Then, just as I had feared, tragedy struck. My mother had a severe, crippling stroke that left her barely clinging to life. For months she remained in the hospital, battling her terrible illness, and during this time she suffered two more strokes. Her illness devastated me. I was an only child and had always been very close to my mother. I did not know how to cope with her condition. I was suddenly immersed in medical decisions, legal considerations, and a host of other problems that left me numb and dazed. When she was finally released from the hospital, my struggle had just begun. During the eleven years that she lived after

her initial illness, she remained in my home, and I cared for her during this time, vainly hoping that she should again be my friend and companion, and my guide in the battles of life. But the stroke had damaged her brain so severely she could barely speak. When she died, I still felt I had failed her somehow, even though her doctor assured me it was time for her to rest. I had not yet learned that death is not an end, but a beginning. This was to be the subject of unrelenting research, finally resulting in the book *What Happens After Death*.

Michael's presence in the sky that fateful day warned me of what was to come. Throughout my entire life, this great archangel has been with me at every moment, letting me feel his presence when I need him the most. His is the voice that sustains and guides me and helps me make the most important decisions of my life.

This book does not contain enough pages to chronicle all my experiences with the Divine. In another chapter I will describe an episode with the Archangel Raphael, and how I learned about the terrible power of the angels on that occasion.

Another angelic encounter, which I related in some detail in my book *The Complete Book of Spells, Ceremonies & Magic*, I had while I still lived in Vienna, where I worked for several years as an associate English editor for the United Nations. This was a period of intense mysticism, when I delved deeply into the mysteries of the Kabbalah. During this time I conducted several kabbalistic rituals, some of which resulted in astonishing experiences. In one of these experiments, I conducted a ritual dedicated to one of the angelic beings belonging to what is known in the Kabbalah as the Sphere of Venus. This entity, known as Hagiel, is a female force identified as the Intelligence of Venus in ceremonial magic. My intention in conducting the ritual was to obtain specific knowledge about love, which falls under the aegis of Hagiel and Venus. The book where this ritual is cited in detail is *Magical Evocation* by the great German kabbalist Franz Bardon.

The ceremony had two important requisites. First, the room where the ritual was to take place had to be suffused with green light, as green is the color associated with the Sphere of Venus. Second, plenty of cinnamon had to be burned throughout the evocation, as this spice is also connected with the Venusian sphere.

Evocation is different from invocation because it asks not only the aid of a spiritual entity like an angel but also its manifestation in physical form during the ritual. This is not as farfetched as it sounds because it uses the mental energies of the person conducting the ritual, which can create a host of images and sounds, all aided and abetted by the person's imagination and powers of visualization.

The ceremony also required the use of a lamp made of copper, the metal of Venus, and seven pieces of heptagonal green glass fitted together around the copper perimeter. Inside the lamp would be placed a green candle whose light, filtered through the glass, would envelop the room in a green haze. In one of the corners of the room a triangular piece of paper with the sigil or signature of Hagiel in green ink was to be placed. It was within this triangle that this angelic being was to materialize.

It was an interesting experiment and I was not sure what would happen. I was not really expecting to see a spiritual entity appear within the triangle, but I thought I might get some interesting spiritual insights. In my view, what I was doing was delving into my own psyche with its huge, largely untapped psychic energies. I was totally unprepared for what actually happened.

I conducted the ritual as Bardon had described it in his book, with the exception of the lamp. I was unable to find the copper or the green glass that it required in Vienna. I did, however, burn large quantities of cinnamon, as the ritual indicated.

Toward the end of the ceremony I heard someone whistling a strange melody that I had never heard before. The sound seemed to be coming from the floor above the room where I was conducting the ritual. That was unlikely, as my apartment was located on the top floor of the building and there was nothing above me except an empty attic. The whistling continued and the music seemed to be moving in a circle over the room. Suddenly, directly over the triangle where Hagiel was supposed to manifest, I heard a thunderous crashing sound, as if someone were trying to come down through the ceiling. Almost simultaneously, I saw the ceiling buckle and begin to crack, as if it were about to collapse. Two things happened at that moment. The whistling stopped and the door that led to the attic slammed with a powerful bang. Forgetting that I was in the middle of an incomplete ritual, I ran out of the door to see who had been in the attic. But when I reached the attic door, I saw that it was securely fastened with a large padlock and a chain, both of which were covered with spider webs. It was clear that no one had entered or left through that door in many years.

Strangely enough I felt quite calm. I knew something momentous had taken place but somehow it did not seem threatening or frightening. I returned to the ritual room and looked at the ceiling. It was as smooth and even as it had always been. There no signs of buckling or cracks on its white surface.

Hagiel did not materialize in the triangle, but that night I dreamt with her. She was dressed in a green satin skirt embroidered with tiny pink roses. She was completely white, not creamy or fair, but snow white. Her skin reminded me of mother-of-pearl, and her long curly hair was tomato red. There is no one with that skin tone or hair

color on this planet. She was naked from the waist up and she was so unutterably beautiful that I could not possibly describe her accurately. Her expression was gentle and affable. She told me that she had tried to be present during the ritual but could not because she needed a green atmosphere to manifest, and that had been missing in the ceremony. All the spirits of Venus, she said, can only exist in green light.

I know she told me many things, but I could not remember them when I woke up. The only thing I remember she said was that one of the flowers that attracts the angels most, and especially the angels of Venus, is the gardenia. Wherever the gardenia grows in profusion, she said, you will always find love.

When my stepsister was married I gave her a bridal bouquet made entirely of gardenias. And even though I never told her of my experience with Hagiel, she and her husband decided to cultivate gardenias. In their family room, there are more than twenty gardenia plants in huge pots along the walls. Theirs is the happiest and most congenial family that I have ever known. They have been together for twenty-five years. They have two wonderful children and a home where there is always harmony and love.

There are many rational explanations for my experience with Hagiel and the phenomena that took place during the ritual. It could all have been imagined by me or, conversely, my own psychic energies could have given form and sound to the various happenings that took place. The power of the human mind is immense and largely unknown. Telekinesis, or the power to move objects with the mind, has already been tested in laboratories. But we must also consider the possibility, as unbelievable as it may sound, that I did contact an outer reality that day, and that there is a spirit known as Hagiel who can be contacted through this ritual.

A ritual is an act during which vast amounts of psychic energies are emitted by the deep unconscious, which can then manifest in a variety of ways. None of this is supernatural, but rather the ability of a human being to transmute matter. An angel is a concentration of cosmic energies of inconceivable power that are part of our unconscious minds, waiting to be released at the opportune moment. Nothing that exists is alien to us. Everything is part of a great whole ruled by immutable laws and intrinsically linked to our collective unconscious.

In many of the depictions of angels that come to us from the Middle Ages or the Pre-Raphaelite period, these celestial beings are shown playing musical instruments. This is perhaps connected with the concept of the angelic choirs that are easily associated with music. That is why music has always been a part of the angelic concept. When George Frederick Handel composed his great oratorio, the *Messiah*, he said he had been surrounded by angels during his work. When he wrote the "Hallelujah," which is the most famous part of the oratorio, he saw how the gates of heaven opened in front of his eyes, revealing to him the glory of God, sitting on his throne and surrounded by angels.

The angels of light are not the only ones who serve as inspiration to human beings during the composition of transcendental music. The fallen angels also love music, into whose mysteries they were initiated when they still resided in the celestial realms. Italian composer Giusseppe Tartini said that his immortal violin sonata, *The Devil's Trill*, had been dictated to him in a dream by the Prince of Darkness himself. Nicolo Paganini, acclaimed by many as the greatest violinist of all times, could play the most complex compositions in only one cord of his violin, making it sound as if several violins were playing at the same time. Many of the people who heard him play believed he was inspired by demonic forces, something that Paganini never bothered to deny.

Angels inspire us and also keep us away from harm. Very often, during times of crisis, we hear a small voice within that quietly guides us out of trouble. Other times we feel an invisible presence that urges us to take a specific path or stops us when we are about to make a wrong decision. Many lives have been saved through this angelic intervention.

During one of my New York seminars, one of the persons in the group related this story. This woman drove to work every day. One morning, as she was getting ready to leave her house, she heard a voice whisper in her ear, "Don't go to work today." She quickly turned around, expecting to see her husband behind her, but there was no one there. She was filled with a sudden premonition, but she shook off her misgivings and told herself she had imagined the whole thing. Without any further hesitation, she got inside her car and began her long drive into Manhattan. She had been driving about ten minutes when she heard the same voice again, this time more forceful and peremptory: "Return home. Do not go to work today." This time the woman doubted no longer and immediately turned around and returned to her house. When her husband saw her come in, he asked her what had happened. She told him her strange experience and he assured her she had done the right thing in obeying the voice. He had also been feeling uneasy since awakening and could not understand why. The woman was nervous the entire day. Later that afternoon, she turned on the television in an attempt to calm her nerves. What she saw on the screen left her numb with horror.

A terrorist group had planted a bomb in one of the Twin Towers in lower Manhattan, precisely in the same building where she worked. She watched, aghast, as several of her co-workers were brought out of the building with blackened faces, one of them wearing an oxygen mask. She realized at once that obeying that small voice had probably saved her life, as she suffered from severe asthma and smoke inhalation would have been deadly to her.

In an even more dramatic incident, a man was changing a tire on the side of the road in North Carolina. One of the bolts that helped hold the tire rolled under the car and the man had to crawl underneath the chassis to retrieve it. At that moment, the jack that was holding the car buckled and fell, trapping the man under the car. Part of the jacket he was wearing was caught under the weight of the car, making it impossible for him to get away. There were only a few inches between his face and the car's underside and he could hardly breathe because of the gas fumes. There was little hope that anyone would stop to help him as he could not be seen by passing cars. Other drivers would assume the car was abandoned and pay no further attention. In desperation, the man began to pray to God and to his guardian angels, asking for help and deliverance. As he prayed, he felt the side of the car under which he was trapped be lifted several feet in the air, freeing him. He immediately rolled out from under the car and stood up on shaky legs, expecting to see someone by his side. There was no one there. As soon as he was freed, the car fell back on its side.

Figure 1: Jacob wrestling with the angel.

Then he saw that the bolt that had fallen under the car was lying neatly on top of one of the tire rims, even though he did not remember picking it up or placing it there. At no time did this man see an angel or anyone else on that solitary road, but he is convinced that his guardian angel saved his life.

Gustav Davidson, the author of *A Dictionary of Angels*, relates in the introduction to his famous work that while he was doing research for the book he was continuously besieged by legions of angels. One particularly terrifying incident took place when he was trekking across a field after visiting a neighboring farm. It was winter time and night had fallen. Suddenly, a large shadowy figure loomed threateningly in front of him, barring his way. Davidson felt paralyzed with terror. Struggling to overcome his panic, he faced the apparition and forced his way past it. The next morning he could not be sure if what he had seen had been an angel, a demon, a ghost, or God himself. According to Davidson, he had several of these experiences as he wrote the book, and he passed from terror to ecstasy, from revelation to other levels of existence, and finally to the conviction that beyond the evidence of the senses lies the reality of worlds of fantasy, which are inconceivable to the human mind.

Davidson's experience with the phantasmagoric figure brings to mind Jacob's struggle with an angel, which lasted an entire night and which is related in Genesis. Biblical authorities cannot agree on the possible identity of the angel mentioned by Jacob. Some believe it must have been the Archangel Metraton, others claim it was Michael, and others are sure it was God himself.

Children, who accept everything they see and hear at face value, are constantly relating their experiences with angels. Many small children play by themselves and laugh at invisible companions, and when their parents ask them why they are laughing they say that they are playing with angels. One of my readers wrote to tell me that his three-year-old daughter plays often with an angel named Muriel. The child consults everything with Muriel and will not do anything that is not approved beforehand by the angel. To get her to eat her vegetables and go to sleep early, her parents must tell her that Muriel wants her to do these things. Except for her Muriel fixation, the girl is a normal three-year-old. The father wanted me to tell him if I knew of the existence of an angel named Muriel and, if such an angel existed, whether she was an angel of God or a fallen angel. Interestingly enough, Muriel is the name of one of the angels cited in the *Pseudepigrapha*. I was able to report to the anxious father that Muriel is the angel of the month of June and one of the regents of the angelic choir known as the Dominions. As such, she is an angel of light. If Muriel walked with his daughter, the child was in celestial hands.

Figure 2: Two small angels (known as "putti") playing with a young woman, who obviously cannot see them. Taken from a painting by W. A. Bouguereau.

Sometimes, children who claim to have discourse with angels begin to forget about them as they grow up. The interaction with other children and their increasing involvement with the material world act as a deterrent to these celestial contacts. Some still retain the memory of angelic faces and crystal voices in the wind, but most of them forget their angelic ties completely. It is almost as if the angels remained by the child's side while he or she needed them most. During one of my book signings at a Borders bookstore in Miami, one of the persons present told the following story.

The son of one of her nieces, who is four years old, asked to be left alone with a newborn cousin. The baby's parents agreed to this peculiar request, but remained hidden behind the door to see what the child wanted to do.

The boy approached the baby's crib and said: "Please talk to me about God because I am beginning to forget him." The baby's parents were astonished at the boy's extraordinary behavior but, respecting the child's privacy, never let him know what they had heard and never questioned him about it.

Modern pediatrics tells us that newborn babies have higher perceptions than was originally thought. For that reason, pregnant women are advised to talk to their unborn babies, to read beautiful books to them, and to listen to classical or soft music during their pregnancies. It is believed that the fetus can

hear outside sounds and can assimilate these experiences, which are then integrated into their developing unconscious minds before they are born. I always try to speak to a newborn baby, and I explain to them the importance of being a good person, of the meaning of morality and ethics, of the observance of divine and human laws. During one of these one-sided conversations with a newborn baby girl, who is a member of my family, the child, who was lying on her stomach facing the wall, lifted her head laboriously and turned to look at me. Her eyes met mine with a steady and knowing glance, filled with such innate wisdom that I was left speechless. The look in those eyes told me that she understood very well what I was saying. This baby was two weeks old at the time. She is now seven years old. She is an unusually bright child, sweet and very religious, and plays Beethoven's sonatas on the piano as if she had been studying music for many years. Her superior intelligence was revealed many years ago, when she gave me that profound and unforgettable look. The idea that newborn babies retain their heavenly links during the early part of their lives is not new and many similar cases have been reported.

The concept of angels manifesting on Earth as human beings is also very old. Often, they may appear to us as mendicants to test our generosity. The Book of Hebrews 13:1 says: "Do not neglect hospitality for through it some have entertained angels unknowingly." Each time a beggar or a homeless person extends his hand to us, we could be facing a divine messenger who is testing our good will in this manner.

Each angelic encounter transforms a person's life forever. But we may often encounter angels, unaware that we are facing a celestial being. How often, unknowingly, have we been protected or guided by these divine guardians? How many times during our lives have we been delivered from a dangerous situation by an invisible friend who never revealed his presence?

An angelic encounter is never fortuitous. There is always a reason for each divine presence among us. But it is also possible to establish contact with an angel consciously, and these are the most important encounters because they establish permanent connections between our cosmic consciousness and our physical awareness. Angelic magic, which we will discuss later on in this book, is one of the most effective ways to have these conscious contacts with the angels.

2

What Is An Angel?

Around 200 B.C., rabbis began to translate the Old Testament from Hebrew into Greek. This translation, which was completed by 300 B.C., became known as the Septuagint. This term is derived from the Latin word *septuaginta*, meaning "seventy," and refers to the seventy (or seventy-two) translators who are said to have been appointed by the Jewish high priest of the time to do the translation for Hellenistic emperor Ptolemy II. The work was undertaken to benefit Greek-speaking Jews who were no longer able to read the Scriptures in the original Hebrew. The Septuagint was in turn translated into Latin, whereupon it became known as the Vulgate, which means "popular" or "common." This Latin version of the Scriptures underwent many revisions across the centuries. The present composite Vulgate is basically the work of Saint Jerome, a Doctor of the Church. It was from the Vulgate that the Scriptures were translated into other languages, including the famous Saint James version of the Bible.

When the Old Testament was translated into Greek, this was the most common language of the time. The Hebrew word for angel is *malakh*, and to translate it the translators had to choose between two Greek words with approximate meaning. One of these words was *angelos*, which means a common messenger, not necessarily celestial. The other word was *daimon*, meaning a spirit that may have both good and evil influences over a person. For example, Socrates believed he was always accompanied by an excellent "daimon" who was his constant guide and helper. But because a daimon could also be a malignant spirit, the Hebrew translators opted for the more prosaic angelos as the proper translation for malakh or divine messenger. From angelos was derived the word angel, which is now commonly used to denote these celestial beings. With the passing of time, daimon became associated with malefic entities and that is how the word demon came into being.

Another Greek word used to denote angels is *exousia*, sometimes translated as Powers and other times as Virtues. These are two of the angelic choirs, and the word is often used in the Greek version of the Old Testament to refer to the angels. For example, whenever Saint Paul spoke of the angels, he referred to them as exousia or Powers.

The study of angels is known as angelology and, contrary to popular belief, these winged beings do not originate in Judaism or Christianity but date as far back as the times of the Babylonians. These ancient peoples lived for many centuries to the south of Mesopotamia. The same area was the site of the latter Chaldean civilization, the country of origin of the Hebrew patriarch, Abraham. The ancient Hebrews' belief in angels was deeply influenced by Babylonian culture.

From the time of the Hebrew exile from Babylonia, around 600 B.C., many Hebrew theologians and artists began to use some of the Mesopotamian religious concepts in their description of the angels. For example, the idea that angels have wings can be traced to the iconography or allegorical paintings of the Mesopotamian gods, many of which had wings. Many of the biblical references to the vestments, physical appearances, names, and hierarchies of the angels can also be traced to Babylonian sources.

The syncretism or identification of deities among different religions is very common and is extended throughout the world. Very often, in ancient times, the gods of one religion became the demons of another. This is typified in the transformation of the great Babylonian goddess Ishtar (Astarte among the Phoenicians) into Ashtoreth, a demonic entity among the Hebrews, repudiated by the prophet Jeremiah. Later, Ashtoreth became known as Astaroth, one of the fallen angels, who is said to be a duke in the infernal regions. The same goddess was known as Isis among the Egyptians, identified with the moon and fertility.

The rejection and demonization of a god of one religion by the religion that followed it was typical of ancient times. Another example is that of Asmodeus, who is still invoked in love rituals, and who was at one time a Persian deva or god. In the Hebrew tradition, Asmodeus, whose true Persian name was Ashmedai, became a demonic entity, accused of having driven Noah to drink. He is believed to be the son of Lilith, Adam's first wife, a ferocious she-demon whose main pleasure consists of destroying small children. Today Asmodeus is said to be the ruler of gambling houses.

The practice of transforming the gods of one religion into the demons of another was also common among the Greeks and the Romans. In some cases, the god of one religion appears also as the deity of another. The Greeks borrowed Astarte from the Phoenicians and transformed her into Aphrodite, who was later called Venus among the Romans.

The dualistic tradition of the Persian religions, especially Zoroastrianism, believed in an eternal conflict between the forces of good and evil. The Hebrews also borrowed this idea, adding a new dimension to their concept of the angels. This is the origin of the vision of the sons of light battling constantly against the children of darkness, angels and demons fighting eternally for the human soul. Centuries later, this angelic vision, enriched by the polytheistic religions, passed from Judaism to Christianity and Islam.

Zoroastrianism

Zoroastrianism was a Persian religion that flourished in the area known today as Iran. It was based on the teachings of the prophet Zoroaster or Zarathustra, who lived around 700 B.C. Zoroaster's beliefs were based on revelations he received as a youth from the god Ahura Mazda. Zoroaster's teachings were very similar to those compiled in the Vedic scriptures of ancient Hinduism, which shows the Indian origins of Zoroastrianism. The Vedas speak of two classes of deities: the Ahuras, who were entities of light, and the Devas, who were dark spirits.

The central god of Zoroastrianism was Ahura Mazda, identified as the creator of the world and the Lord Wisdom. The entities who carried on the decrees of Ahura Mazda were known as the Amesha Spentas, immortal beings of immense light. There were seven Amesha Spentas: the Holy or Incremental Spirit, Good Mind, Truth, Power, Devotion, Health, and Life.

The most important of the Amesha Spentas was the Holy or Incremental Spirit, known as Spenta Mainyu. All evil was caused by Angra Mainyu, who was Spenta Mainyu's twin brother. Angra Mainyu was evil by choice, having chosen to ally himself with Lie, while Spenta Mainyu chose to ally with Truth. The seven Amesha Spentas were the precursors of the seven great archangels of Judeo-Christianity: Michael, Raphael, Gabriel, Uriel, Raquel, Sariel, and Remiel, also known as Jeremiel. These angels appear for the first time on chapter 20 of the *First Book of Enoch*, an apocryphal book that does not appear in the Scriptures.

The rituals of Zoroastrianism were based on the observance of good and the rejection of evil. Fire played a very important part in these rites as it was seen as the manifestation of Ahura Mazda's Truth. Also of great importance was the ritual drink, haoma, very similar to the elixir soma of the Indian Vedas. Zoroaster's teachings were compiled after his death in the Gathas or Psalms, which were an intrinsic part of the sacred scripture known as the Avesta.

The priests of Zoroastrianism were known as Magi. This name was derived from the tribe to which they belonged. As long as Zoroastrianism existed in Persia, the Magi wielded great political and religious power. Their renowned wisdom became legendary in ancient times and extended to Greece, where astrologers were known as Magi. Eventually this word was used to denote wise individuals who had true knowledge of God. It is the source of the term "magic." The three wise kings—Gaspar, Melchior, and Balthazar—who, according to the New Testament, brought gold, frankincense, and myrrh to the baby Jesus, were Magi.

The increasing Muslim persecution drove the vast majority of these high caste priests to migrate to India around the tenth century. Their descendants are known as the Parsi of Bombay in modern times. Therefore Zoroastrianism, which was based on the Indo-European culture, eventually returned to its original Indian roots. That is why the Vedas, the most sacred scriptures of Hinduism, reflect Zoroaster's teachings. For that reason, many of the Judeo-Christian beliefs have Hindu roots, including many of the characteristics of the angels.

Islam

The Muslim religion known as Islam developed its angelic concept based largely on the Judeo-Christian tradition. The Archangel Gabriel, known among Muslims as Jibril, is said to have dictated the Koran to the prophet Mohammed in one single night. It was also Gabriel who gave the famous Black Stone to Ishmael, Abraham's first born, fathered through the Egyptian slave Hagar. Ishmael was the precursor of the Arab races. The Black Stone, which according to many geologists is a meteorite, is kept in the Kaaba, the holy of holies among the Muslims. The Kaaba is housed in the great mosque of the holy city of Mecca. Infidels, those who do not adhere to the teachings of Islam, are forbidden to enter Mecca under penalty of death. Every devoted Muslim must make a sacred pilgrimage to Mecca once during his lifetime to worship the Kaaba. Muslims believe that the Kaaba was constructed originally by Adam and later reconstructed by Abraham and his son Ishmael.

Muslims also have great veneration for the Archangel Michael, known among them as Mikhail. They describe Michael as possessing an immense stature, with emerald wings and saffron-colored hair. To the Muslims, angels are God's servants and are bound to his decrees. They believe in guardian angels and angel scribes, who are said to write down every human action for which human beings have to answer during the day of the Final Judgment.

They also believe in the angel of death, Azrael, and the angels who question human souls on their graves. Islam's angelic tradition comes from the Koran and the teachings of Mohammed, who held the patriarch Abraham in great reverence. Jesus is also venerated by the Muslims, who consider him a great prophet.

Muslims also believe in the Genii, supernatural spirits of great power, who nevertheless belong to a sphere lower than the angels. Genii, better known as Jinn, are made of air or fire and can assume the form of animals and human beings. Jinn may be good or evil. If they are good, they manifest as beings of transcendental beauty. If they are evil, their appearance is hideously ugly. Jinn exist in air, fire, underneath the earth, and in inanimate objects like rocks, trees, and also in ruins. They have the same biological needs as human beings, reproduce sexually, and die, although they may live for thousands of years. Jinn are malicious entities, who often take pleasure in tormenting human beings, punishing their offenses. To a Muslim, every illness, accident, or streak of bad luck is caused by a Jinn. But they also believe that, in spite of their machiavellian tendencies, Jinn may be controlled by a person with magical knowledge. People who know how to control a Jinn are able to realize their most cherished desires through the spirit's help. The awesome prowesses and immense powers of the Jinn are related in full splendor in the famous tales of *A Thousand and One Nights*, specially in such beloved stories as "Aladdin and the Lamp" and "Sinbad the Sailor." The king of the Jinn is Zuleiman and the most famous of the lot is the malicious Iblis, identified by Muslims as the Prince of Darkness. To the Muslims, the Jinn are very real entities, capable of influencing human lives and transforming them for good or evil.

Gnosticism

Gnosticism had very old roots, reaching the heights of its popularity during the year A.D. 200. Its origins are a mixture of Zoroastrianism, the Jewish Kabbalah, and the Egyptian religion. The ancient Christians believed that the founder of Gnosticism was Simon the Magus.

The central teaching of Gnosticism was that the material world is essentially evil and that there is nothing in it that is good or beautiful.

Its principal tenet held that the only salvation of a human being was to liberate his soul from its material prison. According to the Gnostic principles, within each person was hidden a divine seed. The purpose of salvation was to release this seed from its corporeal prison, which was the physical body.

According to the Gnostics, the material world was created by a malevolent entity, known as the Demiurge, Ialdabaoth, who kept human beings imprisoned in matter. The only way to escape the chains imposed by the physical body was through Gnosis, the secret knowledge imparted by the Gnostics. The Demiurge or negative entity was identified as the God of Judeo-Christianity, Yahweh or Jehovah, who was conceived by the Gnostics as a false and evil being. This negative concept of God was based largely on the Gnostics' profound distrust of the teachings of the Old Testament and their hatred of the Jews. To the Gnostics, the Father mentioned by Jesus in the New Testament was not Jehovah but the true god of the Gnostics, perceived by them as the Pleroma or Supreme Creator.

The Gnostics believed in two types of supernatural beings: the Eons, who were beatific forces emanated by their supreme god in fifteen pairs, and the Arcons, who were malevolent entities. Among the Eons were Dynamis (Power), Desire, Depth, Silence, and Wisdom, known as Pistis Sophia. This last Eon conceived a desire to know the unknowable supreme being. Out of this illegitimate desire was born a deformed, evil god who created the universe and who was identified as the Demiurge, Ialdabaoth. This was the first Arcon, who in turn created six more. These seven Arcons formed the seven cosmic planes or planets. The names of the seven Arcons were Ialdabaoth, Sabaoth, Jao, Ailoaios, Oraios, Astanfaios, and Adonaios. According to other Gnostic teachings, there were twelve Arcons who were identified with the zodiacal signs. They were the regents of the material plane and prevented the sparks of light who are the human spirits from returning to the original source, which was the Pleroma. The seven Arcons were also identified with the seven deadly sins and the seven planets: Jupiter (Pride); Moon (Envy); Mars (Rage); Venus (Lust); Saturn (Sloth); sun (Avarice); and Mercury (Lies).

The principal Eon or beneficent god was Abraxas, identified as the supreme being. From Abraxas was emanated the Pleroma. From the Pleroma was emanated the first Eon, and from the first was emanated the second, until all the Eons were created. Because each Eon gave some of its light to the one that followed, each succeeding Eon had less light and less power than the preceding one. Pistis Sophia, who was the last of the Eons to be created, had less light than the rest, and that was why she erred in desiring to know the unknowable, thus emanating the Arcon Ialdabaoth.

Some Gnostic authorities, like Basilides, believed in the existence of 365 Eons, one for each of the days of the year. Later on, perhaps as an act of retaliation on the part of Judeo-Christianity, the Gnostic Eon Abraxas became identified as a demonic entity of great malignity. From his name was derived the word "abracadabra," very popular in the practice of magic.

The Church Fathers considered Gnosticism a heretic sect because of their rejection of Jehovah and because of their teachings, which were contrary to orthodox Christianity. The resultant persecution of Gnosticism culminated in the dispersion of the various Gnostic sects. Eventually, the remaining members of the movement joined the Manicheans or Mandeans, a Persian religion based on the teachings of a sage called Mani, who was in turn profoundly influenced by Buddhist doctrines.

The Mandeans also believed that matter was evil, and exhorted their followers to practice celibacy in order to achieve eventually the extermination of the human race. Gnostic teachings are followed in modern times by small groups of people who practice their magical and mystical rites. Small sects of Mandeans still survive in Iraq and Iran. The Mandeans also believed in the existence of the Arcons, who were conceived by them as the children of darkness, and swallowed the elements of light in human beings.

In angelology an Arcon is a great celestial prince and each region on earth is ruled by one of them. In some mystical traditions they are identified as the Planetary Spirits. In the Kabbalah, the Arcons preside over the heavenly palaces. Among the angelic Arcons are Michael, Raphael, Uriel, Gabriel, and Shemuiel, who is the mediator between the prayers of Israel and the angelic Princes of the Sixth Heaven.

Creation of the Angels

According to canonical sources, all the angels were created simultaneously by God. For this reason angels are immortal but they are not eternal, because eternity is an attribute that belongs only to God. At the end of the universe, after all the suns, stars, and galaxies are extinguished, the angels will also fade away. But as long as the universe exists, their presence in it is permanently assured.

Angels are superior to human beings because they were given a supernal intelligence when they were created. At the moment of Creation, God gave the angels free will. Later on, he presented the same gift to Adam. The angels returned free will to the Creator, but Adam kept it for himself. The angels who retained free will eventually revolted against God. Their sin was pride. These are the fallen angels.

The principal duty of the angels is to carry out God's judgment on Earth and throughout the universe. They also protect the faithful, punish evil, and destroy the power of demonic spirits.

When a person is born he or she is assigned a guardian angel, who remains with that individual as long as he or she obeys God's laws. When a person commits a mortal sin, the guardian angel flees. In the Old Testament they are described as God's messengers, as holy or celestial beings, and as the heavenly host. They also serve as intermediaries between God and humanity.

Angelology teaches that there is a special class of angels known as the Ephemeras, whom are created by God each morning to sing the Trisagion or praises to the Deity. As soon as they finish singing, the Ephemeras return to the divine light.

Angelophany

Angels are incorporeal beings but sometimes they adopt human form to carry out divine decrees. In the Old Testament, they appear for the first time in chapter 3 of Genesis as the Cherubim who guard the gates of Eden with a fiery revolving sword, thus barring the way to the Tree of Life. Later on, in chapter 19, three angels appeared in human form

Figure 3: The Archangel Michael (National Gallery, London).

Figure 4: The Archangel Gabriel with Tobias (The Academy, Venice).

Figure 5: Abraham and the three angels.

Figure 6: Jacob's dream.

to the patriarch Abraham, who was sitting outside his tent. In chapter 22, another angel appeared to Abraham to stop the sacrifice of his son Isaac. In chapter 28, Jacob dreamed of a ladder that reached to Heaven and "God's messengers were going up and down on it." These angelic visitations are known as angelophanies and they have taken place not only in the Bible but to many people in real life. One of the best-known cases was that of Pope Gregory the Great, who saw the Archangel Michael sheathing his sword over the mausoleum of the Roman emperor Hadrian during a terrible plague in Rome. Gregory interpreted the dream as a sign that the plague was soon to end, as it did. To commemorate the miracle, Gregory renamed the mausoleum as Castel Sant' Angelo, the Castle of the Holy Angel, in honor of Michael, and erected a marble statue of the archangel to surmount the structure.

Among the prophets who were visited by angels were Isaiah, Ezekiel, Elisha, Daniel, and Zechariah. An angel announced the birth of Jesus to the Virgin Mary, and the apostles Peter and Paul were also visited by these celestial messengers.

The Bible only mentions three angels by name: Michael, Gabriel, and Raphael, but their numbers reach "myriads upon myriads," according to chapter 7 of the Book of Daniel. A myriad is an innumerable quantity. Many theologians have speculated how many angels were created by God. A very popular quodlib or riddle asks how many angels can dance on the point of a needle. The answer is all of them, as they are pure spirit and do not occupy any physical space.

Around the fourteenth century, a kabbalist calculated that there are exactly 301,655,722 angels in the universe. It is not known how he reached that figure. Albertus Magnus also did some arithmetic on the subject and ended up proposing that there are 6,666 legions in each of the nine angelic choirs and 6,666 in each legion. According to his calculations there are more than 400 millions of angels floating about. But none of these numbers seem very accurate if we consider that each star is an angel, according to Saint John in the Book of Revelation and Clement of Alexandria in his book *The Stromata*. Astronomers tell us that there are billions of stars in our galaxy alone, and billions of galaxies in the universe. This would indicate that if Saint John and Clement of Alexandria are correct, the number of angels in existence runs into the billions of billions, or myriads upon myriads, according to the prophet Daniel.

Because angels were all created at the same time, their numbers are always the same. God does not create angels continuously, with the exception of the Ephemeras. The quantity of angels that exists in our modern times is the same that existed at the moment of Creation.

In spite of the immense amount of angels that are said to exist in the universe, only a

Figure 7: The Virgin Mary and baby Jesus surrounded by Cherubim.

few are known by name. The prophet Enoch lists the names of 150 angels in his book, but other ecclesiastical and nonecclesiastical sources have compiled several thousands.

In this book we are only going to discuss the best known among the angels, including the angels of the Seven Heavens, the zodiacal signs, the planets, and the angelic orders. The angel biographies that form Part IV of this book include close to a thousand angels.

The Angel's Image

Our concept of the angel's appearance, known as its telesmatic image, has evolved throughout the centuries until it has assumed certain definite characteristics that everyone recognizes. This image of the angel is conceived as that of an ethereal being, usually with long, flowing curls, dressed in a gauzy, flowing tunic and a mantle draped over its shoulders.

The angel always has widespread white wings and is surrounded by a halo or shimmering aura. It is usually barefoot or wears Roman sandals. It often has a diadem or golden crown on its head, and may carry a book, a sword, a flower, or play a musical instrument.

Wings and Halos

An angel's wings are a symbol of its divine power and its spiritual essence. The first winged creatures date from ancient Chaldea, in the city of Ur, where the image of an angel was depicted descending to Earth and pouring the water of life upon the head of a king. In Mesopotamia gods were believed to live in the sky and had bird wings.

The Greeks and the Romans absorbed this concept of winged beings, and conceived the messenger of the gods with winged feet. This divine messenger was called Hermes among the Greeks and Mercury among the Romans. The Jews, who lived in captivity under the Babylonians for many centuries, expressed their concept of the angels as winged beings throughout the Old Testament. The Seraphim had six pairs of wings, while the Cherubim had four. The New Testament also describes the angels with wings, and the Gospel according to Saint Luke says that angels flew around the manger during the birth of Jesus. Saint John also describes angels as winged beings in the Book of Revelation. But it was during the reign of the emperor Constantine in the fourth century that angels were first painted with wings. This angelic characteristic continued to appear in Christian art, culminating with the magnificent paintings of these celestial beings during the Renaissance.

There has been much speculation on the size of an angel's wings. Some calculations on these celestial appendages find that an angel of average height would need wings at least thirty feet wide to hold it in the air. Several recent books have made minute estimates of the wings' dimensions, and one of these authors claims that the wing span alone would have to be between 36 and 120 feet for an angel taller than six feet. But these calculations forget to consider that an angel is a spiritual being, without a physical body, and therefore has no weight. If we conceive an angel as a celestial entity whose physical appearance is unsubstantial, then its wings do not need to have specific dimensions because they are only a symbol of the angel's spiritual identity. An angel does not need wings to fly because it can materialize itself at will and move between Heaven and Earth faster than thought. An angel is an idea, a cosmic law, and as such its presence is only as real as it wishes to make it.

The halo or nimbus that surrounds the head or the figure of an angel in many paintings dates from the fifth century. This golden aura, which can also be seen around the figures of Jesus, Mary, and the saints, is a

Figure 8: The halos surrounding the angels are clearly illustrated in this painting by Fra Angelico, "The Coronation of the Virgin" (La Uffizi, Florence).

symbol of the divine light that is believed to emanate from all holy beings. In many medieval paintings of the angels, the halo is delineated as a diffuse golden circle from which extend many rays of light. This circle is often surrounded by another formed by tiny four-petalled flowers. The Greeks also used the halo during the pre-Christian period as symbols of the sun god Helios, later renamed Apollo by the Romans. The Romans also used the halo to surround the figures of their emperors, who were considered divinities.

Angels and Music

Many of the medieval paintings of angels depict them playing musical instruments, among which the harp and the lyre are the most common. This musical concept of the angel is based on the angelic choirs, who sing continuously the Divine Trisagion.

The lyre is believed to be the instrument used by David when he composed the Psalms. The Psalms were not simply prayers dedicated to God, but songs written by David and later sung by him as he played the lyre. That is probably the origin of the lyre as an angelic instrument.

The harp, based on the lyre, was a very popular instrument during the Middle Ages, and that may be the reason why it eventually replaced the lyre as a favorite angelic instrument. The sound of the harp is very ethereal and cannot be compared to any other instrument in the sweetness of its

tone. That is why it is so easy to associate it with celestial entities. The visualization of an angel playing the harp helps us to imagine the celestial choirs singing the music of the spheres in front of the Divine Throne.

Another musical instrument associated with the angels is the trumpet, which is used by the angels to make important announcements like the Day of the Final Judgment. According to the Muslims, the angel of music is Israfel, who will play the trumpet on that dire moment. Another angel associated with the trumpet is Uriel, who is said to rule the angelic choirs who sing praises to the Lord. But undoubtedly it is the Archangel Gabriel who is universally accepted as the divine trumpeter. And it is he, according to the Christian tradition, who will use this sacred instrument to call the souls to divine judgment.

Angelic Symbols

The four best-known angels, Michael, Raphael, Gabriel, and Uriel, carry a distinctive object in their hands that identifies them immediately.

Michael carries a sword and a balance, symbols of justice; Raphael carries a staff, a symbol of wisdom; Gabriel carries a lily, a symbol of purity; and Uriel carries a book or a scroll, a symbol of the divine law. These angels also wear distinctive garbs. Michael wears Roman armor and sandals and his mantle is red and green. Raphael, Gabriel, and Uriel wear tunics of different colors.

Raphael dresses in yellow and violet; Gabriel's colors are blue and orange; and Uriel's tunic is made of the colors of the Earth: olive green, lime, brown, and black. But these great archangels also dress in white and gold, which are the colors associated with the heavenly hosts.

Angelic Strength

According to the Judeo-Christian tradition, the power of the angels is awesome. The Talmud says that Michael can move mountains, and the Book of Revelation tells us that seven angels of God's anger destroyed a third of the stars. According to a Jewish legend, an angel of the Lord held Jerusalem aloft to defend it against Nebuchadnezzar's attack, but God put it back on the ground. The angel Atafiel holds all of Heaven with three fingers. When the angel Hadraniel proclaims God's will, his voice traverses 200,000 firmaments, and if the angel Chayyiel wished to, he could swallow the Earth in one gulp. Other angelic legends tell us that around the thirteenth century, the angels moved Mary's house from Nazareth to Dalmatia and from there to several parts of Italy, setting it finally in the small town of Loretto. In the seventeenth century, German astronomer Johannes Kepler published a work titled *Cosmographic Mystery*, according to which the planetary angels pushed planets in their orbits. These angels were later identified as gravitational forces, leading us to suspect angels may very well be cosmic laws overseen by a Supreme Intelligence. The heavenly host has also been identified with the elements and with other natural forces.

Angelic Contact

Angelic contact with human beings takes place through invocations, evocations, meditations, petitions, and prayers. There is a great difference between these "contacts." A prayer is an act of faith through which a person recognizes divine power and asks for divine guidance; a petition is a special request to God through his angels or ministers to grant the petitioner that which he or she desires; a meditation is contact with a spiritual entity, such as the guardian angel, which is realized through the individual's unconscious mind; an invocation is a direct request to an angelic force, usually through a special ceremony, to help the individual achieve a determinate goal; and an evocation is a request, also through a special ritual, for an angel or any other spiritual entity to manifest physically in front of the person. Invocations and evocations should be conducted within the confines of a protective or magical circle to help balance the psychic energies that are released from the individual's deep unconscious during the ceremony.

I believe that angels are autonomous archetypes of the collective unconscious and as such are made of vast quantities of psychic energies. Because they have been given form and distinctive powers through thousands of

Figure 9: The Archangel Raphael flying over the Earth.

years of visualization, they are real entities with powerful wills and well-defined personalities, and may be released from the deep unconscious, either consciously through a ritual or unconsciously during times of stress. Rituals are markedly effective because the individual is making a concerted effort to contact and release these autonomous energies from the deepest levels of the psyche.

The existence and the power of an angelic archetype to manifest is very real and I was able to ascertain this during another ritual I conducted while I was still living in Vienna. I related this experience in *The Complete Book of Spells, Ceremonies & Magic*, but I want to include it here as a personal testimony of the reality of the angels. During this period I had been studying mysticism for several years, but I did not have much experience with the angelic realm. One day I decided to do an invocation to the angels that I found in a popular grimoire entitled the *Sixth and Seventh Books of Moses*.

The invocation, written in the florid and extravagant language of the Middle Ages, was fascinating, and I decided to use it to invoke the Archangel Raphael. It is said about Raphael that he is the angel who stands in the center of the sun, and he is also known as the divine physician, perhaps because of the episode when he cured Tobias of his blindness. Because yellow is his principal color, I decided to use a yellow candle during the invocation. I knew that all positive

rituals should be done facing the east, as this is the cardinal point where the sun rises every morning. What I did not know is that before every invocation a circle should be traced either on the ground or in the air to protect the person against negative energies.

As soon as I finished reading the invocation to the angels, I felt a strange feeling of dread permeate my entire being. Somehow I felt that I was not alone. My hands began to sweat and my knees shook so badly I could hardly stand. This feeling of apprehension continued to grow until I was in the grip of the most absolute terror. Very slowly I felt the room begin to fill with a powerful energy. There was nothing angelic about it. On the contrary, it was of a terrifying malignity. There are no words with which I can describe the extent of my terror in those moments. I was alone. I had no protection against this invading and pervasive wave of evil. Every prayer that I knew since childhood disappeared from my mind as if they had been erased by a malevolent hand. The only thing that remained untouched was my great faith and trust in God. Clinging to this faith like a life saver, I began to pray to God for his help and blessing. And very slowly, like an ebbing tide, the negative energy that surrounded me began to recede until it disappeared. Exhausted by the ordeal, I lay down in bed and fell asleep immediately. When I woke up, I was in the throes of the most excruciating toothache I have ever experienced. My face swelled up and the tooth felt as if a thousand demons were prodding at it with their tridents. This toothache promptly developed into a serious tooth infection that threatened to turn into septicemia. I spent two weeks in bed, too sick to go to work or move around.

What happened during this experience was that the energies released by the power of the invocation, uncontrolled due to the absence of a protective circle, converged upon me. This awesome psychic energy, without restraint, was too powerful for me to absorb or balance. It then spread rapidly, affecting the most vulnerable part of my body, which was the tooth. The energies of the Archangel Raphael, which represent health and well being, unbalanced, manifested in that which is opposite to health, which is illness.

It was not Raphael who I contacted that day, but his opposite, the archetype of death and destruction.

This experience can be explained away as a hysterical attack, a hallucination, or simply the result of an overactive imagination. But that does not explain the illness that followed as a result.

Feminine or Masculine?

Ecclesiastical authorities tell us that angels are spirits of light and as such they do not possess physical bodies and least of all sexuality. Yet the traditional image of an angel is invariably masculine. In modern times there is an increasing tendency to feminize many of the angels, among them Gabriel and Raphael. But if angels were created spontaneously by God, as Enoch would have us believe, then the question of sexuality is redundant. If an angel does not reproduce its species, why should it need sexual identity? Its telesmatic human image is simply a form an angel may use to facilitate our identification with its essence.

In spite of this apparent asexuality of the angels, the Judeo-Christian tradition abounds with legends about their sexual proclivities. The Talmud mentions the physical union between Eisheth Zenunim, the angel of prostitution, and Samael, who is sometimes identified with Satan. Samael is credited with having had several concubines, including the terrible Lilith.

Genesis also tells us that several of the fallen angels had forbidden relations with the daughters of men. From these unions were born hideous, bloodthirsty giants who devoured everyone in their paths.

In *Paradise Lost*, John Milton's immortal tale of Adam's fall, the Archangel Raphael describes the union between angels. It is softer than softness, he says. And the *Third Book of Enoch*, which literally teems with angels, says that after they finish singing the Trisagion, the angels, in the grip of heavenly bliss, transform their neutral essence into feminine and masculine essences. When angels unite, they simply blend their spirits and become one.

The Zohar, the most important of the kabbalistic treatises, explains that angels can transform themselves and take any form they want. They may appear as males or females. This means that angels do not have a physical form or sexuality, but may adopt it if they wish. This would explain the forbidden relationships between the fallen angels and the daughters of men related in Genesis. These angels did not have corporeal forms but adopted them in order to engage in sexual relations with women.

Angel Food

Do angels eat? In chapter 18 of Genesis, three angels appeared to Abraham and told him that his wife Sarah was soon to bear him a son.

Abraham asked Sarah and one of his servants to prepare food for his angelic visitors. In due time he placed before them dressed meat, bread, milk, and butter, and they ate. This would seem to indicate that when angels assume human form they can eat and perform other human actions, but this is only part of their ability to transmute matter.

Angel food is often identified with the manna that fell from Heaven every day when the Jews were crossing the desert on their way to the promised land. The word manna means "what is this" in Hebrew. That was the question the Israelites asked when they found this celestial substance on the desert sands. Moses answered, "This is the bread that the Lord has given you as sustenance."

According to Exodus, where this story is related, the manna fell from heaven in the form of dew. When it dried it took the shape of grains, which could be used as flour to make bread. Its flavor was similar to honey cakes.

In Psalm 78, which clearly makes reference to this biblical event, David sings: "He rained manna upon them for food and gave them heavenly bread. And they ate the food of the angels."

The prophet Elisha was fed by an angel during his forty-day sojourn in the desert. The prophet was asleep one day when he was awakened by an angel who said, "Arise and eat." Elisha saw in front of him a jug of water and bread baked on hot stones. The prophet ate and drank, and went back to sleep. Shortly afterward, the angel woke him up again and asked him to eat once more, as the journey was going to be long and difficult. Elisha ate and drank obediently. The food prepared by the angel sustained him during the forty days and nights he spent in the wilderness.

According to biblical sources, manna is an angelic food that gives great vitality to human beings, but there is no evidence that angels eat manna or any other food. Manna is eaten by people in the Bible, not by angels. One could say that manna was cosmic energy provided by God to the Israelites and to Elisha so that they could complete their respective journeys. But angels, as spiritual entities, would not need the physical manna. Angels may partake of food when they are with a person, but only to humanize the experience.

The Angelic Presence

There are many individuals who claim to have had conversations and encounters with angels, and describe them as very real at the moment of contact. So many of these cases have been reported that it is estimated that one out of three people has had a similar experience. Marcos, a man who assisted to one of my seminars, said that he once had an automobile accident in a desolate area. His car crashed against a tree and the force of the impact left him unconscious. When he regained consciousness, he found himself dazed and badly wounded. He realized he needed immediate medical attention, but was unable to get out of the car. He began to panic when he saw that there was no one in the vicinity, and that it might be a long time before he was found. Struggling to keep calm, he began to pray to God to send someone to his aid. At that moment, someone tapped on the car's window and he saw a young man with a serene countenance smiling at him through the window glass. "Don't worry, Marcos," he said. "The help you asked for is on its way." As soon as he uttered these words, the young man disappeared.

A few minutes later a police car showed up at the scene and the officers rescued the man from the car wreck. They told him that they were cruising some distance away from the accident when they saw a strange light among the trees and decided to investigate. If it had not been for this light they would not have found Marcos. Who was the young man who came to Marcos and how did he know the man's name? To Marcos, he was a celestial visitor who came to his aid in answer to his prayers.

In another case, a woman who was returning home from work was attacked by a knife-wielding rapist. The man forced his way into her home and threw her to the floor. He placed the tip of the knife against her throat and told her he would kill her if she screamed. The woman began to pray aloud, asking the Virgin Mary and the angels to save her. As soon as she began to pray, the man paled, threw down the knife, and stood up, fixing the clothes that he was beginning to remove. She noticed that he was staring at a point behind her back with bulging eyes. He suddenly turned on his heels and ran out of the house. When the woman turned around, she saw the huge figure of man, dressed in white, with a sword in his hands. Many rays of light emanated from this figure, which slowly faded until there was no one there. This happened in only a few minutes, but she has never been able to forget the experience. This woman is convinced that what she saw was an angel sent by the Virgin to save her from a terrible crime.

There are thousands of cases related by people who claim to have had contacts with angels during crucial times in their lives. This would seem to indicate that angels can take human form to establish contact with a person during special moments. This is the phenomenon known as angelophany.

If an angel can manifest in a physical body, can a human being become an angel? The Bible tells us that three of the patriarchs were transformed into angels. Enoch was transformed into the angel Metraton, the highest-ranking angel in the celestial hierarchy. Jacob, later known as Israel, became the Archangel Uriel. And Elias was transported to Heaven in a chariot of fire, later becoming the Archangel Sandalfon, who is said to be the protective angel of the Earth. The apocryphal books tell us that Saint Francis of Assisi was transformed into the angel Rhamiel, and Saint Anne, the Virgin's mother, into the angel Anas. But we do not know of anyone in modern times who has been transformed into an angel.

To accept that these religious figures have been elevated to the angelic hierarchy is a matter of faith. And not everyone is ready to accept these transformations because angels are perceived as pure spirits who never had a physical body. On the other hand, these angels existed prior to the alleged transformations, so if these indeed took place, the persons involved became part of the angel's substance, merging their spirits with those of the angels.

The Catholic Church gives the title of saint to the three angels who are recognized ecclesiastically. These angels are Michael, Gabriel, and Raphael. Their feast day in the Catholic calendar of saints is September 29. But in reality, a saint is a human being whose love and devotion to God and to humanity, as well as their great purity, has made them worthy of sainthood. The concept of a saint is common to many religions. The Catholic Church bases its decision to canonize a person based on the miracles ascribed to that individual. These miracles have to be proven and sanctioned by the Church.

When this first requisite has been verified by the Church, the person goes through the process of beatification, and later on through canonization, when an individual is declared a saint.

There are many miracles ascribed to Michael, Gabriel, and Raphael, and undoubtedly an angel is a holy being, but this does not make them saints because they were never human beings. They were never beatified or canonized. Furthermore, an angel belongs to a spiritual hierarchy far more exalted than that of a saint, and its power is infinitely superior.

Each angel belongs to one or more of the angelic orders and their titles reflect their position in the celestial hierarchy. Michael belongs to three of the angelic orders. He is a Seraph, a Virtue, and an Archangel, and he is also one of the Princes of the Divine Presence. He is better known as the Archangel Michael, which seems more appropriate, because of his exalted position, than Saint Michael.

Angels may be conceived as concentrations of cosmic energy of great intensity, which control everything that exists. There is an angel behind every idea, every intention, and every action, be they positive or negative, because there are also fallen angels.

In the universal plan, every leaf, every flower, every animal, and every grain of sand has an angel that rules it. Every star and every planet is also ruled by an angel, as we will see later on in this book. These angels are cosmic laws, each of them subject to a higher Intelligence.

If we analyze the names of the angels, we notice that their vast majority ends in "el" or "on." The suffix "el" means "son of God" and "on" means "great."

Among the best-known angels whose name terminate in "el" are Michael, Gabriel, Raphael, Uriel, Anael, Camael, Rhamiel, Ratziel, Zadkiel, Cassiel, and Azrael. The two most exalted angels whose names have the "on" termination are Metraton and Sandalfon, who are also said to be twin brothers. There are many angels whose names do not end in "el" or "on," but they are less common.

In recent years there has been an angel renaissance, culminating in a great quantity of books, films, videos, television, and theatrical productions.

Angel products are increasing in popularity, and we can find angel stationary, angel

oracles, angel jewelry, angel linen, and even angel water in major department stores. Angelic music, some it very beautiful, can be found in every record shop. Increasing reports of angelic encounters are also surfacing all over the globe. What is the reason for our growing fascination with these ethereal creatures?

A possible answer to this question is that we are at the beginning of a new era, one that embraces not only a new century but also a new millennium and a new age, the Age of Aquarius. Every two thousand years a new age dawns on the planet. An age is a span of time—approximately two thousand years—which is measured by the precession of the equinoxes. When priest-astronomers first plotted the skies, thousands of years ago, the first point of Aries, which marks the spring equinox, was seen against the background of the constellation Aries. Two thousand years later, the first point of Aries moved to the preceding constellation of Pisces. These movements appear to be going backward through the constellations. The sign that precedes Pisces is Aquarius, and soon the first point of Aries will be seen against that constellation. That will be the beginning of the Age of Aquarius. There is much speculation as to the actual date when this astronomical event will take place. Most experts agree it will be at the beginning of the millennium.

In astrology, Aquarius is seen as a revolutionary sign, intensely mystical, unpredictable, and explosive. It is a sign of wonderment, of intellectual and technological experimentation. It is the sign that rules the atom and all technical advances. And it will influence the Earth during the next two thousand years.

With the Age of Aquarius, humanity will be experiencing a mystical and spiritual rebirth. The collective unconscious of the human race will expand to encompass new, revolutionary ideas and a new vision of its own divinity and its cosmic destiny. Everything that stands in the way will be set aside or trampled under the Aquarian heel.

The concept of the angel, with its dual cosmic and mystical nature, is a perfect Aquarian vehicle. Angels are our guides of choice in the transcendental odyssey we are just beginning. That is why humanity, awakening slowly from the slumber of two thousand years, begins to perceive the ineffable presence of the heavenly host.

So, what is an angel? An angel is a cosmic force emanated by the Creative Intelligence that created the universe; it is a quantum, a specific quantity of energy, with intelligence, determination, and self-awareness; it is the consciousness of the atom; it is will with purpose, perfection, and logic; it is beauty and it is justice; it is a cosmic law, well defined and manifested; it is control; it is compassion; and it is love.

3

The Celestial Hierarchy

There are various versions of the hierarchy of angels. Among the ecclesiastical authorities who have presented their version of the angelic orders are Saint Ambrosius, Saint Jerome, and Pope Gregory the Great.

Among the Jewish authorities are Moses Maimonides, the Zohar, the Maseket Aziluth, and the Berith Menusha. Other versions come to us from Isidore of Seville, John of Damascus, Dante's *Divine Comedy*, and *The Magus* by Francis Barrett. But the most commonly accepted Christian version is that of Pseudo-Dionysius, written in the sixth century. It was erroneously ascribed to Dionysius the Aeropagite, who lived in the first century. It is said that Dionysius was the first bishop of Athens, who was mar-

tyred by the Romans during the reign of the emperor Domitian. The works that are adjudicated to him are *The Celestial Hierarchy* and *The Ecclesiastical Hierarchy*, but these were written many years later by a group of Neo-Platonists who adopted his name. These anonymous writers became known as Pseudo-Dionysius, or false Dionysius.

These works, which are believed to have been published in Syria or Egypt, were cited for the first time by the Second Council of Constantinople. The writings of Pseudo-Dionysius did not make their appearance in Europe until the sixth century, but they soon became the inspiration of many theologians and Christian writers, such as Saint Thomas of Aquinas, Dante Alighieri, and John Milton.

According to Pseudo-Dionysius there are three angelic orders, each composed of three angelic choirs, making a total of nine celestial choirs. In other versions of the hierarchy the amount of choirs is either more or less. According to Saint Ambrosius and Pope Gregory, there were nine choirs but they were listed in a different order. Saint Jerome listed only six, but Saint Thomas accepted Pseudo-Dionysius' version in his *Summa Theologica*. On the other hand, the Jewish authorities listed ten orders instead of nine because their calculations were based on the ten spheres of the Tree of Life, an intrinsic part of the Kabbalah.

In this book we are going to follow the version presented by Pseudo-Dionysius, but also taking into consideration the kabbalistic concept of ten choirs.

Angelic Hierarchy (Pseudo-Dionysius)

First Order

This order and its three choirs control the balance of the universe and the manifestation of the divine will, which they carry out.

First Choir—Seraphim

Second Choir—Cherubim

Third Choir—Thrones

Second Order

This order and its three choirs represent the power of God and they govern the planets, especially Earth. They also carry out the decrees of the angels of the First Order and oversee the angels of the Third Order.

Fourth Choir—Dominions

Fifth Choir—Virtues

Sixth Choir—Powers

Third Order

This order and its three choirs protects and guides humanity, and brings our prayers to the Divine Presence.

Seventh Choirs—Principalities

Eighth Choir—Archangels

Ninth Choir—Angels

As we can see from this list, the Angels form the ninth and last choir of the Third Order. Even though all the members of the celestial hierarchy are commonly known as angels, there is a specific choir that bears the same name. This means that all divine messengers are angels, but some of them occupy a more exalted position in the celestial choirs.

Seraphim—This is the highest of the heavenly choirs. Jewish tradition describes them as serpents of fire, perhaps because the serpent is a symbol of healing and wisdom. The title Seraphim is composed of SER, which denotes a higher being, and RAPHA, which means "he who heals." Therefore a Seraph is a higher spirit who heals. The name of Raphael, who is known

Figure 10: John's vision of the Virgin's coronation.

Figure 11: The Heaven of fixed stars.

as the divine physician, is composed of RAPHA and the suffix EL, meaning "the son of God." Raphael, therefore, means "the son of God who heals." In spite of his name, Raphael does not belong to the choir of the Seraphim.

The Seraphim are described as shining beings, perfect and incorruptible. Their light is so blinding that none of the members of the other choirs can look at them. A human being would be instantaneously disintegrated if he or she were to come face to face with a Seraph in its true form.

The mission of the Seraphim is to control and direct the divine energies that flow from the throne of God and to inflame the human heart with love for its Creator. For that reason they are known as the angels of love.

The prophet Isaiah is the only one who mentions the Seraphim in the Old Testament. He describes them in the sixth chapter of his book as having four faces, symbols of the four winds and the four elements, and six wings. With a pair of wings they cover their feet, with another pair they cover their faces, and with the third pair they fly. Each wing, according to Isaiah, was the width of the sky.

The Seraphim surround the Throne of God, singing continuously the divine Trisagion: *Holy, holy, holy is the Lord of Hosts, replete is all the world with his glory.* Because they are the closest angels to the Divine Throne and they burn eternally with love

for the Creator, the Seraphim are known as the Burning Ones. The regent princes of the Seraphim are Metraton, Michael, Seraphiel, Jehoel, Uriel, Shemuel, and Natanael.

Cherubim—This is the second choir. The idea of a Cherub as an adorable baby angel with fluffy wings and an ethereal smile is completely erroneous. In art they are known as putti, and their idealized concept comes to us from the Middle Ages. The Cherubim were the angels whom God set at the gates of Eden after the expulsion of Adam and Eve from Paradise. They barred the path of anyone seeking to enter with a whirling, flaming sword.

The word Cherubim comes from the Assyrian *karibu* and means "he who prays or intercedes." Among the Assyrians, the Cherubs were winged creatures with the face of a man or a lion and the body of a sphinx, an eagle, or a bull. The man, the lion, the eagle, and the bull are symbols of the four elements, the four winds, the four cardinal points, and the astrological signs of Aquarius, Leo, Scorpio, and Taurus, respectively. The sphinx is a composite of all four, as it has the face of a man, the feet of a lion, the body of a bull, and the wings of an eagle.

In the Old Testament, in the Book of Exodus, God orders Moses to place the image of a Cherub on each side of the Ark of the Covenant, with widespread wings. The prophet Ezekiel describes them with human bodies, four wings, and four faces, each face looking to one of the cardinal points. The face that looks forward is that of a man; the face on the right is that of a lion; the face on the left is that of a bull; and the face at the back is that of an eagle. As we can easily see, these are the same symbols used by the Assyrians to describe the Cherub. Ezekiel also tells us that these holy creatures cover their bodies with two wings and fly with the other two.

Saint John, in Revelation, describes the Cherubim with six wings instead of four, and covered with many eyes. This description is closer to that of the Seraphim.

In the Jewish tradition, the Cherubim represent the wind and they direct the course of the Merkabah or holy carriage; they also hold aloft the divine throne. Muslims, on the other hand, believe that the Cherubim were formed from Michael's tears, shed for the sins of the faithful. Their name in Arabic is *Al-karubiyan*, which means "those who are closer to Allah."

It is said that from the Cherubim, who are the personification of wisdom, flows a subtle essence of knowledge that they receive directly from God. Among the various titles given to the Cherubim are the Living Creatures, the Winged Creatures, and the Holy Beasts. The regent princes of the Cherubim are Gabriel, Cherubiel, Ophaniel, Raphael, Uriel, and Zophiel.

Thrones—This is the third choir. Their name is derived from the fact that they stand before God's throne. Their mission is to inspire faith in the power of the Creator. It is said that they inhabit the Third or Fourth Heaven. They are the ones that carry out divine justice. Some biblical authorities identify them with the wheels of fire described by Ezekiel in his apocalyptic vision. According to Ezekiel, these creatures are flaming wheels covered with many eyes and they always move in unison with the Cherubim.

In the Kabbalah the Thrones are identified as the Merkabah or holy carriage, which is guided by the Cherubim. Among the various titles given to the Thrones are the Wheels. In the Jewish tradition they are known as the Ophanim and also as the Erelim. The prince regents of the Thrones are Oriphiel, Zaphkiel, Jophiel, and Ratziel.

Dominions—This is the fourth choir. These angels are also known as the Lords. They assign their duties and missions to the angels of the lower spheres. God's majesty is revealed through them. These angels are seldom in contact with human beings, as part of their duties is to maintain the cosmic order. In the Kabbalah they are identified as the Hasmalim. Among their symbols of authority are the scepter and the orb, which represents the world. They often carry swords as symbols of their authority over other creatures. According to the angelic tradition, the Dominions dress in tunics of green and gold. This choir receives its instructions from the Cherubim and the

Figure 12: The vision of the four chariots.

Thrones. Their name is derived from Saint Paul's Letter to the Corinthians where he mentions the Dominions, the Thrones, the Powers, and the Principalities. The *Second Book of Enoch* says that the Thrones are part of the angelic armies. They are said to be channels of mercy and inhabit the Second Heaven. Their regent princes are Zadkiel, Hashmal, Zakariel, and Muriel.

Virtues—This is the fifth choir. As their name indicates, they are the angels in charge of conferring the quality of virtue to human beings. They also confer grace and valor. The Virtues preside over the elements and rule the process of celestial life. They are in charge of the motion of the planets, the stars, and the galaxies, and they control the cosmic laws. This choir also rules astronomy and astrophysics. The Virtues are in charge of nature and the natural laws that rule the Earth, including all natural phenomena. According to Saint Thomas Aquinas, the Virtues are in charge of all miracles and they were the angels who were present during the Ascension of Jesus. The Virtues are associated with the saints and all the heroes who do battle against evil. It is said that the Virtues gave David the strength to overcome the giant Goliath. In the Kabbalah they are known as the Malachim or the Tarshashim. Their regent princes are Michael, Gabriel, Uzziel, Peliel, Anael, Hamaliel, Barbiel, Sabriel, and Tarshish.

Powers—This is the sixth choir. Their principal mission is to maintain order in Heaven and to restrain the fallen angels from destroying the world. They are said to be in charge of the history of humanity and are present during the birth or death of human beings. According to some theological authorities, they preside over all world religions and provide them with the celestial energy to carry on their work. They function through intuition and warn human beings through dreams or premonitions when danger is near. It is said that although all angels were created at the same time by God, the Powers were the first to be emanated from the Creator. This choir has the divine authority to punish and to forgive and also to create by divine will, carrying out God's decrees. Part of the mission of the Powers is to help human beings resist temptation, and to follow God's laws. They also act as guides to lost souls. This choir resides between the First and the Second Heavens and guards the path to the celestial realms. The Powers are also known as Authorities, Potentialities, Dynamis, and Potentates. According to some authorities, most of the rebellious angels belonged to this choir before their fall. One of these fallen angels, called Crocell, told King Solomon that he still hoped to make peace with God and to return to the Powers. The prince regents of the Powers are Gabriel, Verchiel, and Camael.

Principalities—This is the seventh choir. Its principal mission is to guard and protect kings, princes, judges, presidents, governors, and other world leaders, granting them the illumination to rule with wisdom and justice. They also protect the nations, all world organizations, and all religious leaders. Their symbols are the scepter, the cross, and the sword. These angels are also known as Princes because of their association with heads of state. They are identified in the Kabbalah as the Sarim. Their regent princes are Anael, Cerviel, and Rekiel.

Archangels—This is the eighth choir. Their main duty is to intercede on behalf of humanity and its sins so that these may be forgiven by God. They are constantly at war with Satan and his hordes to protect the world against their continuous assault. According to Jewish tradition, Archangels are closely associated with the planets. Other authorities claim that Archangels rule the signs of the zodiac. Pseudo-Dionysius described them as the bearers of God's decrees. Archangels are mentioned in both the Old and the New Testaments. According to the Epistle of Judah, when Michael was battling Satan over the body of Moses after the Lawgiver's death, he did not pass judgment over the prince of hell, but instead told him: "The Lord rebukes you."

There is a great confusion about the Archangels and the angels that do not be-long to this choir but whom are given this title. The confusion started because in the beginning of angelology there were only two classes of angels: Archangels and Angels. It was through the scholarly efforts of Saint Thomas Aquinas, Saint Augustine, and Pseudo-Dionysius that the various angelic orders were properly classified. During those early times, the most exalted angels were called Archangels, a custom that persists in modern times. But not all the high-ranking angels are Archangels. For example, Zadkiel, Camael, Casiel, Azrael, and Asariel, who are among the regents of the signs of the zodiac and wield great power in the celestial hierarchy, are not Archangels but are often referred to by this title. All of these angels belong to spheres superior to that of the Archangels. The regent princes of this choir are Metraton, Michael, Raphael, Uriel, Gabriel, Barbiel, Barachiel, and Jehudiel.

Angels—This is the ninth choir. Its principal mission is to act as intermediaries between God and humanity. Although all the heavenly host are called angels, this is a specific choir. Among them are found the guardian angels. The Angels are the celestial choir who are closest to human beings, and they labor incessantly to guide and protect the human race. According to the *Book of Enoch*, there is a school of Angels in the Sixth Heaven, where they are instructed by the Archangels. The patriarch claimed to

Figure 13: The angels reading the prayers that have reached the Seventh Heaven.

have visited this celestial school during his apocalyptic vision of Heaven. All the Angels Enoch saw had the same faces and were identically dressed.

Among the themes that the Angels are said to study in this school are astronomy, Earth ecology, oceanography, as well as terrestrial vegetation and human psychology. The regent princes of the Angels are Gabriel, Chayyiel, Adnakiel, and Faleg.

According to kabbalistic authorities, especially Moses Maimonides, the celestial hierarchy is divided into ten choirs, instead of nine. These choirs are based on the ten spheres of the Tree of Life. It is difficult to identify the Hebrew names of the choirs with their Christian counterparts, especially because they are listed in a different order. The following list gives my personal version of the identification between the Hebrew and the Christian classifications of the angelic choirs and is based on my studies of the Kabbalah. In the kabbalistic version of the choirs, these are not subdivided into orders.

Celestial Choirs According to the Kabbalah

1. Chaioth ha Quaddosh—Powers
2. Ophanim (Auphanim)—Thrones
3. Erelim (Arelim)—Principalities
4. Hasmalim (Chasmalim)—Dominions
5. Seraphim—Seraphim
6. Malachim—Virtues
7. Elohim—Archangels
8. Bene Elohim—Angels
9. Cherubim—Cherubim
10. Ishim—Souls of the Saints

Each of these choirs is part of the attributes of the spheres of the Tree of Life, which are known as Sephiroth. As we can see, the angelic choirs in the Kabbalah are listed in a different order than those given by Pseudo-Dionysius. I give them here because they are important in the practice of angelic magic, which we will discuss in chapter 10.

The various angelic orders and choirs are of great importance to human beings because everything in creation is ruled by angels, including life and death.

According to the Book of Jubilees, when God created the universe, on the very first day of Creation, he gave life to all the spirits who are his servants. Among these were the angels of the Divine Presence, the angels of Sanctification, the angels of the fire element, the angels of the winds, the clouds, the snow, of darkness, of thunder and lightning, of cold and heat, of the four stations, and of all his creatures on Heaven and Earth. But according to the *Book of Enoch*, the angels were not created on the first but on the second day of Creation. Of these two supreme authorities, Enoch would seem to have the edge, as he claims to have visited the celestial realms and received detailed information from the angels on all celestial events. Enoch even claimed to have interceded with God on behalf of the fallen angels, who wished to be forgiven. God denied Enoch's request.

In the film "City of Angels," we are introduced to a charming angel of death who becomes fascinated with human life and ends up falling in love with a woman. Every day all the angels gather by the sea shore and listen intently to a sound only they can hear. This sound is the holy Trisagion, sung by the angelic choruses in Heaven. It is difficult not to empathize with the plight of this angel, who wishes so much to be human that he is willing to sacrifice his eternal life as a celestial being. But what the film does not tell us is that this fallen angel would be condemned to become one of the silent Watchers, imprisoned forever in one of the darkest halls of the Second Heaven. This is the same place where the original fallen angels, the ones described in Genesis and for whom Enoch interceded in vain, spend all eternity.

Two other films on the subject of angels present these celestial beings as rather disreputable characters. In "Michael," we meet a roguish version of the great Archangel, whose main characteristics are said to be purity and incorruptibility. In the film, Michael is presented as dirty and unkempt and having intimate relations with women. Since angels are forbidden to have carnal knowledge of women this would immediately cause Michael to be expelled from Heaven and be-

come one of the fallen angels. In the film "Prophecy," the Archangel Gabriel is seen as an apostate angel, ferociously jealous of God's love for humanity. He not only hates human beings but openly disobeys God's commands, eventually becoming a heavenly pariah. But in one of the most famous of the heavenly legends, which I will relate in detail in another chapter, Gabriel disobeys God not because he hates humanity but because he loves it so much he is willing to incur the divine wrath in order to protect it. This transgression on our behalf cost Gabriel several hundred lashings with a whip of fire. Films are made for our entertainment and amusement, but adequate research would render them far more impacting and enduring. Whether or not we accept the existence of the angels, to adhere to traditional sources in their depiction seems only fair.

Through each angelic choir, human beings receive a celestial gift, if we are only willing to accept it.

- From the Seraphim we receive the gift of faith and love for God.
- From the Cherubim we receive illumination, power, and wisdom.
- From the Thrones we receive knowledge about our own creation and how to direct our thoughts to divine matters.
- From the Dominions we receive assistance in the banishing of our

enemies and are taught how to achieve salvation.

- From the Powers we are also taught how to control enemies and all obstacles.

- From the Virtues we receive divine power to triumph in life.

- From the Principalities we are taught how to control our environment

and how to acquire secret or supernatural knowledge.

- From the Archangels we receive the power to control all creatures on land or sea.

- From the Angels we receive the power to manifest the divine will.

For these multiple reasons, the holy books exhort humanity to know the angels.

4

The Seven Heavens

The concept of the Seven Heavens is part of the Judeo-Christian tradition, but can also be found in the teachings of Islam. The Persians and the Babylonians also believed in Seven Heavens, which were the multiple abodes of their deities. The Persians, in particular, conceived the Seventh Heaven as the place where the Creator sat on an immense white throne, surrounded by Cherubim. This idea, which was later borrowed by Judaism and Christianity, indicates that the origin of these celestial realms can be traced to these ancient peoples or perhaps even earlier. But certain Jewish accounts, like that of Enoch, tell us that there are more than seven heavenly spheres. According to Enoch, there are ten heavens. It was in the Tenth Heaven

that the patriarch saw the face of God. On the other hand, the Zohar says that there are as many as 390 heavens and 70,000 worlds. One of the many Jewish legends asserts that there are 955 heavens, a quantity that may not be so exorbitant considering we are told that there is an angel for every grain of sand. This would bring the angelic census to a stratospheric amount and they must reside somewhere. To avoid these exaggerated accounts, both the Jewish and the Christian authorities have settled for the more modest concept of seven celestial spheres, each of which is of a prodigious immensity.

It is said that the Seven Heavens are suspended over the Earth in concentric circles. Its constitution is spiritual, rather than physical, and they are better conceived as

Figure 14: Angels before the Throne of God.

states of consciousness or, conversely, as other planes of existence. According to Louis Ginzberg in his book *Legends of the Jews*, the First Heaven is the lowest in hierarchy. It is like a curtain that hides the firmament and the stars during the day. At night, the angels open the curtain to reveal the immensity of the universe and the First Heaven. In this concept, human beings can only see part of the First Heaven, which is the universe and which hides the other six heavens from human eyes.

The following list gives a description of the Seven Heavens and what may be found therein.

First Heaven

Its name in Hebrew is Shamayim or Wilon and its regent prince is Sidriel, although some authorities dispute this and ascribe the regency of this realm to Gabriel. All the stars, planets, and galaxies are found in the First Heaven, each of which has its own ruling or protective angel. Earth, for example, is ruled by Sandalphon. Gabriel rules the moon and Raphael rules the sun. The First Heaven is the abode of Adam and Eve. According to Enoch, it is in this heaven where the snow, the clouds, and the morning dew are kept. It was also here that Enoch saw the two hundred angels that rule the stars, a singularly small quantity of angels if we consider that there are billions of stars in our galaxy alone.

Second Heaven

Its name in Hebrew is Raquia and its regent prince is Barakiel. Again there is some argument about the rulership of this heaven, and both Raphael and Zakariel are mentioned as possible regents. According to Islam, Jesus and John the Baptist reside in the Second Heaven. When Moses visited the celestial mansions, he first passed through this sphere where he came face to face with the angel Nuriel, who is over 300 feet tall. This would make Nuriel one of the smallest angels when we consider that there are some who are said to be bigger than the entire solar system. During this encounter with Moses, Nuriel was accompanied by fifty of the heavenly hosts, all of them formed of fire and water. This heaven is also the realm of the planets.

In the Jewish tradition, the fallen angels are imprisoned in the Second Heaven for their transgressions against God and humanity. The other rebellious angels are kept in several of the celestial realms, in separate areas reserved for them. In this heaven Enoch saw many human sinners, covered with chains, while they awaited the day of the Final Judgment. The fallen angels who had forbidden relations with women are kept in a special area of the Second Heaven, where they are scourged daily for their sin.

Third Heaven

Its name in Hebrew is Shehaquim and its regent prince is Baradiel, although some authorities dispute his regency and say that Anael is the angelic ruler of this heaven. According to Enoch, it is in this heaven that the angels produce and store great quantities of manna, the heavenly nourishment that God sent to the Jews during their forty-year journey through the desert. Manna is also the food of the souls of the saints.

This divine honey is brought to the Third Heaven by celestial bees under the supervision of the Archangel Michael. Saint Paul is said to have visited this heaven, where he heard such terrible words that he dared not repeat them. Saint Paul was no friend of the angels, and he often accused them of breaking the divine laws. Maybe that is the reason why the angels of the Third Heaven received him with such a lack of civility. On the other hand, Hell is said to be located in the northern regions of this sphere. This area is filled with terrifying monsters. It is more plausible that the insults leveled at Saint Paul came from this region instead of the angelic realm. It should not be surprising that Hell should be located in a part of Heaven, because both the Greeks and the ancient Hebrews believed that Heaven and Hell were side by side. A rabbinical commentary on Psalm 90 says that Paradise is at the right of God and Hell to his left. Enoch says that Paradise and the Tree of Life are in the Third Heaven. When God visits Paradise he rests by the shadow of this Tree. Among the regent princes of Paradise are Michael, Gabriel, Zotiel, Zefon, Johiel, and Azrael, who is one of the angels of death.

Fourth Heaven

Its name in Hebrew is Machonon and its regent princes are Michael and Zahakiel. It is said that the celestial Jerusalem is in the Fourth Heaven, together with the Temple and the Altar of God. It was in this heaven that the prophet Mohammed met with Enoch. According to an old legend, it is in the Fourth Heaven that the sun and the moon cross the sky in their respective chariots.

Fifth Heaven

Its name in Hebrew is Mathey and its regent prince is Zadkiel, although some authorities claim that it is Sandalphon who rules this heaven. Sandalphon is also Earth's regent and is universally known as the angel of tears. In a separate area of this sphere are found some of the fallen angels, including the Grigori, also known as the Guardians of the Towers of the four cardinal points. Several of the Grigori, together with their Chief Salamiel, were punished because they rejected their Creator. The prophet Zephaniah said he had visited the Fifth Heaven, where he had a glimpse of the angels known as the Lords, who belong to the choir of the Dominions. All these angels wore crowns on their heads and each of them sat on a throne seven times more resplendent than the sun. The Angel of Vengeance is also found in this heaven. Enoch said that it is in this heaven that the angels sing the holy Trisagion every evening. During the day they are silent so that God may hear the prayers of Israel.

Sixth Heaven

Its name in Hebrew is Zebul and its regent prince is either Gabriel and Zadkiel, as most authorities are not sure of the rulership of this heaven. It is in the Sixth Heaven where all natural disasters, such as hurricanes, plagues, earthquakes, floods, tornadoes, and other acts of God, are kept. It is also here where the Guardian Angel of Heaven and Earth resides, who is made of fire and snow, according to the Muslims. It is said that it is in the Sixth Heaven that angels study astrology.

Seventh Heaven

Its name in Hebrew is Araboth and its regent prince is Michael, although some authorities assign it to Casiel. According to the Judeo-Christian tradition, God's abode is in the Seventh Heaven, and it is in this sphere where the spirits of human beings not yet born live. In the Seventh Heaven the prophet Isaiah heard God formulate the plan of the life of Jesus on Earth. It is also the abode of the Seraphim, the Powers, and the angel Zagzaguel, Prince of the Divine Law.

Angelic Princes

The principal source of the names of the regent princes of the Seven Heavens is the *Third Book of Enoch*, which is part of the *Pseudepigrapha*.

This book describes the strict protocol of Heaven, the interrelationship between the angels of the various choirs, and the mutual respect and homage they share with each other. The power and majesty of the great angels is described at length, especially the princes of the celestial choirs, who are presented in ascending order, as well as the exalted spirits who are closest to the Divine Presence. It is the great Archangel Metraton, into whom Enoch was transformed eventually, who reveals to Enoch the secrets of the angelic hierarchy and the structure of the heavenly host who are called the Celestials.

Each regent prince presides over one of the hosts, composed of 496,000 myriads of angelic ministers. All these angels ride on celestial horses and when they meet their regent prince face to face, they dismount and lay prone at his feet. All the prince regents wear crowns and have mantles draped over their shoulders. All of them also carry scepters.

Each prince takes off his crown and pays homage at the feet of the prince regent of the choir higher than his. For example, Sidriel, prince regent of the First Heaven, takes off his crown and lays at the feet of Barakiel, regent of the Second; Barakiel pays

Figure 15: The Heavens.

the same homage to Baradiel, regent of the Third Heaven; Baradiel honors Zahakiel, regent of the Fourth, in the same manner; and this protocol is observed through the Seventh Heaven.

Under the aegis of the prince regents of the Seven Heavens are the following Sarim, or angelic princes:

Gallaliel—who is in charge of the sun.

Ophaniel—who is in charge of the moon.

Rahatiel—who is in charge of the constellations.

Kokabiel—who is in charge of the stars.

Superior to all the regent princes are the Princes of the seventy-two Kingdoms of the Altitudes, which correspond to the seventy-two nations of the Earth. Michael, regent prince of the Seventh Heaven, removes his crown of glory and pays homage at the feet of these seventy-two princes.

Superior to the Princes of the seventy-two Kingdoms of the Altitudes are the Guardians of the Gates of the Seven Palaces that are in Araboth, the Seventh Heaven. And the seventy-two princes remove their crowns and pay homage at the feet of these higher beings. The Guardians of each of the seven palaces pay the same homage to the Guardians of the superior palaces.

The Guardian of the Seventh Palace removes his crown of glory and pays homage at the feet of the four great princes who guard the four encampments of the Shekinah.

Superior to the four Guardians of the four encampments of the Shekinah is Tagas, who leads all the Celestials. And the four Guardians remove their crowns and render homage at his feet.

Superior to Tagas is Barattiel, who holds the Seven Heavens with three fingers. Tagas pays dutiful homage at his feet.

Superior to Barattiel is Hamon, a terrible prince, greatly feared because of his awesome powers. Hamon is in charge of leading the holy Trisagion. Barattiel renders homage at his feet.

Infinitely superior to Hamon are the angelic princes who have the honor of adding the four letters of God's holy name to their own. This name is known as the Tetragrammaton and it is composed of the letters YHVH, commonly spelled out as Jehovah or Yaweh. The first of these exalted spirits is Tatrasiel YHVH and Hamon removes his crown and lays at his feet.

These superior beings are nine:

1. Tatrasiel YHVH
2. Atrugiel YHVH
3. Naaririel YHVH
4. Sasnigiel YHVH
5. Zazriel YHVH

6. Gevuratiel YHVH

7. Arapiel YHVH

8. Asroilu YHVH

9. Gallisur YHVH

Each of these great princes removes his crown and pays homage at the feet of the prince superior to him.

Superior to Gallisur YHVH is Zakzakiel YHVH, who inscribes the merits of Israel in God's crown.

Superior to Zakzakiel YHVH is Anapiel YHVH, who is in charge of the keys to the seven palaces of Araboth and whose majesty and glory transcends all the realms of the Seventh Heaven.

Superior to Anapiel YHVH is Soterasiel YHVH, who guards the four gateways of the river of fire that runs through Araboth. None of the celestial princes may enter or leave the presence of the Shekinah without his permission.

Superior to Soterasiel YHVH is Sokedhozi YHVH, who weighs the good deeds of human beings on a balance in front of the Creator.

Superior to Sokedhozi YHVH is Sehanpuryu YHVH, who has the power to extinguish the river of fire that runs through Araboth.

Superior to Sehanpuryu YHVH is Azbogah YHVH, the most beloved and terrible prince, who knows the secrets of God's Throne, provides the physical bodies to souls at birth, and gives them eternal life when they die.

Superior to Azbogah YHVH is the dual spirit Soperiel YHVH, who manifests as two separate entities. One of these has the power to give life and the other to take it away. This is the spirit who is in charge of the Book of the Living, those to whom God has granted the gift of life.

Superior to Soperiel YHVH is Rikbiel YHVH, who is in charge of the wheels of the Merkabah or Divine Chariot that transports the Shekinah.

Superior to Rikbiel YHVH is Hayliel YHVH, who is so immense in stature that he could swallow the world in one gulp. This angel is in charge of the holy creatures who sing the divine Trisagion, and whom he leads with a fire whip.

Superior to Hayliel YHVH is Kerubiel YHVH, who is the regent of the Cherubim. His body is made of burning coals and his stature surpasses the length and width of the Seven Heavens. His face is made of flames, his eyes are like sparks of fire, and his eyelashes are like bolts of lightning. He is a righteous and majestic prince whose presence is revered by myriads of angelic legions. He wears a crown inscribed with God's name from which emanates the light of a thousand suns. The Shekinah's rainbow is extended over his shoulders and all his body is covered with eyes. He is surrounded by wings from head to foot and his presence is always preceded by thunder and lightning. The Cherubim, who are under his rule, are the servants of the Shekinah and her Glory rests on their backs. For that reason their faces shine with God's glory and they are covered with sapphires, which is the stone sacred to the Shekinah. Kerubiel YHVH organizes their numbers in exquisite formations and exhorts them constantly to carry on God's will because God's glory rests eternally over their heads.

Superior to Kerubiel YHVH is Ophaniel YHVH, who is the ruling prince of the Ophanim or Thrones. This angel has sixteen faces, four on each side of his head; a hundred wings on each side of his body, and 8,766 eyes from which rush forward many bolts of lightning. All those who dare look at him face to face are burned to ashes instantly. He is the tallest of all the angels. His body has a height of a journey of 2,500 years and no one knows the extent of his powers except God himself. The Thrones, who are under his rule, are clothed with sapphires and emeralds and their radiance extends throughout the Seventh Heaven.

Superior to Ophaniel YHVH is Seraphiel YHVH, a great celestial prince full of praises and divine splendor, who is the supreme regent of the Seraphim. His face is that of an angel, but he has the body of an immense eagle. The sapphire that reposes over his head is as large as the Earth. His body is covered with millions of eyes that shine like stars. His crown reflects the light of God's Throne and his height is that of a journey of 502 years. The Seraphim, who are under his rule, are instructed constantly by him to praise God unceasingly with psalms, prayers, and continuous majesty. The Seraphim are made of fire. It is said that each day Satan, who at one time belonged to the choir of the Seraphim, joins Samael, the Angel of Destruction, and together they write Israel's sins on tablets, which they give to the Seraphim to bring to God's Throne. If these tablets were to reach the Creator, he would have to destroy Israel for trespassing the Commandments. But the Seraphim know that God does not desire to destroy Israel and they never give him the tablets, which are destroyed in the river of fire that runs in front of God's Throne. Michael, who is the Prince of the Seraphim, is guardian and protector of Israel, which may explain this protective action of the Seraphim on behalf of Israel.

The highest in rank of the celestial princes is Radweriel YHVH, whose majesty is exalted above all the ministering angels. This divine prince is in charge of the holy archives, where the scrolls with God's laws and decrees are kept. Radweriel YHVH places these scrolls directly into the hands of the Creator, who then gives them to the Divine Scribes so that they may read them in front of the Great Celestial Council. The power of this divine spirit is so awesome that angels are formed with every word he utters. This is difficult to comprehend, as Enoch, who gives us the descriptions of the great angels, also says that God created all the angels simultaneously.

There are four celestial princes, known as the Guardians and the Holy Beings. These are divided into two Guardians and two Holy Beings, and they always surround God's majesty. These are the Divine Counselors, with whom God holds a holy conclave before he passes judgment or makes a decision about human beings.

According to Enoch, there is a river of fire in the Seventh Heaven. Before they sing the holy Trisagion, the angels bathe in this river and dip their tongues in its flames to be worthy of singing the divine praises. After this ritual purification, they don tunics of blinding light and proceed to sing the Trisagion.

The fire whip, which was already mentioned, is used to punish the angels when they do not discharge their duties with sufficient speed and to remind them that in spite of their exalted ranks, God is still above them. In the *Third Book of Enoch*, the Archangel Metraton told the patriarch that in one occasion Elisha (Aber) arrived in front of God's Throne. Upon seeing the great light emitted by Metraton, who sits to the right of the Creator, he murmured in astonishment: "There are two powers in Heaven!" This is a great offense to God, whose most important quality is union, as he is only One from whom all things proceed. As soon as he uttered these sacrilegious words, Elisha was banished from the Divine Presence and Anapiel YHVH, who is in charge of the keys of the Seven Palaces of Araboth, struck Metraton with sixty lashes of fire to put him in his proper place.

The Seven Heavens are identified with the seven planets, each of which is ruled by a celestial prince. The Seven Heavens are also identified with the Greek Olympus and divided into 196 provinces, each of which is ruled by an Olympic Spirit. From these identifications we can see that to the ancients the Seven Heavens were in reality our solar system, while God was the universe.

5

The Divine Presence

The two most detailed descriptions of Heaven are found in the Book of Revelation, also known as the Apocalypse, and the apocryphal *Books of Enoch*. According to Genesis, Enoch was the son of Seth, Adam's third son. Methuselah, Enoch's son, is the biblical personage of greatest longevity, having lived 969 years. Methuselah was Noah's grandfather and died the same year of the universal deluge. Enoch did not live half as long as his son, but he also enjoyed a long life, which lasted 365 years, the same length of days as the solar year.

Although the biblical tradition says that Enoch wrote hundreds of books, the most popular of these is the one known simply as the *Book of Enoch*, which is divided in three parts: the *First*, the *Second*, and the *Third*

Book of Enoch. In these three books, the patriarch relates his apocalyptic visions, including his visits to the celestial mansions and the rebellion of some of the members of the heavenly hosts, which were later to be known as the fallen angels.

Enoch says that some of the rebellious angels, terrified of the punishment that they would surely receive from God for their transgressions, asked him to intercede on their behalf. Enoch, who was a scribe, immediately wrote the angel's petition and read it several times before falling asleep. He then had a dream where he was transported to Heaven by a great whirlwind. The first thing he saw was an immense crystal rampart surrounded by tongues of fire. He crossed the flames and found himself in front of a magnificent palace, also made of crystal. Its ceiling was crisscrossed by light-ning bolts and rushing stars and flaming Cherubim. Above this awesome spectacle there was a firmament of clear waters. Daz-zling fire columns surrounded the walls of this palace and its gates were also framed with roaring flames.

Enoch entered this formidable fortress and found that it was simultaneously incan-descent, like fire, and freezing, like ice. The pleasures of life did not exist therein. Terror-stricken, the patriarch fell face down on the shimmering floor, shaking uncontrollably. He was then transported to a second palace, larger than the first. Its gate, which was opened in front of him, was also formed of tongues of fire. This structure was more dazzling than the one he had just visited and was made entirely of fire, from the floor to the ceiling, and stars and lightning bolts also crossed overhead.

From his position outside the gate, Enoch could see a great Throne inside the palace, carved of the purest crystal. This Throne had wheels of blazing suns and it was en-compassed by a myriad Cherubim. From beneath the Throne rushed forth a fire so brilliant it blinded the patriarch. God's Glory was seated on this Throne and his vestments were whiter than snow and brighter than the sun.

None of the angels who surrounded the Throne could look at the Creator because of the blinding radiance emanated by his pres-ence. No living being could behold him. A blazing fire encircled him and another fire of great splendor burned before the Throne. Legions of celestial beings surrounded God's Glory, but he had no need of atten-dants. The highest spirits of his heavenly court were always by his side, remaining in his Presence eternally.

During this time, Enoch remained pros-trated on the ground, unable to move or speak. Then God himself asked the patri-arch to come forward. One of the celestial beings who surrounded the Throne lifted Enoch from the ground and brought him to the Holy Presence. Enoch lowered his head before the Creator and heard him pass judg-ment on the rebellious angels. Enoch's inter-cession was acknowledged, but the petition was denied. The fallen angels were con-demned to expiate their sins against God and humanity through eternal captivity.

Enoch's description of God's abode was written approximately two hundred years before the birth of Christ. Modern histori-ans do not believe that Enoch was the au-thor of this apotheosic account because the legendary patriarch is said to have lived 5,000 years before Christ. But whoever wrote the story had a great influence on the authors of the Gospels of Saint John and Saint Matthew, who accepted it as a divinely inspired vision.

An apocalyptic vision is a divine revela-tion and the name of its author is not as important as the message it reveals. Belief in the Scriptures and what we are told by the apocryphal books is a matter of faith. The human spirit chooses the path it will follow, be it guided by faith or by logic. But there is a thin line between faith and logic that must be counterbalanced by intuition. And very often, intuition rejects cold rationalization in favor of faith, and when this happens we are seldom led astray. There are things that defy logical explanations and, in spite of the historical arguments, the Judeo-Christian world still reels under the profound impact of Enoch's story. We wonder at its majesty and dare to hope that someday we may also find ourselves facing that Throne of crystal and fire.

The Book of Revelation, which Christian tradition adjudicates to the apostle Saint John, was written approximately eighty years after Christ, probably in the small island of Patmos where its author was exiled.

In chapter 4 of Revelation, John describes the Divine Presence as follows:

After these things I looked, and behold,
a door standing open in Heaven.
And the first voice which I heard
was like a trumpet speaking with me,
saying: "Come up here, and I will
show you things which must take
place after this."

Immediately I was in the Spirit;
and behold, a throne set in Heaven,
and ONE sat on the throne.

And He who sat there was like a jasper
and a sardius stone in appearance; and
there was a rainbow around the throne,
in appearance like an emerald.

Around the throne were twenty-four
thrones, and on the thrones I saw
twenty-four elders sitting, clothed
in white robes, and they had crowns
of gold on their heads.

And from the throne proceeded
lightnings, thunderings, and voices.
And there were seven lamps of fire
burning before the throne, which
are the seven spirits of God.

Before the throne there was a sea of
glass, like crystal. And in the midst
of the throne, and around the throne,
were four living creatures full of eyes
in front and in back.

The first living creature was like a lion,
the second living creature like a calf,
the third living creature had a face like
a man, and the fourth living creature
was like a flying eagle.

Figure 16: The apocalyptic procession.

And the four living creatures, each having six wings, were full of eyes around and within. And they do not rest day or night, saying: "Holy, holy, holy, Lord God Almighty, who was and is and is to come!"

Whenever the living creatures give glory and honor and thanks to Him who sits on the throne, who lives forever and ever,

the twenty-four elders fall down before Him who sits on the throne and worship Him who lives forever and ever, and cast their crowns before the throne, saying:

"You are worthy, O Lord, to receive glory and honor and power; for You created all things, and by Your will they exist and were created."

This vision of John's was clearly inspired and deeply influenced by Enoch's account of God's Throne and the Divine Presence. The description of the Throne and the fire and crystal that surround it, as well as the "thunderings and lightnings," are all part of Enoch's vision. The four living creatures with six wings are clearly Enoch's flaming Cherubim, although John's account makes them more similar to the traditional depiction of the Seraphim. The twenty-four elders of John's vision may be identified with the celestial beings described by Enoch.

In spite of the undeniable similarities between Enoch and John's vision of the Throne and God's Presence, John is more descriptive of the heavenly abode and the living creatures that inhabit it. The four faces on these beings were later adjudicated to the four astrological triplicities: the creature with a face like a lion represents the sign of Leo; the calf (bull) represents Taurus; the eagle is a symbol of Scorpio; and the man represents Aquarius. They also represent the four elements: fire, earth, water, and air, respectively. Christianity identifies the living creatures with the four evangelists: the lion is Saint Mark; the calf or bull is Saint Luke; the eagle is Saint John; and the man is Saint Matthew.

Creation

One of the most fascinating explanations of the Creation of the universe is the one given by the Kabbalah. What makes the kabbalistic concept of Creation so astonishing is that it adheres in principle to what astrophysics tells us about this momentous event. In my book *A Kabbalah for the Modern World*, I make an extensive comparison between the kabbalistic vision and the cosmogonic theories of modern science.

Figure 17: The Creation of Light.

The Kabbalah teaches that the universe was created by God, an omniscient, omnipotent, and indefinable being who exists beyond the cosmos.

Before creation, there was Nothing, only empty space. That immense vacuum was the Divine Presence, unknowable and incomprehensible. The Kabbalah calls it the AIN, Nothingness. But although it is Nothing, this Presence is immanent, conscious, and all-knowing. It is Nothing because it has no form or physicality; it is pure Intelligence.

AIN, the Divine Presence, wished to manifest as matter and have form. To achieve this manifestation It transformed Its essence from Nothing into Something. This Something is called AIN SOPH and is pure light. It is total light, dazzling and blinding light that extends beyond the confines of the created universe and millions of other universes. AIN SOPH is endless, infinite, and eternal. It is God manifested, without measure or limitations, a concept impossible to comprehend by the human mind.

To express his essence in a physical form, God concentrated one single point of his infinite light and sent it through the vacuum of space. This point of concentrated light is called AIN SOPH AUR or Golden Light.

The most important of God's characteristics as AIN is his unity. This means that there is no division in his essence. He is All, while being Nothing. Matter, on the other hand, is expressed through duality. This duality is the first manifestation of God in the physical world. He continues to be ONE, but expresses his essence in dual form to create the universe. These two characteristics of matter are known as positive and negative and can be found in everything that exists. Night and day, black and white, feminine and masculine, electron and proton—the whole universe is expressed in this duality.

To achieve material manifestation in dual form, God expressed his essence as masculine and feminine, while still remaining ONE. This unity of God in the material world is recognized in the Jewish daily prayer known as the Shema: "Hear O Israel, the Lord our God is the Eternal. The Eternal is ONE." The greatest offense to God is to deny this unity. In the Book of Isaiah, he says to the prophet: "There is no other God but I. I know of no other." That is, God is the only Creator. All the deities worshiped by other religions are the same God of the Scriptures, with other names.

When he manifested his essence in dual form, the feminine aspect of the Creator restricted her light, leaving an empty space within herself so that the point of light from the AIN SOPH AUR would go through her, thus creating the world of matter. As the ray of light from the AIN SOPH AUR moved through space, it formed a series of concentric circles, each of which condensed the light as it descended. These circles are known as spheres or receptacles of divine light and may be identified with various philosophical and spiritual concepts. Physically, they gave birth to the galaxies, the stars, and the planets, and eventually to the solar system and Earth. In kabbalistic terminology these spheres are known as Sephiroth, and together they form the glyph called the Tree of Life. There are ten Sephiroth and they represent the created universe.

This kabbalistic concept teaches that the universe and everything that exists came into being from one single point of the divine light, which gives us an approximate idea of the awesome magnitude of God's power. Modern astrophysics tells us that the universe was created through a single point of concentrated matter, which then exploded into what is commonly known as the Big Bang. This is entirely in harmony with the kabbalistic view of Creation, which was conceived thousands of years before the Big Bang theory.

This divine light is the manifestation of God in the material world. It is life and awareness. Beyond the physical world, where matter ceases to exist, there is only the unfathomable mystery of God before Creation, which is his true essence.

But the Kabbalah tells us much more. As he sent his light catapulting throughout space, there was so much energy in this light that it could not be contained by the circles or spheres. These dispersed, causing the energy to rush vertiginously through the vac-

uum without balance or control. This disseminated light fell into a chaotic pool known as the abyss. The broken spheres became known as the cosmic shells, where the divine light became obscured and totally impregnated in matter. This darkening of the primordial point is the cradle of all evil and is at the root of every destructive action in the material world. In the Kabbalah, this first imperfect creation is known as the Qliphoth and is the dark side of the Tree of Life, which represents the universe and the Earth. This fall of the light into the abyss may be equated with the fall of the rebellious angels. In astrophysical terms it is known as chaos and can be identified with the laws of quantum physics.

After this cosmic catastrophe, God sent another point of light through space, this time contained and well balanced. This is the actual creation, of which human beings are an intrinsic part. But the divine energies that are still imprisoned in matter must be rescued and returned to their divine source. To accomplish this mission, God created Adam and Eve, but through their sin of disobedience they prolonged the separation between the initial light and the Creator. According to the Kabbalah, this mission is now relegated to the human race, who must transmute the cosmic shells into sparks of light. This can only be accomplished by transcending our human weaknesses, which are an expression of the darkening of the divine light. Each good action transforms the innate evil in us created by the initial fall, causing the darkness within to be turned back into light. The darkened light can be identified with the evil forces that permeate our world, leading humanity into every kind of destructive action.

To help human beings in this awesome task, God sends his divine messengers to the world in an effort to dispel the destructive forces that surround us and keep us away from our divinely appointed task. All the sacred books, from the Bible and the Koran to the Vedas and the Avesta, were also divine instructions given by God to certain chosen people who then passed them on to the rest of humanity to help us achieve our cosmic destiny. The created universe is known in the Kabbalah as Adam Kadmon, the body of God.

The Shekinah

In the first chapter of Genesis, before the creation of Adam and Eve, God says: "Let Us create man in Our image." And then he proceeds to create man and woman. It is clear through this phrase that God was not alone in this moment because he says "us" and "our image." According to the Kabbalah, God was speaking to the Shekinah, who is the feminine aspect of the Creator. As we have already seen, God's manifestation in the material world was accomplished through duality. This duality is typified in Adam and Eve, who were created in God's image, male and female, the Divine King and his Shekinah.

The mystery of the Shekinah is also expressed in the concept of the Holy Spirit. In the Gospel according to Saint Luke, Jesus says that God forgives every sin, except an offense against the Holy Spirit. This Holy Spirit is the Shekinah, God's beloved, the Mother of the Holy Trinity. God's love for the Shekinah is self-love, for he and she are ONE.

The Shekinah is the Cosmic Mother, often identified with the forces of nature. All the goddesses of every religion, past and present, are aspects of the Shekinah, and all the various avatars of the Virgin Mary are seen as representations of God's feminine principle on the material plane.

God the Father and God the Mother are a cosmic unity. Their union is an act of love on a cosmic plane, similar to the union of two lovers on the physical world. The sexual pleasure shared by a man and a woman is an imperfect copy of the cosmic bliss shared by God and his Shekinah. Its physical duration is also infinitesimal compared with the eternal and pure ecstasy of divine union. This ecstasy without end is known in Buddhism as nirvana.

The Shekinah is known in the Kabbalah as the Divine Bride but she is also the Mother and the Sister to humanity. She is the architect of Creation because it was through her voluntary act of restricting her light that the universe came into being. This

Figure 18: The Queen of Heaven.

action was undertaken through the Word, the sound, emitted by God the Father at the moment of Creation. This Verb, known as God's Word, was conceived and gestated by the Shekinah in the same way a woman conceives and gestates a child. That is why in Christianity Jesus is identified as the Verb made into flesh because he was conceived by Mary through the power of the Holy Spirit, who is the Cosmic Mother.

In *The Divine Comedy*, Dante Alighieri makes a reference to the Shekinah. This work is a poem written in tersa rima and is divided in three parts: Inferno, Purgatory, and Paradise. In the tenth canto of Paradise, Dante says that God's Bride arises early in the morning to sing her praises to her divine consort that he may love her.

Part of the human tragedy is what is known in the Kabbalah as the Shekinah's exile. Because of Adam and Eve's sin, and their failure to rescue the divine light from its prison of darkness, the Shekinah must remain on Earth, separated from her divine spouse. She unites with him only on Fridays at midnight, which is the ideal time for human couples to unite in love. At this hour, the Divine Presence, Father, Mother, ONE, are united and extend their blessing over all lovers.

In the same way that God's spirit manifests his/her essence as male and female, so does the human spirit. Because the Shekinah is in exile and separated from her male counterpart, the human spirit is likewise separated at birth in two parts, and only the male or the female part is born. The second half may be born later in another body, or may remain in the spiritual plane, awaiting the return of its twin soul after its brief sojourn on Earth. This belief is found in other religions and is known as the concept of twin souls. It is said that if the two halves of the same spirit meet on Earth, something which is not very common, they recognize each other immediately and they will never separate.

According to this concept, the powerful attraction called love takes place because the person we feel attracted to reminds us, unconsciously, of our other half. That is the reason why it is possible to love more than one person in a lifetime. Each of those persons awakens echoes in our spirits of our true and everlasting love, our twin soul. This also explains unrequited love, when we fall in love with someone who does not return our affection. This happens because although that person reminds us of our twin soul, he or she is also looking for the other aspect of their soul, which we do not resemble. The total union with our twin soul can only take place when the Shekinah is reunited for all eternity with her divine consort.

According to the *Third Book of Enoch*, after God exiled Adam and Eve from the Garden of Eden, the Shekinah remained in Eden and established her residence over one of the Cherubim under the Tree of Life. Many angels descended from Heaven continuously to minister to the Shekinah and to carry out God's decrees on Earth. The light emitted by the Shekinah was 365,000 times more brilliant than the sun and was extended throughout the planet. Those who were closest to her and basked in her light were free from all illness, disaster, or danger. For that reason, Adam and Eve and their descendants pitched their tents outside the gates of Eden to remain forever under the protection of the Shekinah's light. But the generations that followed Adam and Eve deviated from God's laws and began to worship graven images of gold and precious stones, forsaking the faith of their fathers. The angelic ministers, outraged at these offenses, denounced them in front of the holy Throne and asked that the Shekinah be removed from Eden so that the faithless human race could not bask in her Glory. After hearing their impassioned plea, God hearkened to the request of his angels and took the Shekinah out of Eden, bringing her to Heaven, accompanied by the enraptured singing of the angelic host. But the Shekinah must return to Earth to continue her exile, and this will not end until the original light of Creation returns to its divine source. Each act of kindness, love, and compassion shortens her stay on Earth and rescues some of the sparks of light that are mired in darkness.

The mystery of the Shekinah is encoded in the four letters of the Tetragrammaton, or holy name of God. These four letters, transliterated as YHVH, are rendered—erroneously—as either Jehovah or Yahweh. According to Enoch, all the angels have the four divine letters inscribed in their hearts.

As we have seen, astrophysics is in accordance with the Kabbalah when it theorizes that the universe came into being through a concentrated point of light. A well-known astronomer paraphrased Genesis by saying: "In the beginning there was light—and plenty of it." But what scientists cannot explain is where this initial energy came from. Some astrophysicists attempt to explain this conundrum by asserting that the energy was always there, an explanation that is not logically acceptable because the universe is based on the laws of cause and effect. If everything has a cause and an origin, why not Creation?

Many astronomers and astrophysicists, faced with the increasing and undeniable evidence of a Supreme Intelligence at work in the universe, have opted to express their belief that the cosmos is the result of a divine plan. Paul Davies, a renowned mathematical physicist from Adelaide University in Australia, wrote in *The Mind of God*, one of his many books about the mysteries of the universe, that our presence on Earth is not the result of a coincidence. In his opinion, we are supposed to be here. The impli-

Figure 19: The Virgin Mary and baby Jesus surrounded by angels.

cation is that there is a cosmic plan at work and that we are an intrinsic part of that plan. What that plan is and how we fit in it is something that science cannot yet tell us. Kabbalah says that we are here to transcend matter, to do good, and in this manner help purify the imprisoned light of the Creator. But it is simplistic to imagine that we are here simply to observe a strict moral code and be kind and just. Being righteous and ethical has far deeper implications. A righteous and ethical individual functions for the good of society in general. A perfectly harmonized society would work in unison for the advancement of humanity and all living things on this planet. This would mean advancements in science, economics, ecology, social reforms, and spiritual evolution. Such a society would rescue the light of the intellect from the darkness of ignorance and moral degradation. In time, it could reach out to the stars and the universal light from where it came.

The *Book of Enoch* describes the Divine Presence as light of blinding intensity. The ceiling of the celestial palace is rent by the passage of myriad stars and lightning bolts. If we stop to consider this description, we can see that what Enoch described is the cosmos.

The most powerful source of light in the universe proceeds from gamma rays, which are billions and billions of times brighter than the sun. In May 1997, astronomers detected a gamma ray burst that they believe originated at a distance of more than seven billion light years away, far beyond our galaxy. In spite of this immense distance, the gamma ray radiation could be detected by several observatories, suggesting that they must have been powered by a catastrophic explosion of awesome proportions. Astronomers calculate that the gamma rays had been travelling toward Earth from the time the universe was half its present age of approximately fourteen billion years. This was the first time these gamma "bursters" had been detected. But on December of the same year a second burst of gamma rays was discovered, this time about twelve billions of light years away. This time scientists were able to pinpoint the source of the radiation, Galaxy K, which has been receding from Earth at astonishing speeds. The energy emitted by the gamma burst from this galaxy is said to be several hundred times greater than the explosion of a supernova, which is the most violent cosmic blast known to astronomers until now. More disturbing still, astronomers say that these gamma bursts are not uncommon and more than 2,000 have been detected since 1991. The powerful explosion detected in December 1997 might have destroyed the human race had it occurred around 3,000 light years from Earth. And scientists believe that because of their random distribution throughout the universe, some of these gamma ray blasts must be relatively close to Earth.

The source of the gamma ray bursts has astronomers in a bit of a quandary. Some theorize that they may be the result of an apotheosic collision between two neutron stars, while others suggest that they may be caused by the violent coupling of two black holes. Within our own galaxy, and too close for comfort, there are at least four known neutron stars that could explode in this manner, wiping out all life on Earth in a matter of seconds.

At the time of the December event, one of the astrophysicists at the University of California at Berkeley, Dr. Alexei V. Filippenko, said that while gamma ray bursters are definitely a potential threat to life on Earth, his group did not see a statistical likelihood of one going off near us for many millions of years. He spoke too soon. On August 27, 1998, Earth was hit by a powerful blast of electromagnetic radiation that stripped atoms of their electrons, disrupted radio transmissions, and caused temporary shutdowns on at least seven spacecrafts. The source of this blast was largely due to gamma rays and other cosmic particles, this time emitted by a magnetic flare on a star some 20,000 light years away. If the explosion had been 3,000 light years away, instead of 20,000, Earth as we know it would have ceased to exist. What this event tells us is that gamma ray explosions could come at any moment, not several million years from now.

What kind of light is so powerful that it can be seen billions of light years away? Our own sun can blind us if we stare at its light for only a few minutes. Gamma rays much further away from us than the sun would not simply blind us but would disintegrate us and absorb us into their light. Some people believe that the gamma rays are the ultimate expression of God's light in the universe, and that it is this light that is perceived during deep states of meditation. There is also speculation about the existence of a gigantic source of gamma rays, similar to a central sun, in the middle of the universe. It is believed that this unfathomable light is the entrance to the tunnel of light described by people who have had near-death experiences. Still others assert that gamma rays are the entrance to the celestial mansions described by Enoch. As farfetched as these speculations may sound, we should consider that Enoch's description of the celestial realms is largely symbolic, and that he was referring to states of consciousness rather than to a physical place. But the physical and the spiritual can both be explained in astrophysical terms through the field of quantum physics that deals in subatomic particles and all forms of radiation, of which light is an intrinsic part.

The ancient kabbalists would say that gamma ray bursts are the divine sparks of light mired in darkness—uncontrolled energy, threatening and destructive, in the grip of negative forces that seek only the cataclysmic annihilation of the cosmic order and the triumph of chaos in the universe. The chaotic behavior of subatomic particles is the main subject of quantum physics.

According to the Kabbalah, this unbalanced energy that surrounds us in the form of gamma ray bursts may eventually disintegrate us unless we complete our appointed mission on this planet and rescue the divine light from the darkness of chaos.

6

Paradise

The word paradise is derived from the ancient Persian *pairidaeza*, and means "enclosure." It later came to mean a pleasure garden with parks and animal sanctuaries and, conversely, a place or state of bliss. For this reason, it is sometimes associated with Heaven. The ancient Hebrews, who lived for many centuries in Persia, used the word to describe the Garden of Eden, the original abode of Adam and Eve.

According to Genesis, from the Garden of Eden flowed a river with four tributaries. These four currents are named in the Bible as the Tigris, the Euphrates, the Gihon, and the Pison rivers. The last two could have been the names of the Nile river and the Persian Gulf in ancient times.

According to Genesis, God told Adam that he could eat from the fruits of all the trees in Eden, except those from the Tree of Good and Evil. If he were to eat from that tree, he would die. That means that Adam and Eve were created immortal. When the serpent tempted Eve into eating from the forbidden fruit and Adam ate of it also, God punished them by exiling them from Paradise and taking away their immortality. Genesis tells us that God "dressed" Adam and Eve in tunics of skins before driving them out of the Garden of Eden. These tunics of skins were mortal, physical bodies because before they ate of the Tree of Good and Evil, they were made of pure spirit, as was God himself.

Figure 20: The Archangel Raphael instructing Adam and Eve.

Once Adam and Eve were invested with a material form and exiled from Paradise, they lost the gift of immortality and became doomed to die, as God warned Adam would happen if he ate from the tree. Their place of exile was the physical world, where Eve would know the pains of childbirth and Adam would toil the earth in sweat, and eat bread with hardship until he returned to the dust from which he was created.

From this we can see that Paradise is not of this Earth, and belongs to the realms of the divine. It is not Heaven, but can be found there. According to Saint Paul, Paradise is in the Third Heaven. And the Book of Revelation gives humanity the hope of returning there if we can only triumph over material temptations. Then we can eat of the fruit of the Tree of Life, which is also in Paradise.

The Tree of Life is mentioned in Genesis. When Adam and Eve ate of the Tree of Good and Evil, God said to his Shekinah, "Behold the man has become like one of Us, to know good and evil. And now, lest he put out his hand and take also of the Tree of Life, and eat and live forever . . . therefore the Lord God sent him out of the Garden of Eden to to till the ground from which he was taken" (Gen. 3:22). Therefore the fruit of the Tree of Life imparts the gift of immortality. But God did not forbid Adam and Eve to eat from the Tree of Life originally, for he said that they could eat the fruit of every tree, except that of the Tree of Good and Evil. They could eat

of the Tree of Life because they were already immortal. It was only when they ate of the forbidden fruit, and were divested of their immortality, that God drove them out of Eden so they would not be as God with both immortality and the knowledge of good and evil, which can be equated with the gift of intelligence and reason, the ability to differentiate between things.

In the context of Revelation, we can see that Paradise is a place reserved for the spirits of the saints and those persons who have achieved purification through their control of worldly temptations. It is important to understand that when we speak of Heaven or Paradise we are referring to other dimensions and states of being, not to physical places. When Saint Paul speaks about the Third Heaven he is referring to exalted states of the human superconsciousness once it has transcended the material world.

In *Paradise Lost*, John Milton describes the expulsion of Adam and Eve from Eden in a poem made of twelve cantos or chapters. *Paradise Lost* is intrinsically Christian and tells the story of the first disobedience of humanity, its temptation, its fall, and the promise of redemption through Jesus Christ. In the poem, Satan is the adversary of humanity. It begins with an invocation to the celestial muses and goes on to describe in detail the battle between the angels, Satan's expulsion from Heaven, the creation of Hell and of Satan's children who, according to Milton, are sin and death. The book ends with Adam and Eve's exile from Paradise. In losing Paradise, what Adam and Eve are really losing are God's grace and divine ecstasy.

As we saw in the preceding chapter, Dante describes Hell (Inferno), Purgatory, and Paradise with great visual power. Dante's guide during his visit to Hell and Purgatory is the Roman poet Virgil. His guide in Paradise is Beatrice, Dante's beloved. When Dante saw Beatrice for the first time, she was only nine years old and it is doubtful that he ever spoke to her during her lifetime. He loved her always from a distance and in silence, but his great passion for her is expressed throughout his work. After her death at the age of twenty-five, he continued to love her and to idealize her. This love reached its culminating point in *The Divine Comedy* where he envisions her as his celestial guide through Paradise.

In Dante's vision, Heaven is Paradise, and he describes it as surrounded by a wall of flames. Outside this fiery wall are two rivers that erase the memory of all sins and strengthen the memory of every good action.

Dante's Paradise is based on the Ptolemaic cosmic concept, very popular during his time, where the Earth is in the center of nine heavens or celestial spheres, which revolve over it from a great height. These spheres are placed over each other and the speed of their motion is relative to their distance from Earth. Each heaven is governed by one of the angelic choirs and exerts its own special influence over the material world.

Dante's Seven Heavens are represented by the seven planets known in the Middle Ages: Sun, moon, Mars, Mercury, Jupiter, Venus and Saturn. The Eighth Heaven is the sphere of the stars and the Ninth is the Primum Mobile or First Cause, which rules the motion of the heavens from east to west. Far beyond the Nine Heavens is the Empyreum, which is God's abode and that of his saints, a sphere where there is neither time nor space, and where everything is Light.

In December of 1998, the Discovery Channel aired a program on unusual psychic experiences that have baffled scientists. One was the story of an eight-year-old girl who made a drawing of nine concentric spheres flanked on the outside by four angels on the four cardinal points of the drawing. Many smaller angels were drawn around the spheres, all of them with grieving faces. In the center of the spheres was a large black dot that they seemed to surround. It was disturbingly similar to Dante's description of the celestial spheres and Earth, and Gustave Doré's famous illustration of this part of Dante's Paradise was used as a comparison by some of the experts who analyzed the drawing. The child's mother, who related the experience, said the girl came to her, drawing in hand, and asked her point-blank if she was going to die. The mother smiled and told her daughter this was not going to happen, and the child ran away happily and said no more. But three days later the girl died of a ruptured appendix, leaving her mother and a host of experts astonished at her presentiment of her own death and the detailed drawing of the Nine Heavens and the four angels who are said to rule the four cardinal points. One may conjecture that the child might have seen Gustave Doré's illustration of the nine spheres, but why did she draw the four angels, and why did she ask her mother if she were going to die three days before this actually happened? Many similar visions have been recorded all over the world and there seems to be no logical explanation for them, other than the fact that human beings seem to have a subtle connection with other realms of being, or non-being, which so far cannot be explained by science.

The angels, according to Dante's concept, are incorporeal spirits of pure form and total intellect who were created immortal by God. They have the power of will, as do humans, but they have subjugated it to the service of their Creator. Each angelic order is superior to the one beneath it, which they illuminate with their celestial light, inspiring their inhabitants to love God. According to Dante, the vast majority of angels are in continuous contemplation of the Divine Light but some are in charge of the movement of the celestial spheres through the power of their minds.

Both Milton and Dante's visions, expressed in these two immortal poems, reflect their profound knowledge of the Judeo-Christian traditions. Both works are deeply interrelated with the biblical and apocryphal books, including Genesis, the Prophets, Revelation, the *Book of Enoch*, and the Kabbalah. Therefore, even though both works are classified as fiction, it is a fiction based on Christian faith and its many legends.

Hell and Purgatory

Like Paradise, Hell may be seen as a state of conscience, and the torments endured by the condemned souls reflect the horror of the evil acts committed during their human lives, whose memory is their worst punishment. In the Christian tradition, Hell is a mixture of the Jewish *Sheol*, a tenebrous cavern where all spirits go upon death to await the Day of Final Judgment, and the Greek *Gehenna*, where the spirits of evil persons are punished for their sins.

The Christian concept of Hell is also very similar to the Hades of Greek mythology, a somber underground world ruled by the god Pluto. The Christian images of hellfire come from the New Testament, especially Revelation, where Hell is described as a boiling lake of fire and brimstone, which Saint John calls the second death.

The most interesting aspect of the Christian concept of Hell is that only the rebellious souls are condemned to its eternal

Figure 21: The gates of Purgatory.

torments. These are the adamant spirits who refuse to repent from their past sins. This implies that in repentance lies the redemption of the human spirit.

When a sinner repents from his past actions on Earth, his spirit is not condemned to burn forever in the lake of fire and brimstone. Instead, the soul is sent to Purgatory, where it is eventually purified of all sins. How long a soul remains in Purgatory depends on the gravity of his past actions. But if he is truly repentant, his sins will be erased in time by his sufferings in Purgatory, regardless of how terrible they may have been.

In Dante's vision of Purgatory, there is a place called Limbo, a Latin word that means "edge" or "border." The name comes from an ancient belief that Limbo is situated at the edge of Hell, a place between Hell and Purgatory. In Catholic theology, Limbo is the resting place for those souls who have been excluded from Paradise, even though they did not sin. According to this concept, there are two Limbos: the one inhabited by the souls of the just who are awaiting redemption through Jesus Christ, and the one reserved for children who died unbaptized. Among the just awaiting redemption are those who lived before the birth of Jesus and were not Christians. In Limbo can also be found those who did not have time to repent before they died. Dante envisions in Limbo the Greek philosophers, like Aristo-

tle, who did not know Jesus and were not baptized. Limbo is like a waiting room, a place of spiritual suspension, where souls enjoy serenity and natural happiness but that cannot be compared with the supreme bliss of Heaven.

According to Christianity, Purgatory is a state of repentance where the souls of the dead are purified from their venial or lesser sins or receive temporal punishments for their mortal sins.

A sin is a theological term that describes every evil action. It must not be confused with crime, which is a legal word that refers to the serious infraction of the laws that societies impose upon their members. It also differs from vice, a moral term that defines the degrading behavior of an individual in detriment to himself and others. A sin is an act that offends God and breaks his laws. It may be a crime, a vice, or an action not punishable by human law but unacceptable by divine judgment. For example, cruelty and malevolence, jealousy and greed do not break any human law, but they are all sins in the eyes of God.

All the major religions believe in the concept of sin, but differ in their interpretation of its meaning. The doctrine of karma, according to Hinduism, teaches that every human action results in retribution, if it is evil, or recompense, if it is good. This is accomplished through new incarnations. The good actions help the spirit to liberate itself from the influence of the world of the senses and the bad actions degrade it, anchoring it with stronger ties to the wheel of karma and a continuous cycle of incarnations. Only when the spirit ceases to act or to desire does it break its ties to the karmic wheel and cease to incarnate, joining the divine fountain of light that is its true origin.

Judaism, Christianity, and Islam teach that sin is an offense to God. In the Old Testament, sin is a rebellious act against one or more of God's laws. The first sin was Adam and Eve's act of disobedience and its effects are still being felt by their descendants, the human race. According to Christianity, the original sin affected humanity so deeply that every human being is born a sinner and this tendency to sin is profoundly ingrained in our natures. The passion and death of Jesus Christ erased the original sin from our spiritual slates, but did not diminish our inclination to sin. In Christianity, we can sin not only by action but also by every thought and inclination that is opposed to divine law.

According to the Bible, there are seven mortal sins. These are Pride, Avarice, Gluttony, Lust, Envy, Rage, and Sloth. Of these seven sins, Pride is the one that most effectively separates humanity from divine grace. In Christianity, the remission of sins is possible only through Jesus Christ, whose death and ultimate sacrifice liberates the repentant sinner from the jaws of sin.

Purgatory, where souls are cleansed from their sins, is a state of intense spiritual suffering, but contrary to Hell, it is only a temporal suffering.

According to the Roman Catholic Church, the purification experienced by a soul in Purgatory is accomplished through fire. The Greek Orthodox Church does not define the type of purification undergone by souls in Purgatory, and considers it a state of tribulation.

The Heavenly Court

The *Book of Enoch* tells us that every morning God passes judgment on humanity in the heavenly court, accompanied by his Angelic Ministers. Only the Angelic Princes who bear the holy letters of God's name, YHVH, may participate in the divine proceedings. Surrounding the Divine Presence are the two Guardians and the two Holy Beings who act as divine counselors. Radweriel YHVH places in the hands of God the scrolls where the divine decrees are written. The Creator then gives the scrolls to the holy scribes so that they may read them to the Celestials. Soperiel YHVH then opens the books of life and death.

God is arrayed in a garment of righteousness, whiter than snow and more resplendent than a million suns. His hair is white as wool. Each action on Earth and in the whole universe is carefully described, and perfect

Figure 22: Purified souls in the sun sphere.

judgment is passed on it. God's judgment is perfect because it is based on Justice, Mercy, and Truth. Mercy is at his left, Justice at his right, and Truth in front of him. These three virtues are represented by the three columns of the Tree of Life.

The Divine Throne is held aloft by the holy creatures known as the Hayyoth, belonging to the Angelic Order of the Powers. Each of these beings holds the throne with three fingers. Facing the Throne is a curtain inscribed with all the human generations and every action of every person to the last generation. This means that although God granted the gift of free will to human beings he knows, because of his omniscience, what each person will do throughout his or her life.

According to Enoch, when God sits on his Throne of Judgment, he decides who will live and who will die on that day. The Angels of Mercy are on his right, the Angels of Peace are on his left, and the Angels of Destruction are in front of him. The Angels of Mercy grant the gift of life to human beings. The Angels of Destruction bring about death. The Angels of Peace ensure that there is balance in the judgment.

A scribe is below the Throne and another scribe is above it. The Seraphim, clothed in glory, surround the Throne with walls of lightning on its four sides, and the Ophanim surround the walls with tongues of flame. In front of the Throne are the heavenly hosts of the Seventh Heaven, led by Michael, and their numbers are 496,000 milliard armies and each army is made of 496,000 angels of light. A milliard is the equivalent of a billion.

All the angels sing the divine Trisagion. When they finish singing God's praises, the angels are transformed into sparks and flames of light. Some adopt female forms and the same amount adopt male forms, and they all tremble with love and awe at the glory of God.

When a human soul arrives at the Divine Presence and receives his grace, a ray of light emanates from the Divine Mercy and shimmers in front of the soul. The spirit falls down immediately at the feet of God and all the Angels of Destruction move back a step because that soul has received God's pardon.

Even though there is a perfect balance in God's judgment, he always inclines toward Mercy because it is upon this virtue that he has established his Throne.

There are seventy-two Angelic Princes who bear God's holy name and they are all present during each judgment. The great Archangel Metraton, who is the Guardian Prince of this world, is also present because it is he who intercedes for humanity and asks God's Mercy for our sins.

The Final Judgment

The end of the human history is known as the Day of the Lord and the Day of Final Judgment, when both the living and the dead will be judged according to their actions. That apotheosic moment marks the return of the souls of the elect to Paradise. Both Judaism and Christianity believe in that awesome event, which will be announced by the sound of Gabriel's trumpet.

The concept of a Final Judgment comes from Zoroastrianism. Many of the elements of Zoroaster's vision about the end of time, which was conceived as a battle between the forces of good and evil, were adopted by Judaism, and later absorbed by Christianity and Islam. The angels are an intrinsic part of this apocalyptic scene. And although it is God who passes judgment on humanity and the fallen angels, it is the angels of light who will carry out his decrees on this supreme day.

According to the New Testament, the Final Judgment will be carried out by Jesus Christ, seated at the right of God the Father. This moment is known as the Second Coming of Jesus and the Final Judgment as a manifestation of his eternal victory over evil.

The Catholic Credo mentions this Judgment and also the resurrection of the flesh. The idea of the resurrection of the physical body after death can be found in Egyptian mythology, in Zoroastrianism, in Judaism, and in Islam. In Christianity, the concept of the resurrection of the dead is based on the resurrection of Jesus. The Gnostics, who were branded as heretics by the medieval Church, rejected the idea of the resurrection of the body because they believed that Heaven was a spiritual realm and the human body had no place in it.

The Book of Revelation is the last book of the New Testament and it is divided in two parts: seven epistles written by Saint John to the seven cities of Asia Minor and a series of prophetic visions about the Final Judgment. The book describes in detail the great battle that is to take place between the Archangel Michael and the heavenly host against Satan and the fallen angels. At the end of this celestial war, Michael throws Satan and the rebellious legions toward Earth. Revelation describes the seven angels who are in charge of carrying out the preliminaries of this last day. Each angel has a trumpet and each time he blows it, terrible calamities rain upon Earth. Among the many angels that take part in this devastation are the seven angels of the plagues who empty the cups of God's ire over the world. There are also the angels of the four winds, the angel crowned with a rainbow, the angel of the bottomless pit, the angel of the Epistles, the angel of harvests, and the angel who announced the fall of Babylon. The Seraphim and the billions of angels that surround God's Throne complete this terrifying vision of the heavenly host on Judgment Day.

According to Revelation, when human beings appear in front of God's Throne to receive the Final Judgment, those who are not inscribed in the Book of Life will be thrown to the lake of fire, which will be the second death. After Judgment Day, God will create a new Heaven and a new Earth. A new Jerusalem will descend from the heights, gloriously arrayed like a bride for her spouse. God will remain with the new humanity and death and sorrow will end forever.

The Tree of Life

The Judeo-Christian tradition teaches that the ultimate reward of the elect souls and of the saints is to eat from the fruit of the Tree of Life, which is in Paradise. This confers the gift of eternal life, which belongs only to God, but which human beings can attain through the purification of their sins.

The Tree of Life in the Kabbalah is a glyph or design made of ten spheres known as sephiroth, each of which represents one of God's characteristics and powers, as well as a part of the created universe. The Tree is also a symbol of the human body. Collectively, the ten spheres are a sort of cosmic archive where everything that exists has been encoded. Each sphere or sephira is ruled by one of the many names of God, one of the angelic choirs, and one of the great archangels. The spheres are also adjudicated a great many attributes, such as colors, numbers, planets, perfumes, flowers, herbs, and stones. Human endeavors or interests are also represented in each sphere.

Kabbalah teaches that if one knows the names of God, the choirs, the archangels, and the attributes of each sphere or sephira, it is possible to access the immense cosmic energies within that sphere and achieve anything one might desire.

On the reverse side of the Tree of Life there is another tree known as the Qliphoth, formed of ten adverse or negative spheres. These chaotic sephiroth are unbalanced and are diametrically opposite to the harmonious forces of the Tree of Life. These are considered malefic and represent the infernal legions. Each virtue, symbolized by one of the sephira of the Tree of Life, has a corresponding vice in the opposite sephira of the Qliphoth. The two trees are like two sides of the same coin. The last or tenth sphere of the Tree of Life, known as Malkuth, represents the Earth or material world. This last sphere is the First Sephira of the Qliphoth. For that reason, the material world is part of both trees because the sphere of Malkuth fell from grace through Adam and Eve's fall. Because the world of matter rests on top of the Qliphoth, or infernal tree, the influence of its demonic forces is felt continuously on Earth.

The Prince Regent of the Qliphoth is Samael, the angel of poison and death, often identified with Satan and who rules the first sphere corresponding to Earth. That is the reason why Jesus called Satan the prince of this world. The second sphere is ruled by one of Samael's four wives, Eisheth Zenunim, known as the harlot. Of the union between Samael and Eisheth Zenunim is born Chiva (who is not to be confused with the Hindu god Shiva), who represents the third sphere. The seven remaining spheres correspond to the Seven Hells inhabited by demons that represent every vice and crime committed by humanity.

Another of Samael's four wives is the hellish Lilith, sworn enemy of childhood, who is the destroyer of small children. The secret kabbalistic tradition teaches that Lilith was Adam's first wife, to whom she bore one hundred children each day. This account is found in the apocryphal *Book of Adam and Eve*. This tradition also teaches that Lilith and not Eve was the real mother of Cain. After Adam's fall, Lilith was set loose upon the world, where she will continue to unleash her demonic rage against children until the end of time and Judgment Day.

The Tree of Life represents cosmic states in different degrees of evolution and its power is universal. It is possible, through knowledge of the Tree, to eat of its divine fruit and thus acquire eternal life. To accomplish this it is necessary to know how to apply this wisdom, and this is only possible through the names of God and the archangels associated with each Sephira or sphere. The table on page 96 gives the name of each sphere, the name of God associated with it, the angelic choir, and the archangel that rules it.

In the angelic magic of the Kabbalah, the forces of the spheres, including the names of God, the choirs, and the archangels, are invoked to achieve things in the material world. Those readers interested in the magical aspects of the Kabbalah are directed to my book *A Kabbalah for the Modern World*, which gives an in-depth explanation on the subject.

The Names of God

The best known of the names of God is undoubtedly the Tetragrammaton or Great Name of Four Letters. These four letters, as we have already seen, are YHVH. Other transliterations of the Hebrew letters that form the name—Yod, He, Vau, and He—are sometimes given as IEVE, YHWH, or IHVH. Many biblical authorities pronounce this name as Yahweh and the Christian word as Jehovah, but in reality the exact pronunciation of this most holy name of God is unknown. In biblical times, only the high priest of the temple knew the pronunciation of the name, which was uttered only once a year. Because Hebrew does not have any vowels and is composed entirely of consonants, in order to know the pronunciation or the meaning of a word, a series of small dots are placed underneath the consonant that is followed or preceded by a vowel sound. The dots indicate which vowel pertains to what particular word. For example, if we were to write the word "house" without vowels, we would write it as "hs." These two letters could encode any number of words, such as house, his, has, hose, hoes, or hues. It is impossible

The Tree of Life

Sephira	God's Name	Choir	Archangel
1. Kether	Eheieh	Seraphim	Metraton
2. Chokmah	Jehovah	Cherubim	Ratziel
3. Binah	Jehovah Elohim	Thrones	Zaphkiel/Cassiel
4. Chesed	El	Dominions	Zadkiel
5. Geburah	Elohim Gebor	Powers	Camael
6. Tiphareth	Jehovah Elo Ve Daath	Virtues	Raphael
7. Netzach	Jehovah Tzabaoth	Principalities	Anael
8. Hod	Elohim Tzabaoth	Archangels	Michael
9. Yesod	Shaddai El Chai	Angels	Gabriel
10. Malkuth	Adonai Ha Aretz	Ishim (Blessed Souls)	Sandalphon

Among the most important attributes corresponding to the various spheres are the following:

Attributes of the Tree of Life

Sephira	Title	Planet	Color	Incense	Stones
1. Kether	Crown	The Cosmos/Uranus	White	Ambergris	Diamond
2. Chokmah	Wisdom	The Zodiac/Neptune	Grey	Musk	Turquoise
3. Binah	Understanding	Saturn	Black	Myrrh	Sapphire
4. Chesed	Mercy	Jupiter	Blue	Cedar	Amethyst
5. Geburah	Justice	Mars	Red	Tobacco	Ruby
6. Tiphareth	Beauty	sun	Yellow	Olibanum	Amber
7. Netzach	Victory	Venus	Green	Roses	Emerald
8. Hod	Glory	Mercury	Orange	Storax	Agate
9. Yesod	Foundation	moon	Violet	Jazmin	Moonstone
10. Malkuth	Kingdom	Earth	Brown/Citrine/Olive/Black	Dittany of Crete	Quartz

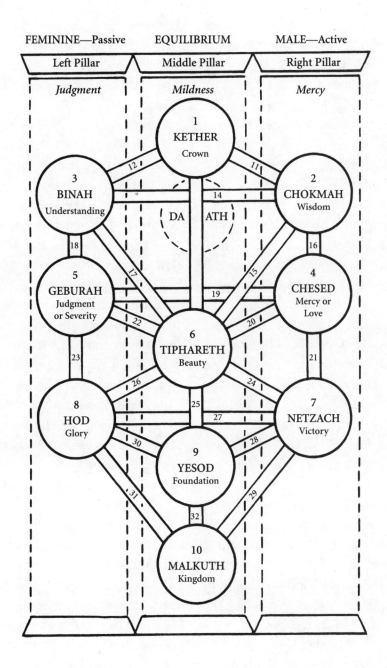

Figure 23: The Tree of Life and the Paths.

to know the word indicated by the consonants "hs" without the vowels, which Hebrew resolves by the use of the dots underneath the appropriate consonant.

In the case of the Tetragrammaton, the dots that would reveal the pronunciation of the name have been lost across the centuries. In biblical times, the scribes that copied the Scriptures, wishing to preserve the secret of the name, substituted the dots of the correct pronunciation with the punctuation of another of God's names, Adonai, which means "Lord" in Hebrew. From this erroneous transcription of the name comes the equally erroneous pronunciation of the Tetragrammaton as Jehovah. This holy name is said to mean "He Who Is."

Among other well-known names of God are Elohim, translated as the Lord God, and Jah, the name that is used in the Hallelujah or praises to the Creator. "Hallel" means "praises," "u" means "to," and "Jah" means "God." Another name mentioned in the Scriptures is the one given by God himself to Moses when he spoke to the Lawgiver from the burning bush. In Hebrew this name is Eheieh Asher Eheieh, and means "I am that I am." Eheieh by itself means "I am." This is the name of God adjudicated to the first sphere of the Tree of Life. The name Tzabaoth, which appears often in the Scriptures, means "Lord of Hosts." We often find in the Scriptures a combination of names, such as Jehovah Elohim or Jehovah Tzabaoth. Each name or title refers to a different aspect of God and one of his specific virtues. Sometimes the names are hidden in the middle of a sentence in the original Hebrew.

God has so many names that it is practically impossible to know them all. Hebrew scholars believe that the first five books of the Old Testament, known collectively as the Torah (or the Pentateuch, in the original Hebrew), starting with the first letter of the first word of Genesis and ending with the last letter of the last word of Deuteronomy, form the longest of the names of God.

But it is undoubtedly the Tetragrammaton, YHVH, which encompasses the Creator's glory and his great majesty and power. That is why the Scriptures say that God and his name are One. That is, YHVH is God himself. To know God's name is the equivalent of knowing God and to be worthy of his grace and protection. This is expressed in Psalm 91 where God says, "I will set him on high because he has known My name."

The *Third Book of Enoch* and the *Sixth and Seventh Books of Moses* reveal many of the divine names. Enoch even provides a list of seventy of God's names that may be pronounced but admonishes that there are many more that must never be enunciated. The seventy names that may be invoked, according to Enoch, are given in the following list. Each name is followed by the letters of the Tetragrammaton, YHVH.

The Seventy Names of God

1. Hadiriron YHVH of the Hosts, holy, holy, holy
2. Meromiron YHVH
3. Beroradin YHVH
4. Neuriron YHVH
5. Gebiriron YHVH
6. Kebiriron YHVH
7. Dorriron YHVH
8. Sebiroron YHVH
9. Zehiroron YHVH
10. Hadidron YHVH
11. Webidriron YHVH
12. Wediriron YHVH
13. Peruriron YHVH
14. Hisiriron YHVH
15. Ledoriron YHVH
16. Tatbiron YHVH
17. Satriron YHVH
18. Adiriron YHVH
19. Dekiriron YHVH
20. Lediriron YHVH
21. Seririron YHVH
22. Tebiriron YHVH
23. Taptapiron YHVH
24. Apapiron YHVH
25. Sapsapiron YHVH
26. Sapsapiron YHVH (This name is identical to the preceding one but the pronunciation seems to be different; maybe the preceding name should be pronounced Shapshapiron, but this is not made clear by Enoch.)
27. Gapgapiron YHVH
28. Raprapiron YHVH
29. Dapdapiron YHVH
30. Qapqapiron YHVH
31. Haphapiron YHVH
32. Wapwapiron YHVH
33. Pappapiron YHVH
34. Zapzapiron YHVH
35. Taptapiron YHVH
36. Apapiron YHVH
37. Mapmapiron YHVH
38. Sapsapiron YHVH
39. Napnapiron YHVH
40. Laplapiron YHVH
41. Wapwapiron YHVH (identical to #32)
42. Kapkapiron YHVH
43. Haphapiron YHVH

The names #44 to #70 are followed by the name Jah. This name is seen as the "greater YHVH" because it forms the first half of the Tetragrammaton, Yahweh or Jehovah.

44. Taptabib, who is JAH, the greater YHVH
45. Ababib JAH
46. Qapqabib JAH
47. Sabsabib JAH
48. Babbabib JAH
49. Sapsabib JAH
50. Gabgabib JAH
51. Rabrabib JAH
52. Harabrabib JAH
53. Pabpabib JAH
54. Habhabib JAH
55. Ababib JAH (identical to #45)
56. Zabzabib JAH
57. Sabsabib JAH (identical to #47)
58. Hashabib JAH
59. Tabtabib JAH (identical to #44)
60. Wesibib JAH
61. Pabpabib JAH (identical to #53)
62. Basbabib JAH
63. Papnabib JAH
64. Lablabib JAH
65. Mabmabib JAH
66. Nupkabib JAH
67. Mammambib JAH
68. Nupnubib JAH
69. Paspabib JAH
70. Sassib JAH

This list is divided in two classifications: the names ending in "on" and those ending in "ib." The only name that does not follow these classifications is #3 Beroradin. The termination "on" means "great," but the meaning of "ib" or "in" is not made clear by Enoch. The repetition of some of the names is also not explained by Enoch, but it is assumed that they should be pronounced in the order in which they are given.

The Sixth and Seventh Books of Moses

The first five books of the Old Testament, Genesis, Exodus, Leviticus, Numbers, and Deuteronomy, are known collectively as the Pentateuch. Jews know them as the Torah or the Law. They are traditionally ascribed to Moses, who was the recipient of God's revelation at Mount Sinai. Some scholars disagree with the idea of Moses as the author of the Pentateuch because some of the events related in these books took place at least two hundred years before the birth of the Lawgiver. Certain details of Moses' childhood appear in other legends, notably that of Sargon, which would seem to indicate that they were borrowed and added by latter scribes to the Mosaic account.

The esoteric tradition says that Moses wrote not five but ten books. The other five books ascribed to Moses have been compiled in two volumes: the *Sixth and Seventh Books of Moses* and the *Eighth, Ninth and Tenth Books of Moses*. The most important of these two works is the *Sixth and Seventh Books of Moses*, which also includes a section on the magical uses of the Psalms.

The *Sixth and Seventh Books of Moses* is a compilation of rituals, invocations to the angels, magical seals, sigils, and talismans supposedly received by Moses from the angels. This work was published originally in German in 1849, and its author, Johann Scheibel, claimed that the rituals and magical seals given in the book were taken from Hebrew sources, especially the Talmud. Some sections of the book are very old, dating from the fourteenth and sixteenth centuries. Unfortunately, many of the holy names of God and other Hebrew inscriptions are almost illegible and have suffered much through subsequent translations. In spite of these corruptions, many of the seals and inscriptions, including the Semiphoras and the Shemhamphora, are often engraved in metal and sold as talismans for protection and invocation. These so-called Mosaic talismans are very popular but their authenticity is dubious.

The Semiphoras and the Shemhamphora

The Semiphoras, as given in the *Sixth and Seventh Books of Moses*, are seven of the holy names of God, which are said to confer great powers on those who use them. Each name or Semiphora is used for a different purpose.

The book gives two versions of the Semiphoras: Adam's Semiphoras and Moses' Semiphoras.

The Shemhamphora is a name of God composed of seventy-two letters and is said to be one of the most powerful names of the Creator. This name is hidden in chapter 14 of the Book of Exodus in the original Hebrew text. It is to be found in three of the versicles of this chapter, which contain the seventy-two letters of the holy name. Seventy-two of the angels of the Divine Presence are associated with this holy name. The Shemhamphora is usually depicted as a wheel formed by seventy-two leaves and on each of these is inscribed part of the holy name.

Following are the seven Semiphoras of Adam. I decided not to include Moses' Semiphoras here because they are very similar to Adam's Semiphoras and are more difficult to decipher. The transliteration of the divine names from the original Hebrew is not very clear in these passages and undoubtedly there were errors in the transcriptions.

Adam's Semiphoras

First Semiphora—The name of God in this Semiphora is Jove, possibly a corruption or abbreviation of Jehovah. It is pronounced in moments of dire need, to ask God's help in the solution of a serious problem.

Second Semiphora—The name of God here is Yeseraye, possibly a corruption or abbreviation of Eheieh Asher Eheieh, the name revealed by God to Moses from the burning bush. This name means "God without beginning or end" and it is used to invoke the angels that they may grant any petition.

Third Semiphora—The name of God here is Adonai Tzabaoth and it is used to invoke the powers of the four winds and to call upon the souls of the dead.

Fourth Semiphora—The name of God here is Layamen Iava Firi Lavagellayn Lavaqiri Lavagola Lavatsorin Layfialafin Lyafaran. It is not clear whether the transliteration was exact in this lengthy name, and therefore its accuracy is uncertain. This name is invoked to have control over all spirits and animals.

Fifth Semiphora—The name of God here is Lyacham Lyalgema Lyafarau Lyalfarah Lebara Lebarosin Layararalus. Again,

LETTER OF THE TETRA-GRAMMATON	THE ASSOCIATED THREE-LETTER NAMES (READ TOP TO BOTTOM)																	
Y	K	L	H	H	M	I	H	L	A	H	K	A	L	M	O	S	I	V
	L	A	Q	R	B	Z	H	A	L	Z	H	K	L	H	L	I	L	H
	I	V	M	I	H	L	O	V	D	I	Th	A	H	Sh	M	T	I	V
H	M	K	L	I	V	L	A	R	Sh	I	H	N	Ch	M	I	N	P	L
	N	V	H	Ch	Sh	K	V	I	A	R	A	Th	H	L	I	L	H	V
	D	Q	Ch	V	R	B	M	I	H	Th	A	H	V	H	I	K	L	V
V	N	N	O	H	D	V	M	O	O	S	L	V	M	H	I	R	Ch	A
	I	N	M	Ch	N	H	I	Sh	R	A	L	V	I	H	I	H	O	N
	Th	A	M	Sh	I	V	H	L	I	L	H	L	K	H	2	O	M	I
H	M	H	I	R	Ch	A	M	D	M	O	I	V	M	H	I	N	P	M
	V	I	B	A	B	I	N	M	Ch	N	H	M	Tz	R	I	M	B	V
	H	I	M	H	V	O	Q	B	I	V	H	B	R	Ch	L	M	I	H

Figure 24: The seventy-two names of God in accordance with the Shemhamphora. Each name consists of three letters, shown here in the Latin alphabet but originally written in the Hebrew alphabet.

The Cabula.

Shewing at one View the Seventy-two Angels bearing the name of God Shemhamphora.

Angel names (row 1)
Vehuiah, Jeliel, Sitael, Elemiah, Mahasiah, Ielahel, Akhaiah, Cahethel, Haziel, Aladiah, Lauviah, Hahaiah, Iezalel, Mebahel, Hariel, Hakamiah, Loviah, Caliel

Angel names (row 2)
Lauviah, Pahatiah, Nelchael, Ieiaiel, Melahel, Hahuiah, Nithhaiah, Haaiah, Ierathel, Seehiah, Reiiel, Omael, Lecabel, Vasariah, Iehuiah, Lehahiah, Chavakiah, Menadel

Angel names (row 3)
Aniel, Haamiah, Rehael, Ihiazel, Hahahel, Michael, Veualiah, Ielahiah, Sealiah, Ariel, Asaliah, Mihael, Vehuel, Daniel, Hahasiah, Imamiah, Nanael, Nithael

Angel names (row 4)
Mebahiah, Poiel, Nemamiah, Ieilael, Harahel, Mizrael, Umabel, Iahhel, Annauel, Mehael, Damabiah, Menkl, Eiael, Habuiah, Rochel, Ibamiah, Haaiel, Nevamaih

Figure 25: The seventy-two angels who reign over the Shemhamphora.

the accuracy of this name is not certain. It is invoked to have control over harvests and all earthly vegetation.

Sixth Semiphora—The name of God here is Letamnin Letay Logo Letasynin Levaganaritin Letraminin Letalogin Lotafalosin. As in the last two Semiphoras, its accuracy is questionable. It is invoked to have control over the four elements—air, fire, water, and earth. It is used when one of these threatens the life or property of an individual. This Semiphora is said to be extremely useful in cases of fire, floods, earthquakes, hurricanes, and tornadoes.

Seventh Semiphora—The name of God associated with this Semiphora has been lost

Figure 26: A design associated with the Shemhamphora; from the *Sixth and Seventh Books of Moses.*

Figure 27: The seventy-two names of God from the Shemhamphora; from the *Sixth and Seventh Books of Moses.*

because of poor translations and transcriptions. All that is known about it is that it was used originally to ask God's protection against the elements. The Sixth Semiphora, which is used for similar cases, can be used instead of the Seventh.

The problem associated with the corruption of the divine names through poor translations and transliterations is found in many of the apocryphal books, the ancient grimoires or books of angelic magic, and the *Pseudepigrapha*. Only the best-known names of the Deity have escaped the deterioration caused by bad translations and repeated editions across the centuries. In spite of this, there is so much power in each of the divine names that even when mispronounced or misspelled they can still be the source of many miracles.

7

The Angelic Language

According to the Jewish tradition, Hebrew is the language most commonly used by the angels to communicate with humanity. The Talmudic commentaries and several of the apocryphal books, like the Book of Jubilees, say that not only the angels but God himself uses this language. The Apocalypse of Saint Paul states clearly that Hebrew is the chosen language of God and his angels. All of this changed, however, with the building of the Tower of Babel around 2247 B.C. Chapter 11 of Genesis relates how Noah's descendants decided to erect a tower on the valley of Shinar in Babylon. Their intention was to build a tower that would reach to Heaven. But this presumption offended God, who disrupted the construction of the tower by causing a confusion of tongues among the builders, who found themselves unable to understand the speech of their neighbors. God then dispersed these people, speaking different languages, to the four corners of the Earth. This is the biblical origin of the profusion of languages on the world. The word Babel comes from Babylon, where the tower was erected. It literally means "confusion."

Maybe because of the explosion of languages on Earth, angels developed the ability to speak multiple tongues. Gabriel, Metraton, and Zagzaguel are said to speak as many as seventy languages. The Talmud, which is the Jewish book of rabbinical commentaries on the Old Testament, says that Gabriel taught Joseph these seventy languages in the

Figure 28: The Tower of Babel and the confusion of languages.

course of one evening. The angel Kirtabus is said to be a master of all languages.

According to the angelic tradition, these celestial beings have their very own language which, although very similar to Hebrew, has its own special characteristics. Like Hebrew, the angelic script has no vowels, which are also indicated by punctuation beneath the appropriate letters. Each of the letters of the angelic alphabet terminates in a small circle. It is not certain why they have this form, but it is believed that the circles serve to contain the immense angelic energy that is hidden in the letters.

There are several versions of the angelic script. The best known are the Angelic Alphabet, the Malachim Alphabet—also known as Angelic or Royal Script—and the Alphabet of the Passing of the Waters. These three versions, as given in this book, come from *The Practical Kabbalah (La Kabbale Pratique)* by the French kabbalist Robert Ambelain.

If we compare the Hebrew alphabet with the three versions of the angelic script, we can appreciate the similarities between them. The Hebrew alphabet is composed of twenty-two major letters, beginning with Aleph and ending with Tav or Tau. Both the Angelic Alphabet and the Alphabet of the Passing of the Waters also have twenty-two letters and begin with Aleph and end with Tau. But the Malachim Alphabet begins with Aleph and ends with the letter Resh. It

also has twenty-three letters instead of twenty-two and their order changes after the letter Nun. The reason why there are twenty-three letters in this alphabet is that the letter Samekh is included twice. The Malachim Alphabet is the one most widely used in kabbalistic magic to write letters to the angels in their own script.

In order to compare the Hebrew and the Angelic alphabets, one must remember that Hebrew is written from right to left. The three versions of the angelic script must also be read in this manner. The Hebrew alphabet shown here has been written from left to right to make it easier for the reader.

Following is a transliteration of the Hebrew letters into our Roman alphabet:

Hebrew letter, Roman letter

1. Aleph, A
2. Beth, B
3. Gimel, G
4. Daleth, D
5. He, H or E
6. Vau, V or U
7. Zain, Z
8. Cheth, Ch
9. Teth, T
10. Yod, Y or I
11. Caph, C
12. Lamed, L

The Misterious Characters of Letters deliver'd by Honorious call'd the Theban Alphabet.

A' B C D E F G H I K L M

N O P Q R S T V X Y Z

The Characters of Celestial Writing.

Lamed Caph Jod Theth Cheth Zain Vau He Daleth Gimel Beth Aleph

Tau Shin Res Kuff Zade Pe Ain Samech Nun Mem

The Writing call'd Malachim.

Caph Jod Theth Cheth Zain Vau He Daleth Gimel Beth Aleph

Pesh Kuff Zade Pe Ain Samech Samech Schin Tau Nun Mem Lamed

The Writing call'd Paſsing the River.

Lamed Caph Jod Theth Cheth Zain Vau He Daleth Gimel Beth Aleph

Tan Schin Resh Kuff Zade Pe Ain Samech Nun Mem

Figure 29: Four versions of the angelic alphabet, which is very similar to the Hebrew alphabet. From top to bottom: Theban, Celestial, Malachim, and Passing the River.

Aleph (A)	Beth (B)	Gimel (G)	Daleth (D)	Heh (H)	Vav (V)
א	ב	ג	ד	ה	ו
Zayin (Z)	**Cheth (Ch)**	**Teth (T)**	**Yod (Y)**	**Kaph (K)**	**Lamed (L)**
ז	ח	ט	י	כ	ל
Mem (M)	**Nun (N)**	**Samekh (S)**	**Ayin (O)**	**Peh (P)**	**Tsaddi (Ts)**
מ	נ	ס	ע	פ	צ
Qoph (Q)	**Resh (R)**	**Shin (Sh)**	**Tau (T)**		
ק	ר	ש	ת		
Final כ	**Final מ**	**Final נ**	**Final פ**	**Final צ**	
ד	ם	ו	ף	ץ	

Figure 30: The Hebrew alphabet consists of twenty-two letters with five additional letters. Each letter has a special numerical significance as well.

13. Mem, M

14. Nun, N

15. Samekh, S

16. Ayin, O

17. Pe, P

18. Tzaddi, Tz

19. Qoph, Q

20. Resh, R

21. Shin, Sh

22. Tav or Tau, T

It will be noticed that although the Hebrew alphabet has no vowels, these have been introduced in the transliteration of the

Hebrew letters. This has been done to facilitate the use of the angelic scripts, which have the same meaning as Hebrew. To write a message to an angel in one of the angelic scripts, all that one has to do is substitute the Roman letter of each word of the message for the corresponding letter in the angelic script chosen.

My father, who was a man of profound mysticism and a great biblical scholar, taught me the importance of an exhaustive scrutiny of the Scriptures. By scrutiny he meant the seeking of hidden messages in the Bible, particularly the Old Testament. Although he knew that most of the original meaning had been lost in the many transla-

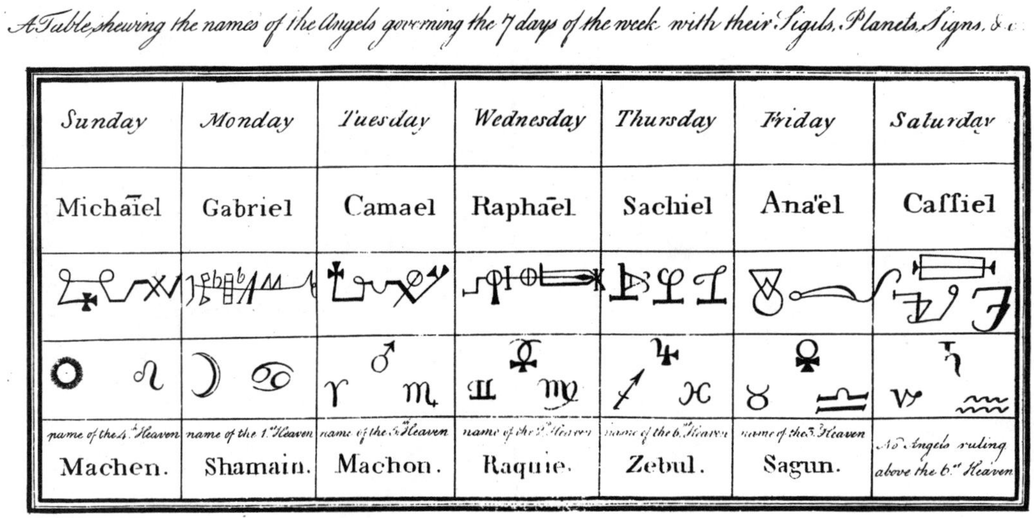

A Table, shewing the names of the Angels governing the 7 days of the week, with their Sigils, Planets, Signs, &c.

Sunday	Monday	Tuesday	Wednesday	Thursday	Friday	Saturday
Michaël	Gabriel	Camael	Raphaël	Sachiel	Anaël	Caffiel
name of the 4.ᵗʰ Heaven Machen.	name of the 1.ˢᵗ Heaven Shamain.	name of the 5.ᵗʰ Heaven Machon.	name of the 2.ⁿᵈ Heaven Raquie.	name of the 6.ᵗʰ Heaven Zebul.	name of the 3.ʳᵈ Heaven Sagun.	No Angels ruling above the 6.ᵗʰ Heaven

Figure 31: The seven archangels and the Seven Heavens they are associated with, along with their sigils, planets, and signs.

tions of the Holy Book, he believed that much hidden truth was still to be found by those who sought it diligently. One of the things he insisted upon was the observance of God's commandments, not just the ten we are so familiar with but all the precepts that are delineated in the first five books of the Old Testament, especially Leviticus and Deuteronomy. There are 613 of these precepts and among them is the kosher law concerning forbidden foods. But although some meats, such as beef, lamb, and fowl, can be eaten according to these precepts, my father, who was a strict vegetarian, believed that God does not want us to eat any form of animal flesh. He based his belief in several biblical passages, especially Isaiah 65:17 where God describes a new Creation. In Isaiah 65:25, God says that in this new Earth the lion and the lamb shall feed together, the lion shall eat straw like the ox, and no one will hurt or destroy in his holy mountain. This, therefore, means that God does not wish us to hurt or destroy anything and that includes all forms of life. Furthermore, the Sixth Commandment states clearly that we must not kill, and it does not specify what or whom. That is what my father meant by scrutiny of the Scriptures, looking for a deeper meaning within. God suffers us to eat meat because of our ignorance of this ideal state that is to come. In time, we will know better.

Perhaps because of his great asceticism, my father received many revelations from the angels. I would like to share with you two of these angelic messages. The first is a prayer to God written in the form of an acrostic using the first and last names of the person. This prayer must be created by the individual, in a spontaneous form, as it comes from his or her own heart. This prayer will then become that individual's personal prayer to the Creator. Later the prayer is rewritten in one of the angelic scripts, sealed, and kept in a safe place. To illustrate how such a letter may be composed, I will give a simple example. If a person named Ann Smith wished to write a letter to God using her name, she could write it in the following manner.

A lmighty God,

N ever have you ceased to love me.

N one of my prayers have you left unanswered.

S ave me from my own weaknesses and constant doubts.

M ay your mercy follow me always.

I n your light may I walk all the days of my life,

T o find peace, love and the serenity to fulfill my destiny.

H allowed be your name forever.

This prayer would then be transcribed into the angelic script and sealed in an envelope. The original would be used as a personal daily prayer to God. This is only one example of the many prayers that can be composed using a person's name.

The second angelic revelation that I want to give you here was received by my father from the Archangel Michael. It is a petition to Michael and is extremely effective. This letter must be written to Michael only once a year, on a person's birthday. There can only be one thing asked of the archangel and the letter must be short and very clear as to its intention. To write it, you must have fasted for twenty-four hours and abstained from alcohol, drugs, tobacco, and sexual activity, also for twenty-four hours. Once these preliminaries are observed, write the letter on an unlined piece of white paper. Then place a small glass with a little water in front of yourself and soak a piece of red cloth in the water so that all the liquid is immediately absorbed into the cloth. The red cloth is then placed over your eyes and you may proceed to meditate on the petition to Michael. When some of the water has evaporated from the cloth, both the letter and the cloth are placed in an envelope and sealed. The envelope is addressed to Michael Arch and below the archangel's name is written the capital and the country that are directly opposite to the country where the person was born. For perfect accuracy, this is ascertained by using the nearest longitude and latitude of both countries. This information can be found in any atlas. The letter must have a return address and must be certified to ensure its return to the sender. When the letter is returned by the postal authorities of the other country, it is a sign that Michael received the message.

When I wrote a petition to Michael for the first time, I sent the letter to Karachi because the opposite longitude and latitude of Puerto Rico, where I was born, are in the middle of the Indian Ocean and I thought that Karachi was the place closest to that specific area. I did not realize at the time that there are many small islands in the Indian Ocean and that the closest to the correct longitude and latitude was the island of Mauritius. My petition to Michael had been to hear from a Norwegian friend with whom I had lost contact for a long time. Shortly after the postal authorities in Karachi returned Michael's letter, I received a letter from my friend, sent from Mauritius. What was a Norwegian doing in Mauritius, of all places? My friend said that he was on a holiday cruise and the ship had to change its course and dock in the small island because of bad weather. What made him write that letter from Mauritius after such a long silence I will never know. What I do know is that Michael answered my petition and, in so doing, also let me know where to send him any future letters.

The most effective way to write a petition to the Archangel Michael is by using one of the angelic alphabets. This is not absolutely necessary but it would be of added help. The seal or signature of Michael, as it appears in the accompanying illustration (Figure 31, page 112), would also be helpful at the beginning of the message. These aids would make the petition more powerful and effective.

8

The Angelic Regents

The supernatural powers of the angels, which is known as angelic magic, is based on cosmic and natural laws. One could define an angel as a quantum of energy, as a cosmic force invested with pure conscience and created to preserve the order of the universe. Electricity, magnetism, inertia, gravitation, momentum, cohesion, adhesion, and a host of similar universal laws could easily be identified with angelic forces. Natural elements such as water, fire, air, and all natural phenomena could likewise be identified with angels. All these forces seem to follow immutable cosmic laws that determine their actions and behavior. Like them, the angel is immutable and inviolate and fixed in its capacity as preserver of the divine laws. It is also faithful and steadfast, and its will is irrevocably subjugated to God's will. The angel acts only in accordance to this supreme will and wishes only to serve it. It is this faithfulness and constancy of the angels that gives them their immense power, which is rooted in God's own power.

Because of the transcendental power ascribed to the angels and their cosmic characteristics, the angelic tradition has invested them with control over the planets, the stars, and the natural elements. This is the origin of the concept of the planetary angels and their supposed ability to transmute matter.

As we saw earlier, there are seven great archangels, which in the Middle Ages were said to rule the seven planets and the twelve signs of the zodiac. In modern times, with the discovery of Uranus, Neptune, and Pluto, three new archangels, Uriel, Asariel,

Planetary Angels

Archangel	Zodiac Sign	Planet	Day	Color	Main Stone
Camael	Aries	Mars	Tuesday	Red	Diamond
Anael	Taurus	Venus	Friday	Green	Emerald
Raphael	Gemini	Mercury	Wednesday	Yellow	Agate
Gabriel	Cancer	moon	Monday	Silver	Pearl
Michael	Leo	sun	Sunday	Gold	Ruby
Raphael	Virgo	Mercury	Wednesday	Grey	Sapphire
Anael	Libra	Venus	Friday	Pink	Opal
Azrael	Scorpio	Pluto	Tuesday	Wine	Topaz
Zadkiel	Sagittarius	Jupiter	Thursday	Ultramarine	Turquoise
Cassiel	Capricorn	Saturn	Saturday	Black	Onyx
Uriel	Aquarius	Uranus	Saturday	Violet	Amethyst
Asariel	Pisces	Neptune	Thursday	Blue-green	Aquamarine

and Azrael, have been added to the original seven to account for the rulership of these planets. The above table presents the planetary angels that are now said to rule the zodiac and the planets.

As can be seen from this table, each of these angels rules a sign of the zodiac and a planet, with the exception of Raphael, who rules both Virgo and Gemini, and Anael, who rules Taurus and Libra.

The zodiac signs are divided into four triplicities, each of which falls under the aegis of one of the four elements. Each element, in turn, is ruled by one of the four great archangels—Raphael, Michael, Gabriel, and Uriel.

Triplicity—Element, Archangel

Gemini, Libra, Aquarius—Air, Raphael

Aries, Leo, Sagittarius—Fire, Michael

Cancer, Scorpio, Pisces—Water, Gabriel

Taurus, Virgo, Capricorn—Earth, Uriel

The twelve zodiac signs are also placed in the order of the four elements and the four cardinal points, as follows: Fire/South; Earth/North; Air/East; and Water/West. These form three groups or triplicities:

Zodiac—Element, Cardinal Point, Archangel

Aries—Fire, South, Michael

Taurus—Earth, North, Uriel

Gemini—Air, East, Raphael

Cancer—Water, West, Gabriel

Leo—Fire, South, Michael

Virgo—Earth, North, Uriel

Libra—Air, East, Raphael

Scorpio—Water, West, Gabriel

Sagittarius—Fire, South, Michael

Capricorn—Earth, North, Uriel

Aquarius—Air, East, Raphael

Pisces—Water, West, Gabriel

In chapter 9 we will discuss the four great archangels and the four elements in greater detail. The four triplicities and the four elements are closely linked with the Cherubim described in the vision of Ezekiel, who describes them with four faces: the face of a bull (Taurus/Earth); the face of a lion (Leo/Fire); the face of an eagle (Scorpio/Water); and the face of a man (Aquarius/Air).

Guardian Angels

The guardian angels protect not only people but also nations, cities, religions, and institutions. The guardian angels of nations are known as Ethnarcs.

The concept of the guardian angel exists in many religions and cultures and can be traced to the Assyrians and the Babylonians. In ancient times they were known as Keribu, the origin of the word "Cherub," and were said to guard palaces and temple gates. The Romans believed that men and small children were guarded by spirits known as Genii, while women were protected by Junos, an idea undoubtedly inspired by Juno, Jupiter's irascible wife, who was the guardian of the home. Muslims believe humanity is

Figure 32: A guardian angel.

protected by the Malaika and by the Jafaza, who are said to keep away evil spirits. The Japanese believe in guardian spirits known as Kami. And the American Indians also believe in protective spirits that remain with them throughout their lives.

The Christian tradition teaches that a guardian angel is assigned to every human being at the moment of birth. According to the Catholic Church, we are assigned two guardian angels, one who is good and another who is evil. These two angels sit upon each of our shoulders and try to influence our actions. The day of the guardian angels is celebrated by the Church on October 4. The Archangels Michael, Raphael, and Gabriel, the only angels recognized by name by the Catholic Church, are honored on September 29.

The guardian angels are believed to guide human beings and to steer us in the path of goodness throughout our lives, but they do not interfere with human free will. They only indicate the right course but do not force us to follow it. Each person is called to make that decision on his own because God wants us to walk in the right path because we choose to, not because we must. The divine gift of free will makes that choice our own.

The guardian angels belong to the ninth angelic choir, that of the Angels, and they use a variety of ways to influence a person. Among these are intuition, telepathy, dreams, and that small, inner voice that sometimes we hear and that never steers us wrong. Sometimes a guardian angel may use another person to send a message, and can manipulate the circumstances of everyday life to assist an individual in times of need. Other times they may choose to take the form of a human being, an animal, or simply appear in the traditional guise ascribed to them by religious tradition: a radiant being, dressed in dazzling white raiment, with widespread snowy wings.

The guardian angels protect, but they cannot intervene in human destiny, which has already been decided before each person's birth. He can only safeguard us from making wrong decisions and try to keep us away from evil actions, but each person's life is predestined, like Saint Augustine taught. This may be blamed on what is known as the karma of previous lives, according to Buddhism, but the end result is the same. The guardian angel cannot change a person's destiny. That is why sometimes small children die of incurable diseases or in a tragic form. In these cases, most mystical and religious traditions agree that this spirit came to Earth for a short time. When good people, who follow the divine laws, experience tragic or overwhelming events in their lives, this is also seen as part of their destinies or their karma.

The guardian angel protects us and guides us, but always within the laws that rule our destinies and our free will. But when a person deviates from God's laws, the guardian angel abandons that person and no longer guides or protects him. Also, because of the accumulation of negative energies in the world created by evil human actions and the imbalance created by the original Creation, a human being may be sometimes surrounded by powerful destructive forces that threaten to destroy him. These may prove too strong for the guardian angel, who does not always win every battle. For that reason, it is important to establish a strong contact with our guardian angels, and that may be accomplished by calling him to our side often. Meditations, invocations, prayers, and ritual purifications also help to strengthen our spiritual link with our guardian angels.

Each person is said to have two protective angels: the archangel who rules his zodiac sign and his personal guardian angel, who fortifies his spirit and steers him in the good path. But each person also has an evil genius, a malefic spirit, who incites him to break both human and divine laws and to destroy everything in his path, including himself. This evil spirit preys on personal weaknesses, which it endeavors to multiply in order to hasten individual self-destruction. It particularly thrives on rage, intolerance, hatred, and vengeance. When a person has self-destructive tendencies or shows a markedly antisocial behavior, he or she is said to have an "evil genius." This evil genius

reflects the malefic spirit who afflicts that person.

In the mystical tradition, this destructive force is known as the "Dweller on the Threshold," which induces human beings to commit evil acts. It may be seen as the embodiment of a person's baser instincts. In Freudian psychology, the amalgamation of the lower instincts is known as the Id. Jung called it the Shadow.

There is a constant struggle between the guardian angel, who may be seen as a person's higher self, and the dark angel, who may be identified with the human lower instincts. Each individual decides who will win this never-ending struggle through his own actions. If he chooses an evil course, he becomes the willing slave of his evil genius. If he opts for the path of righteousness, the guardian angel helps him achieve salvation. Unfortunately, the circumstances of human life are such that they preclude such a simple and direct decision. Most people are constantly torn between the natural desire to do good and the temptation to do evil. And so the battle rages on between the two angels.

The ancient Chaldeans, who were the originators of our modern astrology, believed that the guardian angel of each person resides in the eleventh house of the zodiac, while the dark angel may be found in the sixth house.

According to an esoteric tradition, the best way to ensure the guardian angel's triumph

The Regent Princes of the Four Altitudes

FIRST ALTITUDE (East)	SECOND ALTITUDE (South)	THIRD ALTITUDE (West)	FOURTH ALTITUDE (North)
Alimiel	Aphiriza	Eliphaniasai	Barachiel
Barachiel	Armon	Elomina	Capitiel
Gabriel	Genon	Gedobonai	Deliel
Helison	Geron	Gelomiros	Gebiel
Lebes	Gereimon	Taranava	Gedi

over the dark angel is to find out the name of the guardian angel and to invoke it in times of need or dire temptation. To discover this name, the person must fast and abstain from sexual relations and all addictive substances for twenty-four hours. The next morning, at sunrise, he must bathe and dress in white. He then faces the east with a small glass vessel in his hands filled with olive oil, a few bay leaves, frankincense, and myrrh. Placing his lips over the oil, he asks his guardian angel to reveal his name. He repeats this petition seven times. The name of the angel will then come to his mind. This name must never be revealed. The oil is to be kept in a small bottle and used during meditations or to invoke the help of the angel. It is rubbed over the forehead, the temples, the chest, the hands, and the feet.

The Angels of the Altitudes

Besides the zodiac signs, the elements, and the planets, the angels also rule everything in the universe, according to their hierarchies. For example, an old grimoire known as the *Almadel of Solomon* says that there are four angelic choirs called the Altitudes who are associated with the four cardinal points.

As we have already seen, the four cardinal points are ruled by the four great archangels—Michael, Raphael, Gabriel, and Uriel. But each of the Altitudes is ruled by five different Regent Princes.

The princes of the First Altitude take the appearance of angels and they carry a banner with a red cross. They wear rose crowns and speak in low voices.

The princes of the Second Altitude take the form of small boys dressed in satin. They have reddish faces and wear crowns of red flowers.

The princes of the Third Altitude appear as small boys or tiny women. They dress in green or silver and wear laurel crowns. When they leave, there is always a trace of sweet smells in the air.

The princes of the Fourth Altitude take the form of small boys or tiny men. They dress in green and black, the colors of the earth element. In their hands they carry a plucked bird.

The Altitudes must always be invoked in the proper hour of the day and the correct month of the year.

The twelve months of the year are also ruled by angels.

Month—Regent or Ruling Angel

January—Gabriel or Cambiel

February—Barchiel

March—Machidiel or Malahidael

April—Asmodel

May—Ambriel or Ambiel

June—Muriel

July—Verchiel

August—Hamaliel

September—Uriel or Zuriel

October—Barbiel

November—Adnachiel or Advachiel

December—Anael

The four seasons are likewise ruled by angels.

Season—Regent or Ruling Angel

Spring—Spugliguel, with co-regents Amatiel, Caracasa, Core, and Commisoros

Summer—Tubiel, with co-regents Gargatel, Gaviel, and Tariel

Fall—Torquaret, with co-regents Tarquam and Guabarel

Winter—Attarib, with co-regents Amabel and Cetarari

The information on the regent princes of the months of the year and the four seasons come from De Plancy's *Dictionnaire Infernal* and *The Magus* by Francis Barrett, a noted scholar on angelology and ritual magic who wrote in the early part of the nineteenth century. The source of the many names of angels cited by Barrett and other angelologists is not always clear. It is probable that many of the names come from the Talmud and other rabbinical writings, as well as the apocryphal books and many of the medieval treatises.

As we saw in chapter 3, each of the Seven Heavens is ruled by a Sarim or Regent Prince. But the *Third Book of Enoch* says that there are also sixty-four protective angels who are constantly on guard on the vestibules of the Seven Heavens. Maybe because it is the most accessible and where the main gates to Paradise may be found (though Heaven and Paradise are in the Third Heaven, the gates to them are in the First), the First Heaven is the most closely guarded of all the Heavens. It has twenty-two protective angels. The Seventh Heaven, the most forbidden of the Heavens as it encloses the Divine Presence, has only two protective angels. Following is a list of the protective angels of the celestial vestibules in the Seven Heavens.

Protective Angels of the Seven Heavens

First Heaven

1. Suria
2. Tutrechial
3. Tutrusiai
4. Zortek
5. Mufgar
6. Ashrulyai
7. Sabriel
8. Zahabriel
9. Tandal
10. Shokad
11. Huzia
12. Deheboryn
13. Adririon
14. Khabiel
15. Tashriel
16. Nahuriel
17. Jekusiel
18. Tufiel
19. Dahariel
20. Maskiel
21. Shoel
22. Sheviel

Second Heaven

1. Tagriel
2. Maspiel
3. Sahriel
4. Arfiel
5. Shahariel
6. Sakriel
7. Ragiel
8. Sehibiel

Third Heaven

1. Sheburiel
2. Retsutsiel
3. Shalmial
4. Savlial
5. Harhazial
6. Hadrial
7. Bezrial

Fourth Heaven

1. Pachdial
2. Gvrtial
3. Kzuial
4. Shehinial

5. Shtukial

6. Arvial

7. Kfial

8. Anfial

Fifth Heaven

1. Techial

2. Uzial

3. Gmial

4. Gamrial

5. Sefrial

6. Garfial

7. Grial

8. Drial

9. Paltrial

Sixth Heaven

1. Rumial

2. Katmial

3. Gehegial

4. Arsabrsbial

5. Egrumial

6. Parzial

7. Machkial

8. Tufrial

Seventh Heaven

1. Zeburial

2. Tutrbebial

Angels are also associated with the moon and lunar forces. The phases of the moon are divided into waxing and waning, each one lasting fourteen days. The waxing phase begins after the new moon and the waning phase begins after the full moon. The twenty-eight-day cycle formed by the two lunar phases is known as the twenty-eight mansions of the moon. Each of these days is ruled by a lunar angel. It is important to remember that the first mansion of the moon is the first day of the twenty-eight-day lunar cycle and it begins with the new moon. That is, the first mansion of the moon is the new moon. This waxing phase lasts fourteen days, culminating with the Full moon, which is the fifteenth day of the lunar cycle. From that day onwards the moon begins to wane and the phase lasts fourteen days more, ending the cycle with the next new moon, when the entire process is repeated. Following are the names of the lunar angels who rule each of the twenty-eight mansions of the moon.

Lunar Angels
Waxing Phase

1. Geniel (new moon)

2. Enediel

3. Anixiel

4. Azariel

5. Gabriel

6. Dirachiel

7. Scheliel

8. Amnediel

9. Barbiel

10. Ardifiel

11. Neciel

12. Abdizuel

13. Jazeriel

14. Ergediel

Waning Phase

15. Atliel (full moon)

16. Azeruel

17. Adriel

18. Egibiel

19. Amutiel

20. Kyriel

21. Bethnael

22. Geliel

23. Requiel

24. Abrinael

25. Aziel

26. Tagriel

27. Atheniel

28. Amnixiel

As we have already seen, the most powerful angels in Heaven are known as the Angelic or Regent Princes, better known as the Sarim. The following list was compiled by Gustav Davidson (*A Dictionary of Angels*) from various sources, including the Testament of Solomon, the works of Jellinek, and others. It gives the names of thirty of the most important Sarim or Angelic Princes. These powerful entities are the most refulgent stars in the angelic firmament. Among them are the seven great archangels and the glorious Metraton, who is said to be seated to the right of God on his Throne. Davidson compiled the Sarim in alphabetical order, but I have reorganized them according to their hierarchy in Heaven.

Sarim (Angelic or Regent Princes)

1. Metraton—Chancellor of Heaven; prince of the ministering angels and sustainer of humankind.

2. Michael—Chief angel of the Lord; deliverer of the faithful; tutelary prince of Israel and angel of repentance; one of the seven great archangels.

3. Uriel—Archangel of salvation; regent of the sun and overseer of Tartarus (Hell); one of the seven great archangels.

4. Raphael—Angel of healing, science and knowledge; one of the princes of the presence; the angel who stands in the sun; one of the seven great archangels.

5. Gabriel—Angel of annunciation, resurrection, mercy, and vengeance; ruling prince of the First Heaven; chief of the angelic guards over Paradise; one of the seven great archangels.

6. Anael (Haniel)—Chief of the Principalities and Virtues; one of the seven great archangels; governor of December; said to have transported Enoch to Heaven; one of the seven great archangels.

7. Camael (Kemuel)—Chief of the Powers; personification of divine justice; one of the seven great archangels.

8. Raziel (Gallizur)—Chief of the Supreme Mysteries; preceptor angel of Adam; herald of God; reputed author of the *Book of the Angel Raziel.*

9. Sandalphon—Angel of power and glory; Metraton's twin brother; ruling angel of the Earth, according to the Kabbalah.

10. Zadkiel or Tzadkiel—Angel of divine justice; ruler of Jupiter, and bringer of abundance.

11. Irin—Twin angels who, together with the Qaddisin, constitute the supreme judgment council of the divine court; among the eight exalted hierarchs who are said to be superior to Metraton.

12. Quaddisin—Twin angels who, with the Irin, constitute the supreme judgment council of the divine court.

13. Akatriel—Revealer of the divine mysteries and angel of proclamation.

14. Anafiel—Chief of the angels of the Merkabah or divine chariot; there are six classes of angels of the Merkabah, who guard God's Throne.

15. Phanuel (Raguel)—Archangel of penance; prince of the Divine Presence; often identified with Uriel and Ramiel.

16. Jehoel (Jaoel)—Mediator of the holy name; prince of the Divine Presence.

17. Radueriel (Vetril)—Recording angel who writes in the heavenly scrolls all that happens in the universe; leader of the celestial choirs and creator of the lesser angels.

18. Barakiel (Barbiel)—Ruler of the Seraphim; governor of February.

19. Galgaliel—Chief of the Galagalim or chariot of the Merkabah; chief angel of the wheel of the sun.

20. Rikbiel—Chief of the divine chariot and prince of the angels of the Merkabah.

21. Sopheriel Mehayye—Together with Sopheriel Memeth, keeps the Book of Life and Death; one of the chiefs of the Merkabah.

22. Sopheriel Memeth—Works with Sopheriel Mehayye; one of the chiefs of the Merkabah.

23. Soqed Hozi—Keeper of the divine balance and God's Sword; one of the supreme chiefs of the Merkabah.

Hours Day.	Angels and Planets ruling SUNDAY.	Angels and Planets ruling MONDAY.	Angels and Planets ruling TUESDAY.	Angels and Planets ruling WEDNESDAY.	Angels and Planets ruling THURSDAY.	Angels and Planets ruling FRIDAY.	Angels and Planets ruling SATURDAY.
	Day.	*Day.*	*Day.*	*Day.*	*Day.*	*Day.*	*Day.*
1	☉ Michael	☽ Gabriel	♂ Samael	☿ Raphael	♃ Sachiel	♀ Anael	♄ Cassiel
2	♀ Anael	♄ Cassiel	☉ Michael	☽ Gabriel	♂ Samael	☿ Raphael	♃ Sachiel
3	☿ Raphael	♃ Sachiel	♀ Anael	♄ Cassiel	☉ Michael	☽ Gabriel	♂ Samael
4	☽ Gabriel	♂ Samael	☿ Raphael	♃ Sachiel	♀ Anael	♄ Cassiel	☉ Michael
5	♄ Cassiel	☉ Michael	☽ Gabriel	♂ Samael	☿ Raphael	♃ Sachiel	♀ Anael
6	♃ Sachiel	♀ Anael	♄ Cassiel	☉ Michael	☽ Gabriel	♂ Samael	☿ Raphael
7	♂ Samael	☿ Raphael	♃ Sachiel	♀ Anael	♄ Cassiel	☉ Michael	☽ Gabriel
8	☉ Michael	☽ Gabriel	♂ Samael	☿ Raphael	♃ Sachiel	♀ Anael	♄ Cassiel
9	♀ Anael	♄ Cassiel	☉ Michael	☽ Gabriel	♂ Samael	☿ Raphael	♃ Sachiel
10	☿ Raphael	♃ Sachiel	♀ Anael	♄ Cassiel	○ Michael	☽ Gabriel	♂ Samael
11	☽ Gabriel	♂ Samael	☿ Raphael	♃ Sachael	♀ Anael	♄ Cassiel	☉ Michael
12	♄ Cassiel	☉ Michael	☽ Gabriel	♂ Samael	☿ Raphael	♃ Sachiel	♀ Anael
Hours Night	*Night.*	*Night.*	*Night.*	*Night.*	*Night.*	*Night.*	*Night.*
1	♃ Sachael	♀ Anael	♄ Cassiel	☉ Michael	☽ Gabriel	♂ Samael	☿ Raphael
2	♂ Samiel	☿ Raphael	♃ Sachiel	♀ Anael	♄ Cassiel	☉ Michael	☽ Gabriel
3	☉ Michael	☽ Gabriel	♂ Samael	☿ Raphael	♃ Sachiel	♀ Anael	♄ Cassiel
4	♀ Anael	♄ Cassiel	☉ Michael	☽ Gabriel	♂ Samael	☿ Raphael	♃ Sachiel
5	☿ Raphael	♃ Sachiel	♀ Anael	♄ Cassiel	☉ Michael	☽ Gabriel	♂ Samael
6	☽ Gabriel	♂ Samael	☿ Raphael	♃ Sachiel	♀ Anael	♄ Cassiel	☉ Michael
7	♄ Cassiel	☉ Michael	☽ Gabriel	♂ Samael	☿ Raphael	♃ Sachiel	♀ Anael
8	♃ Sachiel	♀ Anael	♄ Cassiel	☉ Michael	☽ Gabriel	♂ Samael	☿ Raphael
9	♂ Samael	☿ Raphael	♃ Sachiel	♀ Anael	♄ Cassiel	☉ Michael	☽ Gabriel
10	☉ Michael	☽ Gabriel	♂ Samael	☿ Raphael	♃ Sachiel	♀ Anael	♄ Cassiel
11	♀ Anael	♄ Cassiel	☉ Michael	☽ Gabriel	♂ Samael	☿ Raphael	♃ Sachiel
12	☿ Raphael	♃ Sachiel	♀ Anael	♄ Cassiel	☉ Michael	☽ Gabriel	♂ Samael

Figure 33: The angels who reign over each hour of the day and night.
The symbol of the reigning planet is next to the name of each angel.

24. Chayyiel—Chief of the Cherubim (Holy Hayyoth).

25. Shemuil—Intermediary between the prayers of Israel and the Angelic Princes of the Seventh Heaven; one of the great Arcons.

26. Suriel—Moses' instructor and a benevolent angel of death; one of the princes of the Divine Presence.

27. Zophiel (Iofiel)—Chief of the Order of Thrones; one of the guardian princes of the Torah or divine law.

28. Azbugah—One of the eight judgment angels of God's Throne; he dresses in a garment of righteousness the souls of the elect.

29. Yefefiah (Dina)—One of the angels of the Torah or divine law; he taught Moses the mysteries of the Kabbalah.

30. Zagzagel—Angel of wisdom; angel of the burning bush; he is also a chief guard of the Fourth Heaven.

These celestial princes may be propitiated by human beings during difficult moments, according to the things they rule. To propitiate an angel means to ask for his help and guidance, mentioning his name and making an offering of a white candle, frankincense, and myrrh. Angels should only be evoked or invoked with precaution because of the great energies they emit. This will be discussed in detail in chapter 10.

Figure 33 (page 128) shows the angels that rule the hours of the day and night. The astrological symbol next to each angel signifies the planet ruled by that angel. Once the name of the angel who rules each hour is known, it is easier to propitiate it by choosing that specific time to make the petition.

The most famous of the books on angels is the *Book of the Angel Raziel* which, according to traditional sources,was written by Raziel himself. Most angel scholars, however, believe the book to be the work of Jewish kabbalist Eleazor of Worms. The earliest known edition of the book was published in Amsterdam in 1701. Its original title is *Sepher Raziel*. There are copies of the book in the original Hebrew in the New York Public Library, but the British Museum is said to have an English edition in its Sloane Collection. Several sections of the book in English were presented to me by a collector friend several years ago, and the material presented in those few precious pages was mesmerizing. Whoever the author may have been, he certainly knew his angels. Copies in Hebrew are available from a Jewish press in Brooklyn. When I purchased my copy from them, I was told the book is used as an amulet against danger by devout Jews.

The *Book of the Angel Raziel* cites the seven great archangels who stand in front of God's Throne. The names given are Michael, Gabriel, Uriel, Raphael, Phenuel, Israel, and Uzziel. Other sources say that there are anywhere between four and seventy angels facing the Divine Presence, but most angelologists concur that seven is the most accurate number.

One of the most fascinating bits of information given in the *Book of the Angel Raziel* is a list of the angels of the celestial encampments that are found in the Seven Heavens. All the various angelic hosts are named, as well as what each of them rules in the material world and how they may be invoked to acquire unimaginable wealth and everything the human heart may desire.

The segment of the book that I own is called the *Book of Noah* and it gives detailed instructions for the preparation of an iron ring through which the angels of the camps of the Sixth Heaven may be invoked. The names of the angels given only provide the consonants because Hebrew, from which these segments were translated, does not have any vowels. Therefore it is no easy task to read them, even when one is familiar with the angelic names. But among them I was able to detect the names of Gabriel, Asariel, Barakiel, Sopheriel, Muriel, Anael, and Adonael. Perhaps the most poignant part of the segment are the two beautiful hymns that end it. Only an angel could have written them. I would like to share one of them with you.

Second Hymn

He promises His Name.
They praise its power and beauty.
He promises through the treasures of snow.
They praise in flux of fire,
in lustrum clouds and flashing palaces.
He who rules the sky promises,
and their praise sweeps through the armies.
He promises the Mystery of the Flame.
They praise through voices of thunder
and quick flashing lightning.
Earth praises, abyss praises,
waves of the seas praise.
Praise the pristine Name
on the throne in each soul
in each creature
infinitely.

9

The Four Great Archangels

As we have seen, most of the information we have on angels originates from rabbinical sources, such as the Talmud, the Midrash, and the Kabbalah. The Koran and other Muslim holy books speak at length on the subject of angels and their great powers. Some of the most vivid descriptions of these celestial beings come from the Koran, according to which the Archangel Michael has saffron-colored hair and emerald wings. Other well-known sources are the Apocrypha, the *Pseudepigrapha*, Saint Augustine's *The City of God*, and Saint Thomas Aquinas' *Summa Theologica*. Among the less familiar sources are the *Book of the Angel Raziel*, *The Testament of Solomon*, *The Arbatel of Magic*, *The Almadel*, the *Greater and Lesser Keys of*

Solomon, the *Sixth and Seventh Books of Moses*, and many of the medieval grimoires.

Of all the angels mentioned in these books, the most popular and most revered are Raphael, Michael, Gabriel, and Uriel. Uriel is the lesser-known of the four, but his influence in the angelic tradition cannot be ignored.

As we have seen in the preceding chapter, these four archangels rule the four cardinal points and the four elements. The elements and the cardinal points form a wheel, a circle of great power and magnetism that surrounds the terrestrial globe. The first cardinal point starts in the east, where the sun rises every morning, and corresponds to the air element and the Archangel Raphael. Moving to the right on this cosmic circle, following the course of the sun and the hands of the clock, we reach the south, corresponding to the fire element and the Archangel Michael. Still moving to the right, we reach the west, corresponding to the water element and the Archangel Gabriel. And finally, we come to the north, the quarter belonging to the earth element and the Archangel Uriel. If we visualize the planet Earth within this cosmic wheel, we can imagine the four archangels standing on the four corners of the world, forming a giant cross.

Each of the four archangels has his own colors and a specific appearance, according to the angelic tradition. Raphael wears a yellow mantle with a violet lining over a resplendent white tunic. He is barefoot. He represents the dawn and is described as a beautiful adolescent with light blue eyes and pale blond hair that surrounds his head like a halo. Like all the four archangels, his wings are dazzling white, like snow crystals shimmering in the sun.

Michael follows Raphael in the solar cycle. He wears a red mantle with a green lining over Roman armor and knee-high Roman sandals. Michael represents midday and has the appearance of a young man in his mid-twenties. His skin is fair, with golden tones, and his shoulder-length hair is red like a flame, thick, and wavy. His eyes are blue-green.

Gabriel follows next and represents the early afternoon. He wears a blue mantle with orange lining over a snowy white tunic.

He is barefoot. He has the appearance of a man in his mid-thirties. He has light-olive skin, green eyes, and his bronze-colored hair falls below his shoulders.

Uriel, the fourth archangel in the solar wheel, wears a mantle made of the four colors of the earth element: lemon-green, olive-green, reddish-brown, and black. He represents the sunset and early evening. His skin is dark olive, his eyes are dark brown, and his long hair is dark and curly. He is the only one of the four archangels who has a beard. Uriel's appearance is that of a man in his mid to late forties.

It is easy to see from the traditional descriptions of the four archangels that each of them matures as they move along the solar wheel, and their features darken. This happens because the sun marks the passing of the day from sunrise to sunset, and the sky darkens as evening approaches. The angels represent the motion of the sun and the passing of the hours. In one single day they show the four transitions of human life, from birth and early youth, to latter youth, midlife, and full maturity. After the angels leave and night falls, the cycle of death envelops the Earth and human life comes to an end, only to be reborn next day with a new sunrise.

Raphael

Raphael is the Angel of Dawn, Prince Regent of the Second Heaven, and one of the

Prince Regents of the Cherubim and the Archangels. He is Chief of the Virtues and belongs to four of the other choirs: the Seraphim, the Cherubim, the Dominions, and the Powers. He is of Chaldean origin and his first name was Labbiel.

Raphael's name means "God has healed." In the Catholic Church he is known as the "divine physician" and is reputed to have the power to heal all illnesses. He is also the protector of the Earth, which he also heals. It is said of this archangel that he is the regent of the sun and stands in its middle. He is often identified with Ramiel, Raguel, and Raffarel.

Figure 34: The Archangel Raphael and Tobias.

Among the Muslims, he is known as Azrael, the angel of death, who is also the regent of Scorpio. In the *Book of Tobit*, Raphael hides his angelic identity under the name Azariah.

Raphael is the angel who guards the Tree of Life, one of the six angels of repentance, the angel of prayer, of joy, and of light. He is also the angel of science, of medicine, of wisdom, and one of the seven angels of the Apocalypse.

When Solomon asked God to help him in the construction of the temple, the Creator gave him a ring engraved with a pentagram, a star of five points. Raphael was the divine messenger who brought this ring to Solomon. It is believed that the use of the pentagram as a magic and religious symbol originates in this story.

Raphael is often depicted with a staff in one hand and a fish in the other, a symbol of his odyssey with Tobias. In this apocryphal story, Raphael teaches Tobias how to use the heart and liver of a fish to exorcise the infernal spirit, Asmodeus, and how to use the bile of the same fish to heal the blindness of Tobias' father, Tobit.

Raphael is propitiated to heal all illnesses and his help is often asked in everything connected with papers, such as studies, contracts, and books. An easy way to secure his help is by writing the petition on a yellow paper, which is then burned in the flame of a yellow candle. The ashes are thrown to the wind from a high place, as Raphael rules the

Figure 35: The Archangel Michael defeating Satan,
who is represented here as a dragon.

air element. This should always be done during the waxing moon and preferably on a Wednesday, the day ascribed to Raphael in angelic magic.

It is also said of Raphael that he is one of the Guardians, or Grigori, who maintain a constant vigil over the gates of Heaven. He is also one of the guides into Sheol, which according to the Jews is the place where the spirit goes upon the death of the physical body.

Raphael is one of the four great princes who stand in front of God's Throne and, according to rabbinical sources, one of the three angels who visited Abraham in the Book of Genesis. The other two are said to be Michael and Gabriel. Raphael is also the ruling angel of the Sixth Sephira in the Tree of Life, which is the sphere of the sun. He is an amiable, joyful angel who is said to smile constantly.

In recent times there have been rumors that Raphael is a feminine entity, something strongly negated by the biblical accounts, all of which depict him as a male angel. But in reality, angels are spiritual beings without any sexual characteristics. They only assume physical form when they want to be perceived by human beings.

Michael

Michael is the symbol of perfect divine justice. His name signifies "he who is like God." In spite of the fact that there are so many great angels in Heaven, he is still considered the greatest of all the angels in Judaism, Christianity, and Islam. It is said of Michael that he sits next to God on his Throne and is often identified with Metraton and with the Shekinah. He is also identified with Saint Peter, as they both have the keys of Heaven. Some ecclesiastical authorities find parallels between Michael and Saint George because both slew the dragon, a symbol of Satan in Christianity.

The ancient Persians worshiped Michael as Beshter, the protector of humanity. Michael is both uncorrupt and uncorruptible, which means that it is impossible to corrupt or to tempt him to do evil. He is perfect and pure and there is no blemish in him.

Michael is God's favorite angel and the most powerful. The Judeo-Christian tradition teaches that vengeance belongs to God, who dispenses his perfect justice through Michael's scales.

In Christian iconography, Michael is shown wearing tall sandals and Roman armor. He wears a red and green mantle and carries a balance in one hand and a sword in the other. One of his sandals is firmly planted on the dragon's neck, who is Satan, as a symbol of his triumph over God's adversary in the war between the angels.

Michael is one of the Prince Regents of three of the angelic choirs: the Seraphim, the Virtues, and the Archangels. He is also the ruler of the Fourth Heaven, one of the six angels of repentance, the angel of rectitude, of compassion, of sanctification, and Prince of the Divine Presence. He is also the guardian angel of Israel and Germany, and it is said that it was he who gave the tablets of the Ten Commandments to Moses in Sinai.

Like Raphael's, Michael's name originates in ancient Chaldea. He is said to be the author of Psalm 85, which is read in his name to ask him for a miracle. In the sacred teachings, Michael is often identified with the Holy Spirit because of his great purity.

According to the Muslim tradition, Michael's wings are emerald in color and each of his hairs, red like burning coals, are covered with millions of faces, all of which implore God's forgiveness for the sins of humanity. It is said that Michael cries constantly for the sins of the faithful, and from his tears were formed the Cherubim. The Muslims, who know him as Mikail, say that when the great archangel cries, his tears are immediately transformed into precious stones.

Michael is the Prince Regent of the planet Mercury, the sign of Leo, and the fire element. He is Prince of the Light, Prince of the Virtues, Prince of the Archangels, Guardian of Peace, Commander-in-Chief of the Heavenly Hosts, Guardian Angel of the Catholic Church, Guardian Angel of Israel, Angel of the Earth, and Prince of God. He is also the divine archstrategist, who devises all the battle plans in Heaven against the legions of evil. He is the angel who rescued Saint Peter from prison and the prophet Daniel from the lion's den. It will be Michael who will descend from Heaven on the Day of the Final Judgment with the key to the bottomless pit, where he will imprison Satan for a thousand years. He will also weigh the souls on his balance on that momentous day.

The secret name of Michael is Sabathiel. Some traditions envision him in the Seventh Heaven surrounded by the celestial armies. In Christianity he is venerated as a benevolent angel of death through whom it is possible to receive the forgiveness of the Creator and eternal life. According to the biblical tradition, it was Michael who saved Meshach, Shadrach, and Abednego, the companions of Daniel, from the fiery furnace where they were thrown by King Nebuchadnezzar of Babylonia because they refused to worship his idols.

Michael was also the angel who knelt by Mary's side with a lit candle in his hand to announce her coming death. When Mary asked his name, Michael answered, "I am called Great and Powerful." Joan of Arc named Michael as the angel who inspired her to do battle against the English on behalf of the French Dauphin, later Charles VII, a heroic act for which she was burned at the stake.

Michael is the patron of policemen, firefighters, sailors, soldiers, and shopkeepers. An easy way to propitiate this great archangel is by burning a red apple with laurel leaves in the fire while reading Psalm 85. The ashes are placed in a small red bag and carried with the person until the petition is granted. Afterward, the ashes are thrown outside the person's home to ensure Michael's protection. This ritual should be done on a Tuesday during the waxing moon.

Gabriel

Gabriel is the Angel of Annunciation, of Death and Resurrection, of Vengeance and Compassion. Above all, Gabriel is the divine messenger who reveals God's will to humanity. According to the Muslim tradition, Gabriel has 140 pairs of wings. This great archangel stands in the west, where the sun sets, thereby sealing the door where evil dwells. The west is believed to be the door to evil because when the sun sets in this cardinal point, the Earth is covered by the dark mantle of the night, which has always been associated with negative forces.

When a human body dies, God sends Gabriel to Earth to retrieve that person's spirit and guide it, depending on its past actions, to its place of rest. Gabriel also guides all spirits back to Earth for their next incarnation. He is the Angel of Annunciation because he knows when a child is going to be born. Women who desire the gift of maternity ask Gabriel for this favor, and for this reason he is also known as the Angel of Hope. According to an ancient Jewish teaching, Gabriel instructs the child in its mother's womb during the nine months of gestation.

It is believed that terminally ill persons may prolong their lives by asking Gabriel to intercede on their behalf in front of the Divine Throne. During Judgment Day, it will be Gabriel who will sound his trumpet to awaken the souls of the dead.

The *Pseudepigrapha*, which contains the apocalyptic visions of several of the prophets, says that it was Gabriel who revealed to Ezra the Seven Paths through which a soul must pass to reach the Divine Presence. The First Path, according to Gabriel, is terrible and fascinating; the Second is terrifying and indescribable; the Third is a frozen hell; the Fourth is filled with horrific battles. If the soul is pure, it will begin to radiate light as it reaches the Fifth Path; if it is impure, its aura will darken. In the Sixth Path the pure soul will be as dazzling as the sun. When it reaches the Seventh Path, Gabriel guides it to the Divine Throne and the Glory of God. In this narrative it is not clear what happens to the impure souls once they reach the Fifth Path. The last three paths are not described by Gabriel, but it is obvious that the Seven Paths are the ones that traverse the Seven Heavens.

According to the *Third Book of Enoch*, it is Gabriel, and not Michael, who rules the fire element. Enoch also says that Gabriel is the Prince Regent of the Sixth instead of the First Heaven. In the Gospel according to

**Figure 36: The Archangel Gabriel appearing to the Virgin Mary
to announce Jesus' conception (the Annunciation).**

Luke, Gabriel announces to Zechariah the coming birth of his son, who was to be known as John the Baptist.

Gabriel is also said to be a consummate linguist and he was the angel who taught Joseph, Jacob's son, the seventy languages spoken in the Tower of Babel in the course of one single night.

Gabriel's name means "God is my Power." The archangel is often depicted with a lily in one hand, a symbol of Mary's purity, or with a trumpet, a symbol of Judgment Day. According to Jewish tradition, it was Gabriel who destroyed the cities of Sodom and Gomorrah. He is also the angel who revealed to Daniel what will happen during Judgment Day, and the one who wrestled with Jacob during an entire night, although several other angels are also named in this famous biblical encounter. It is also said of Gabriel that he is the angel who ripens all the fruits on Earth.

In one of the best known of Gabriel's stories, the great archangel lost the Lord's favor because he failed to carry out one of the Creator's orders exactly as he had been instructed. In those early times, God was very angry at Israel's continuous offenses and he asked Gabriel to rain coals of fire over the Israelites. Then he was to help the Babylonians destroy the survivors of the divine fire. But Gabriel, filled with compassion toward Israel, chose the laziest angel in Heaven to gather the burning coals. The angel took such a long time in gathering the coals that they were quite cold when Gabriel sent them down to earth and they caused no major damage. Then Gabriel counseled the Babylonians against destroying Israel, leading the Israelites instead into exile in Babylonia. When God discovered Gabriel's disobedience, he was so indignant that he immediately expulsed Gabriel from his Divine Presence. And if we are to believe what Enoch tells us about this heavenly fiasco, Gabriel received several lashes of fire on his celestial back for this offense, and was ordered to remain behind the sacred curtain that protects God's Throne. During several weeks Gabriel was substituted by the angel Dubbiel, protecting angel of the Persians. While Gabriel remained in this forced exile, the Israelites suffered cruelly under the Persian boot, whose guardian angel was now in power in Paradise. But Gabriel, who was waiting for the right moment behind the sacred curtain, made such a brilliant suggestion during one of the Heavenly Councils that he was immediately reinstated to his place in front of the Divine Throne. Perhaps because he lost his exalted position in Heaven, Dubbiel later became one of the rebellious angels.

In Islam, Gabriel is known as Jibril, and it was he who dictated the Koran to the prophet Mohammed. An easy way to propitiate Gabriel is to light a silver candle in his name by the light of the full moon, making the petition. The flame of the candle is then extinguished in a goblet filled with cold mineral water. The water is drunk in one single draught, without removing the goblet from the lips. This is repeated during nine full moons with the same candle. The last night the candle is allowed to burn to its completion. This is said to be especially effective when a woman desires to conceive a child.

Uriel

Uriel is one of the Prince Regents of the Seraphim and the Cherubim and one of the regents of the sun. He is also one of the Princes of the Divine Presence and the Angel of Salvation. His name means "Fire of God."

Uriel is the angel who protects against thunder and lightning, earthquakes, cataclysms, and volcanic eruptions. He is the angel that God sent to warn Noah of the coming deluge. In *Paradise Lost*, Milton describes Uriel as the angel with the acutest eyesight in Heaven, the one who can best foresee the future and from whom nothing is hidden. That is perhaps the reason why his help is invoked by those suffering from eye problems. He is also said to grant increased mental clarity.

Uriel's name is said to derivate from the prophet Uriah. His symbol is a hand holding a flame. Francis Barrett, in his work *The Magus*, says that it was Uriel who taught the mysteries of alchemy and the Kabbalah to human beings.

The *First Book of Enoch* relates how the patriarch was carried through the Seven Heavens by the angels of the Lord. During this awesome journey he saw a chaotic place where there was neither Heaven nor Earth. In the midst of this terrifying scenario he saw seven angels, similar to stars, all tied together, huge as mountains, burning in a vast fire. When Enoch asked what was the meaning of this portent, Uriel, who was his guide in this part of the odyssey, told him that these creatures had broken God's commandments and that they would remain in the burning chasm for ten million years, which was the number of their sins.

In the *Second Book of Esdras*, Uriel is described as the interpreter of this prophet's vision. In the fifth chapter of the book, Esdras reproaches God, asking why he punishes Israel and protects its enemies. Uriel, who is walking by Esdras' side, says that he will reveal God's reasons to Esdras, but only if the prophet can weigh the fire, measure the wind, and bring back the previous day. When Esdras complains that what Uriel demands is impossible, the archangel tells him that if knowing the fire, the wind, and the days, he cannot understand them, how can he possibly understand the designs of God, whom Esdras does not know? Filled with shame, Esdras lies down at Uriel's feet and asks forgiveness for his blind judgment of God's actions.

In spite of his patient labors as guide and instructor of patriarchs and prophets, Uriel

Figure 37: The Archangel Uriel following the fall of Satan.

can also be terrifyingly severe in the punishments he devises for those who offend the Creator. In the Apocalypse of Saint Peter, Uriel chastises those who blaspheme against God by hanging them by their tongues over an inextinguishable fire.

Uriel is the regent of the month of September and may be especially propitiated by those born on that month, whom he protects greatly. He also rules Aquarius and white quartz crystals are offered to him in order to increase their power. To gather Uriel's energy within a white quartz, it is first necessary to purify the crystal by immersing it in sea saltwater for twenty-four hours. It is then rinsed and placed in sunlight for at least six hours to replenish its energies. The quartz is then placed over a bit of earth and surrounded by four burning green candles. When the candles are extinguished, the quartz is placed in a small green bag with a bit of wheat to attract money and prosperity, which are ruled by Uriel.

The Ritual of the Pentagram

As we saw in the preceding chapter, it is said that God gave Solomon a ring engraved with the five-pointed star, known as the pentagram. This is a very popular magical symbol. It represents a human being with open arms and widespread legs.

In angelic magic, there is a very famous ceremony known as the Ritual of the Pentagram, which is used to protect a person and surround him with angelic energy. This ritual invokes the power of the four great archangels, Raphael, Michael, Gabriel, and Uriel, and is based on the teachings of the Kabbalah.

The ceremony, in itself, is simple. The person faces the east and makes the kabbalistic cross in the following manner:

With the right hand he touches his forehead and says: *Atoh* (In the name).

He then brings the same hand to the solar plexus and says: *Malkuth* (of the Kingdom).

He touches his right shoulder and says: *Ve Geburah* (and Power).

He touches his left shoulder and says: *Ve Gedulah* (and Mercy).

He then unites both hands in front of his chest and says: *Leolahm* (Amen).

He then places his thumb between the middle finger and the index finger of the right hand (or left hand if he is left-handed) to form what is known as the ficca (see the illustration on page 143). This is a very ancient symbol used to protect against all forms of evil.

The person points the ficca, arm extended, toward a point slightly higher than his head and traces the Pentagram of Invocation, as shown in Figure 38. As he does this, he visualizes that the pentagram he is tracing is made of fire. When the pentagram has been formed, he points the ficca at the imaginary center of the pentagram and says in a loud and strong voice:

Figure 38: The invoking pentagram.

In the holy name of God,
Yod He Vau He, and the great
Archangel Raphael, I seal this circle in
the east and the air element.

Without lowering his arm he moves to the right until he reaches the south, imagining that the ficca is forming a fiery line connecting from the east to the south. Once he has reached the south, he traces another pentagram at the same level as the first, points the ficca at the center and says:

In the holy name of God, Adonai,
and the great Archangel Michael,
I seal this circle in the south
and the fire element.

Figure 39: The banishing pentagram.

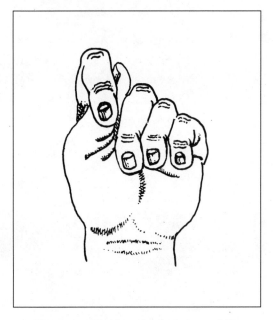

Figure 40: The ficca formation, used for tracing the magical circle, or pentagram.

He then turns to the west, still tracing the fiery line that connects it to the south. At the west, he traces the third pentagram in midair, points the ficca at its center, and says:

In the holy name of God, Eheieh,
and the great Archangel Gabriel,
I seal this circle in the west
and the water element.

He continues to trace the imaginary line of fire until he reaches the north.

Here he forms the pentagram again, points the ficca at its center, and says:

In the holy name of God, Agla,
and the great Archangel Uriel,
I seal this circle in the north
and the earth element.

He continues to move until he reaches the east once more, completing the circle of imaginary fire surmounted by four blazing stars in its four cardinal points. He then opens his arms and says:

In front of me, Raphael;
Behind me, Gabriel;
To my right, Michael;
To my left, Uriel.
Facing me is the flaming pentagram,
and behind me is the six-pointed star.

The six-pointed star is better known as the Star of David, which is formed by two interlaced triangles, one pointing upward and the other pointing downward. The upper triangle represents fire and the lower triangle represents water.

After the pentagrams have been traced, the person visualizes them on the four quarters of a flaming circle. Behind the eastern pentagram he visualizes Raphael, draped in yellow and violet with golden hair; behind the southern pentagram he visualizes Michael, in red and green, hair like flame; behind the western pentagram, he visualizes Gabriel, in blue and orange, with bronze hair; and behind the northern pentagram he visualizes Uriel dressed in lemon and olive green, brown and black, his hair and beard dark as the night. All the archangels stand with widespread wings, more dazzling than the sun.

At this point, the person may petition one or more of the angels for a special favor, or carry out any other ceremony that requires the protection of the angels. During this ritual the person should move only toward the right, in the movement known as deosil. To move to the left is to invite negative energies into the circle.

When he wishes to end the ceremony, the person must retrace the pentagrams in the same order, but this time using the banishing pentagram (see page 143). The words that must be said are:

In the east, after tracing the pentagram:

*In the holy name of God, Yod He
Vau He, and the great Archangel
Raphael, I banish this circle in
the east and the air element.*

In the south, after tracing the pentagram:

*In the holy name of God, Adonai,
and the great Archangel Michael,
I banish this circle in the south
and the fire element.*

In the west, after tracing the pentagram:

*In the holy name of God, Eheieh,
and the great Archangel Gabriel,
I banish this circle in the west
and the water element.*

In the north, after tracing the pentagram:

*In the holy name of God, Agla,
and the great Archangel Uriel,
I banish this circle in the north
and the earth element.*

The angels are now visualized with their backs to the person, as they are now ready to depart. The person now says:

*In the name of the Creator of the
Universe and the great Archangels
Raphael, Michael, Gabriel, and Uriel,
this ritual is ended. I thank you for
your presence during this ritual
and I say Hail and Farewell.*

These words are repeated on the four cardinal points, starting with the east.

Before commencing this ritual, the place where it is going to take place should be sprinkled with saltwater for purification. Frankincense and myrrh should be burned to sweeten the air and to attract the angels. Fasting for twenty-four hours before the ritual is strongly recommended, as well as the abstention from sexual relations and addictive substances. All the rituals of invocation of the angels should only be carried out during the waxing moon.

After the conclusion of the ritual, the person should drink a small glass of sweet wine and eat a small cake or a piece of bread, in order to reestablish contact with the material world. This is known as "grounding" the angelic energies.

This ritual, like all magical ceremonies or meditations, is done to establish a deeper contact with the inner self or unconscious of the individual, also known as a person's holy guardian angel. The four archangels may be seen as archetypes of the collective unconscious of the human race. As such, they have immense power, based on the combined psychic energies of all humanity. It is possible to contact and tap into these energies through ceremonies like the Ritual of the Pentagram. They can then be channeled and integrated into our conscious personality, empowering the individual with their cosmic force. This can be of great help during our daily lives.

Ceremonies like the Ritual of the Pentagram, as well as meditations, breathing exercises, and meditations, are growing in popularity in our modern times. In reality, we are rediscovering our spiritual roots and laying claim to an ancient heritage that has been lost for centuries.

10

Invoking the Angels

An invocation is a petition to God, the angels, the saints, or any supernatural entity that may be able to grant us our desires. It can also be an incantation, a conjuration, or a formal prayer used at the beginning of a church service. In law, it is a formal request from the bench for evidence pertaining to a case other than the one under trial. In short, one makes an invocation to ask for a special concession. And this request is invariably formal. It needs to be presented correctly and through the appropriate channels. This signifies that an invocation to a superior force is more than a simple prayer. It is a formal request, like those presented in a court of law, for a specific action on behalf of the petitioner. It is interesting that a judge should use the word "invocation" when making a request for certain legal actions, especially when God is considered to be the Supreme Judge and the celestial court the highest court of appeal.

As ministers of the Lord, the angels are in a paramount position to grant or deny the petitions made through invocations. But to be considered, these must be presented correctly, and that is where the rituals and ceremonies to the angels come in. Prayers, invocations, and evocations are all rituals, but it is important to determine their differences.

A prayer is an act of communion with God, his angels, or saints. The Psalms are at the core of the liturgy of both Judaism and Christianity since ancient times, and they are still used as prayers to ask God's blessing and his help in the problems of daily life. In the original Hebrew, many of the Psalms have several of God's names hidden among their versicles and are often used in magical rites, as they are believed to possess supernatural powers through which human problems may be solved. The Muslims believe that the Koran also has magical powers and some of its versicles are used in conjunction with certain ceremonies to solve problems. All the sacred books, like the Vedas, the Avesta, and the Tripitakas, are also used in magical ceremonies.

The Christian prayer includes invocation, praises, thanksgiving, petition, confession, and supplication for the forgiveness of sins, and it is based on the Pater Noster, which was given by Jesus to his disciples.

In its strictest definition, a prayer is a spiritual communion with a deity for the purpose of requesting a favor. It is an oral ritual specifically designed to contact supernatural forces.

The ritual dances of the African and American Indian tribes and the meditations of the Buddhist monks in their search for perfection are forms of prayers. And all of them, in one way or the other, help the petitioner establish contact with the depths of the unconscious, which is the key to the sacred mysteries.

To assist in making a prayer more effective, there are many forms of prayer aids, such as the Tibetan wheel and the Catholic rosary, where repetition is believed to be the key to success. The Muslims use prayer rugs and the Jews use phylacteries, small leather cases holding slips inscribed with scriptural passages. One of these is fastened with leather thongs to the forehead and the other to the left arm during morning prayers.

Certain actions are always involved with prayer. Catholics kneel while Jews stand. Orthodox Jews move back and forth during prayer, as motion is believed to infuse the prayer with more power. Muslims kneel with their foreheads on the dust, while facing Mecca. Hindus and Buddhists sit with straight backs, their legs interlaced in the lotus position, their hands folded or their fingers intertwined in complicated positions called *mudras*. The idea is the same in all cases, to reach a Higher Force for a specific purpose.

In a prayer, the supplicant expresses his need or desire to his Deity and lets that Supreme Power decide whether or not the prayer will be answered. During an invocation, the petitioner goes beyond prayer and attempts to contact that Force directly by means of the attributes associated with it. Among these attributes are sacred names, colors, numbers, stones, flowers, herbs, incenses, metals, talismans, and other mystical symbols, as well as the element belonging to that entity. These are all used in special ceremonies dedicated to the Force invoked.

Because it is more direct and dynamic, the invocation is usually more effective than ordinary prayer and the results are seen faster and in a more positive form. As a result of the invocation, the unconscious generates large quantities of psychic energy, which are then channeled consciously by the individual to manifest his desires in the material world. During the invocation, what is desired is strongly visualized so that the images are received by the unconscious and turned into reality. An example of an invocation is the Ritual of the Pentagram, which we discussed in the preceding chapter, and through which the energies of the four archangels are invoked for the protection of the individual. Because of the great amount of psychic energy released by the unconscious during this invocation, a circle of light or fire is also visualized. This keeps the energies concentrated around the person and not corrupted by any negative vibrations that may be lurking outside the circle.

In contrast to the invocation, the evocation is a specific petition to a spiritual entity, like an angel, to *manifest visibly* in front of the person. This requires the use of several of the attributes traditionally ascribed to that particular force, powerful prayers, and most especially a very strong will and determination. An example of an evocation is the Ritual of Hagiel that I described before and which I will give in detail later in this chapter. The evocation works in the same manner as the invocation. All the attributes of the force evoked—its name, the prayers used to evoke it, and the concentrated will of the petitioner—assist in releasing tremendous

amounts of psychic energies from the unconscious. Because the unconscious carries within its depths the telesmatic images of the entity, that is, the presupposed appearance that tradition has ascribed to that force, the energies released are emitted in the visual form of the force. This functions very much in the form of a hologram that appears to be solid but is not. All the knowledge or information that may be imparted by the evoked entity is in reality part of the contents of the unconscious that have been collected since the beginning of time and are in fact engraved in the genetic code. What the person is doing through an evocation is accessing information from within his own higher self through an archetypal form that manifests as a supernatural force.

In the Middle Ages, many books of evocation were written that gave detailed instructions for the evocation of supernatural entities, such as angels, with an emphasis on infernal forces. These books were commonly known as grimoires. Among the best-known ones are *The Great Grimoire*, *The Grimorium Verum*, the *Greater and Lesser Keys or Clavicles of Solomon*, *The Arbatel of Magic*, and *The Grimoire of Pope Honorius*, which in spite of bearing his name was never written by that much-maligned prelate of the Church. The grimoires recommended the use of magic swords and knives to force the entities to materialize visibly outside the circle of protection. Magical squares with the inscribed names of the forces evoked, powerful incenses, and burning crucibles where the names of the forces could be burned to further coerce the spirits to appear were all part of the formidable array of magical weapons used in these rituals by the medieval magicians. The magical rites for the evocation of evil spirits was known as goetic or black magic. Much of the information contained in the grimoires has been discredited by latter studies, mainly because many of the names of the entities had been corrupted by poor translations through the passage of time.

The rites of invocation and evocation can result in astonishing and quite visible manifestations of psychic energies. Some of these, particularly when evil forces are being evoked, can be terrifying. Evil forces manifest in the same manner as positive forces through the release of psychic energies from the unconscious. Evil is present in all of us, and is willfully repressed by an individual for the good of society. As we saw earlier, these negative energies were called the Id by Freud, and the Shadow by Jung. They are archetypal in nature, which means that they can take specific forms and have specific characteristics. Jung called them autonomous complexes because they can exist and function independently of the conscious will of the individual. When an archetype, whether positive or negative, takes possession of the conscious personality, the result may be a tempo-

rary trance when the person behaves and acts as if he were that archetype, or it can be a more powerful outpouring of psychic energy where the individual consciousness is totally overpowered by the archetype. This is the cause of many irreversible psychoses and may be the reason behind many impulsive criminal acts, where the person is unable to control his destructive urges. A well-known case of an archetype totally overpowering the conscious personality is that of Frederick Nietzche, whose obsession with Zarathustra or Zoroaster eventually resulted in the Zoroaster archetype's complete overshadowing of Nietzche's consciousness. Nietzsche in fact *became* Zoroaster and spent the rest of his life in the grip of a powerful psychosis that he was never able to overcome.

To resume, what happens during an invocation or evocation is that the individual establishes direct contact with the collective unconscious, which is a pool or receptacle for everything the human being has done, imagined, or learned since his emergence from the primeval soup. The telesmatic images of the angels or negative forces are part of this huge accumulation of knowledge. Through an evocation, the telesmatic image of an entity, whether positive or negative, is released from the deep unconscious and projected outwardly, making it visible to the individual. This mental hologram has physical characteristics because it is formed of distinctive energies that give it a solid appearance. The entity seems real because it has been formulated and shaped by human imagination through many centuries of visualization. The passage of time has imbued it with sufficient psychic energy to make it apparently solid and with a definite identity.

As I explained earlier, for an evocation to be successful and for the evoked entity to manifest visibly, it is necessary for the person who conducts the ritual to have a powerful will and great powers of visualization, as well as the capacity of total concentration. The person must also be able to withstand the shock of *seeing* a supernatural force manifest visibly in front of him without losing his equanimity and self-control. He must always remember that what he is seeing is an outpouring of the contents of his own psyche and that he should be able to control these energies at will. For this reason, the rituals of evocation are not easy to carry out. Invocations are preferable because they do not call for physical manifestations, making the released energies far safer and more easily accessible.

In the case of the angels, we are dealing with entities that have well-defined personalities, easily identifiable with cosmic laws and cosmic dimensions. The *Book of Enoch* describes some of the angels as beings so huge that they extend beyond the galaxies. The seven great archangels are identified by Enoch as stars created by God at the moment of Creation. This indicates that to Enoch the angels are cosmic forces with intelligence and purpose, something that some astrophysicists, like Australian Paul Davies, are beginning to suspect. In his book *The Mind of God*, Paul Davies says that he has no doubts that the universe is ruled by intelligent and purposeful cosmic forces, and he is not the only well-known scientist who has expressed this belief.

The best form to contact an angel directly and to tap into its huge reservoir of cosmic energies is through invocation and other rituals that help establish direct contact with the deep unconscious. This is commonly known as angelic magic.

Ritual to Learn the Name of Your Guardian Angel

Because the angel is a cosmic entity of great power it is always advisable to prepare mentally and physically before contacting him. This is not superstition but simple logic. All the energy that is released from the unconscious must be as pure as possible in order to use it more effectively. For that reason it is always recommended that the person contemplating such contacts should fast and abstain from sexual relations and addictive substances such as alcohol, drugs, caffeine, and nicotine for at least twenty-four hours before any ritual. Bathing and dressing in white are also advised because white is a symbol of light, which comprises the entire solar spectrum. The burning of incense, specially frankincense and myrrh, helps in concentration, as does the use of soft and ethereal music during the ritual.

To learn the name of your guardian angel, open a previously chosen book, which may be the Bible or a dictionary. This ritual is conducted facing the east, which represents the positive and creative forces of the universe. After the book is opened, close your eyes and place your index finger on the right-hand page. On a piece of white unlined paper, proceed to write down the first letter of the word directly under your finger.

This is repeated three, four, or five times, depending upon your intuition. If you decide to open the book three times, you will write down three letters; if you open the book four times, you will write down four letters; if you open the book five times, you will write down five letters.

Most of the letters you will jot down will be consonants because there are more consonants than vowels in the alphabet. If the letters are all consonants, choose any of the five vowels (a, e, i, o, u) in the order dictated by your own intuition, to place between any of the consonants. If the letters are a combination of vowels and consonants, you may or may not add any more vowels, again according to your intuition. After you have done this, add the termination EL or ON to the letters because most of the angelic names end with one of these two suffixes. Well-known examples of angel names end-

ing in EL or ON are Michael, Gabriel, Raphael, Uriel, Sopheriel, Metraton, and Sandalphon.

For example, if you decide to open the book three times and the letters you jot down are H R M, you may decide to add two As and one I to form the name HARAMI. To this, add the termination EL and the angelic name you have created will be HARAMIEL. That is the name of your guardian angel, revealed to you by the angel himself through your own intuitive powers. On the other hand, if you chose to open the book five times, and the letters you wrote down were DGALU, you may decide to add only the vowel I to form the name DIGALU, to which you add the termination EL to form DIGALUEL. This will then be the name of your guardian angel. Conversely, you may decide to use the termination ON instead of EL, and the name would then be DIGALUON. If four letters are chosen, like ATRZ, you may decide to add just the vowel I to form the name ATRIZ, to which you add ON to form ATRIZON or EL to form ATRIZEL. The vowels chosen and the place where they are to be inserted is decided by you, guided by your own intuition and your guardian angel, who reveals his name in this manner. When the name of the angel is known, thank God and the angels and end the ritual. You are now able to call upon your personal guardian angel at any time you may need his help and protection.

Ritual of Invocation of the Planetary Angels

According to the angelic tradition, the Planetary Angels rule the seven planets of antiquity among which were included the sun and the moon. As we saw earlier, Neptune, Uranus, and Pluto were not included among the seven because they had not yet been discovered. The Planetary Angels are commonly identified as the Seven Princes who stand in front of the Divine Presence and are also identified as the seven stars created by God at the beginning of Creation.

Each of the Planetary Angels rules certain human interests and is ascribed a series of attributes and characteristics, such as planets, colors, numbers, metals, days of the week, incenses, flowers, stones, and other things. In a preceding chapter I gave a list of the names, planets, and days of the angels. I will now give some of the additional attributes of the Planetary Angels and the things they rule. Some of the colors and other attributes of the angels, in their planetary capacity, vary from their traditional attributes. This is markedly so in the case of the four great archangels, Raphael, Michael, Gabriel, and Uriel, whose attributes in the solar wheel are different than those given here. It is important to remember that the following attributes are only used when the angels are invoked in their planetary capacity.

The Seven Planetary Angels

1. Michael—He rules Sunday, the sun, abundance, money, mental power, spiritual illumination, and growth. Color as a Planetary Angel: yellow, gold; Number: 6; Trees: pine, walnut, date, oak; Incenses: frankincense, copal, vanilla, cinnamon, heliotrope; Plants: laurel or bay, eyebright, mistletoe, chamomile; Flower: sunflower, yellow chrysanthemum; Stones: peridot, citrine, sardonyx, ruby, diamond, tiger's eye, amber, topaz; Element: fire; Metal: gold; Sign: Leo.

2. Gabriel—He rules Monday, the moon, all liquids, intuition, dreams, women, short trips, and changes. Color as a Planetary Angel: violet, silver; Number: 9; Trees: coconut palm, hazel, weeping willow; Incenses: camphor, orris root, ylang-ylang, galbanum, jasmine, eucalyptus; Plants: white or purple lilies, melons, pumpkins, beans, yams; Stones: moonstone, beryl, alexandrite; Element: water; Metal: silver, platinum; Sign: Cancer.

3. Camael—He rules Tuesday, Mars, energy, war, all human difficulties, adversaries and enemies, rage, destruction, surgery, magnetism, willpower; Color as a Planetary Angel: red; Number: 5; Trees: mahogany, ash, holly, fig; Incenses: asafetida, dragon's blood resin, tobacco, spearmint, mustard, pepper, cumin; Plants: cactuses and all thorned plants, dandelion, John the Conqueror root, ginger, bamboo; Stones: ruby, garnet, bloodstone, rodochrosyte, carnelian; Element: earth; Metal: iron, nickel, steel; Signs: Aries, Scorpio.

4. Raphael—He rules Wednesday, Mercury, illnesses as well as good health, businesses, papers, books, contracts, lawsuits and legal trials; buying and selling; neighbors, literature; Color: orange; Number: 8; Trees: almond, magnolia; Incenses: anise, gum arabic, sandalwood, lavender, storax; Plants: marjoram, rue, ferns, mandrake, parsley; Stones: fire opal, carnelian, agate; Element: air; Metal: quicksilver, aluminum; Signs: Gemini, Virgo.

5. Sadkiel (Zadkiel)—He rules Thursday, Jupiter, prosperity, triumph, long journeys, expansion, generosity, banks, loans, executives and persons in charge, and gambling; Color: electric blue; Number: 4; Trees: olive, cedar, maple, juniper, all true oaks; Incenses: nutmeg, pine resin, clove, sarsaparilla, hyssop; Plants: sage, marjoram, purple betony, liverwort, flax; Stones: sapphire, azurite, sodalite, lapis lazuli, amethyst, turquoise, labradorite, thunderstones, meteorites; Element: fire; Metal: tin, zinc; Signs: Sagittarius, Pisces.

6. Anael—He rules Friday, Venus, love, marriage, the arts, music, pleasures, young people, beauty, joy, dances, entertainment, and social gatherings; Color: emerald green; Number: 7; Trees: apple, cherry, pear, orange, lemon; Incenses: benzoin, valerian, sandalwood, cinnamon, lavender, storax; Plants: vervain, myrtle, red roses, tulips, hibiscus; Stones: emerald, opal, malachite, jade, rose quartz, chrysocolla, amazonite, peacock ore; Element: air; Signs: Taurus, Libra.

7. Cassiel—He rules Saturday, Saturn, the elderly, inheritances, agriculture, real estate, debts, properties, death, and wills; Color: black or navy blue; Number: 3; Trees: cypress, elm, yew, acacia, ebony; Incenses: myrrh, patchouli, spikenard, cassia; Plants: violet, mullein, nightshade, white lilies, opium poppy; Stones: onyx, obsidian, hematite, jet, diamond; Element: earth; Signs: Capricorn, Aquarius.

As I mentioned earlier, it is important to remember that these attributes and correspondences are ascribed to these angels in their planetary aspects.

In astrology, the angels who rule the signs may differ from the above. Scorpio, for example, is ruled by Azrael; Pisces is ruled by Asariel; and Aquarius by Uriel. In the kabbalistic Tree of Life, Michael and Raphael exchange their regencies and Michael is associated with the sphere of Mercury while Raphael is associated with the sun. These correspondences are observed during kabbalistic rituals. The differences in the attributes and correspondences ascribed to the angels in different systems should not confuse the reader. What must be remembered is that each ritual calls for its own corre- spondences and as long as these are fol- lowed, the ritual will be effective.

The Ritual

Before conducting an invocation to any of the Planetary Angels, you must first decide what you wish to accomplish. Then choose the angel who rules that particular need or desire and its various attributes or corre- spondences. The ritual should be conducted on the day and hour ruled by the angel dur- ing the period of the waxing moon. A table with the planetary hours was given in a pre- ceding chapter. The angels are usually in- voked at 1 A.M., 8 A.M., 3 P.M., and 10 P.M. of the angel's day.

Begin by purifying yourself during the twenty-four hours before the ritual, as ex- plained earlier. Then sprinkle saltwater around the room where the invocation is to take place, to dispel any lingering negative vibrations. Burn a mixture of the incenses ascribed to the angel on several pieces of charcoal and pass them around the room. Then visualize a circle of light around the room, starting and ending at the east. You must always move deosil, that is, to the right, around the ritual area.

Then place a yellow candle in the east, a green candle in the south, a blue candle in the west, and a green candle in the south, as symbols of the four elements: air, fire, water, and earth, respectively. This is important because everything that exists is based on the four elements and this helps in the man- ifestation of what is desired.

When you are conducting this ritual, you must be dressed in white or in the color of the angel you wish to invoke. You should also stand on a large piece of cloth in the angel's color. Several of the angel's attrib- utes, such as its plants, flowers, metal, and stones, should be placed on this cloth to es- tablish a better contact with the uncon- scious, which will recognize the significance of the attributes, making the contact with the angel more easily accomplished. Over the cloth should also be placed a small glass of wine and a small cake or bread roll.

When everything is in readiness, face east and say the following:

In the name of the Creator of the universe, by whom we have both been created, I ask you, great Archangel _____ (here the name of the Archangel to be invoked is mentioned) *to grant that this which I desire* (the desire is here expressed) *and which falls under your regency, be manifested and realized in the material world in a natural and positive form, for my benefit and without any danger to myself or to any other person.*

This is repeated on the four cardinal points. Then return to the east and say:

May this bread that I offer to you
aid me in the manifestation of what
I ask in joy and prosperity
in the material world.

Then eat the bread or cake with reverence, visualizing that what you have asked has already come to pass. Then raise the glass of wine and say:

May this wine that I offer you aid me in
the manifestation of what I ask in joy
and prosperity in the material world.

Then drink the wine with reverence, visualizing that what you have asked has already come to pass. Replace the empty glass on the floor, open your arms wide, and say:

I give thanks to the Almighty Creator
and the Archangel _____
for granting my desire,
and I say Hail and Farewell.

Repeated this in the four cardinal points and visualize the circle as fading from the room, leaving a great sense of peace and well-being in yourself. The candles are extinguished and later disposed of. The angel's attributes are then wrapped in the cloth and placed under the person's bed or in a place where they can be seen daily, making sure that nobody else touches them.

This ritual is very effective and, if conducted with strength and determination, what is desired will come to pass shortly thereafter, and in such a natural way that you may be inclined to think that the ritual had nothing to do with it, and that it would have happened any way. The reason for this is that everything that is strongly visualized and concentrated upon during a ritual has easy access to the unconscious, which will then manifest in the material world what was expressed ritualistically.

As I mentioned earlier, music is very helpful during rituals because it aids the concentration and uplifts the mind. The music chosen must have an ethereal quality. The music of the New Age, which tends to use synthesizers, is ideal for rituals of invocation.

Ritual for the Guardian Angel

This ritual is more like a meditation during which an attempt is made to establish contact with your guardian angel. Before doing this ritual, you must have learned the name of your guardian angel, by following the instructions given earlier. As usual, a twenty-four-hour period of purification is required. Dress in white and sit facing the east with your legs crossed, in the semi-lotus position. Place a white quartz in front of you, one behind you, and one on each side. The crystals should be cleansed before the ritual by immersing them in saltwater for twenty-four hours, then rinsing them and placing them by sunlight for at least six hours. In front of you should also be a glass of cold mineral water. A lit white candle should be placed behind the glass.

Begin the ritual by breathing deeply through the nose while counting to four. Hold the breath, also counting to four, and exhale through the mouth slowly, also on a count of four. This form of breathing, which is known in yoga as Pranayama, is repeated six times to relax the body and to prepare the mind for the meditation.

After the breathing is completed, visualize a ray of light being emitted by the quartz crystal in front of you. This light moves to the quartz on the right, and then to those behind and to the left of you, ending at the front. This forms a circle of bright imaginary light that completely surrounds you.

The mind is then emptied of all thoughts and you concentrate on the light of the candle that can be seen through the glass of water. Begin to count backward slowly from ten to one. This will place you in the alpha state, which is a state of light trance used to access the energies of the unconscious. Close your eyes and visualize the image of the candle flame in the center of your brow.

When the flame is clearly seen in the mind's eye, begin to invoke the name of your guardian angel. Pronounce the name of the angel seven times, slowly and in a loud voice, with your eyes still closed. As the name is repeated, you will feel that your consciousness is rising above your physical body until you will have the sensation that you are floating several inches off the ground. This apparent levitation will not affect your body, only your mind. It is a form of astral projection.

When the angel's name has been repeated seven times, you will feel the presence of your guardian angel around you in the form of a great source of light and love, immensely comforting and relaxing. This force will fill the petitioner with a great sense of peace and an indescribable joy. In this state of ecstasy, you will receive several messages from the angel that will reach your mind from within, as if someone infinitely wise and loving were speaking to you from the depths of your soul. You may then ask any questions you may desire of your angel and the angel will answer you. This is what is known as the Conversation with the Holy Guardian Angel.

The presence of the angel remains for only a few moments and then it will begin to fade away slowly. As the angel leaves, you will feel that you are descending from your floating position until you find yourself well grounded in your body. When this happens, rest for a few moments and then begin to count again, this time from one to ten, to come out of the alpha state. At the count of ten, open your eyes, and the ritual is ended. It is advisable to have a notebook and a pen on the side and to write all the messages received from the angel, as they may be otherwise forgotten.

The candle is then extinguished, the circle of light is dispersed, and the crystals are put safely away to be used in another occasion. The water is drunk, as it is filled with great cosmic energies.

This ritual is very simple but very powerful, and a great sense of peace will remain with you for several days.

To Help Another Person at a Distance

Before attempting to contact an angel on behalf of another person, it is important to remember that every human being has the right of free will and that we are not permitted to infringe upon this right and try to alter that person's life without their permission. We may send angelic energy to someone who is ill, who has serious problems, or who is experiencing a severe crisis so that this energy may help that individual transcend his problems or be healed from any given illness. But this energy should never be used so that the person would do something that we wish them to do and that the person would not do on his own. If you are certain that your intention is to help and not to coerce an individual, then you can proceed with the ritual.

This ritual requires a photo of the person who is to be helped. This photo is placed facedown on a round mirror, which rests upon a white cloth. One of the seven Planetary Angels must be chosen for the ritual, depending upon the person's problem. The list of these angels, which I already gave, mentions all the various human situations ruled by them. For example, if the person is ill, the angel chosen may be Raphael, who is the angel of healing, or Michael, who represents life and vital strength.

If the angel chosen is Raphael, the photo is surrounded with eight orange-colored candles, the number eight and the color orange being attributes of Mercury and this archangel. If Michael is chosen, six yellow candles are chosen, the number six and yellow being among the attributes of the sun and this archangel in his planetary aspect.

Place one of the stones associated with the chosen angel over the photo to help establish contact with this force. As petitioner, close your eyes and visualize the person radiantly healthy and full of energy and life. As soon as the person is visualized in this manner, pronounce the name of the angel several times, depending upon his allotted number—six times for Michael and eight times for Raphael. This will help channel the angel's energy to the person who is ill. Open your eyes and visualize a ray of light descending from the archangel to the stone that rests upon the photo. This light traverses the stone and is concentrated upon the person's image. The mirror is used to send the energy to the person.

This ritual should be conducted on the day and hour of the chosen archangel, during the waxing moon. One or several of the archangel's incenses should be used before starting the ritual. Purification is advised, as during all angel rituals, as is the cleansing of the room with saltwater and the visualization of a circle of light around the area.

The ritual may be repeated several times in severe cases, but it should only be done once a week. Since the period of the waxing moon lasts only two weeks, the ritual can only be done twice within one month. It is recommended that the stone be left over the photo until the person's situation has been resolved.

Meditation for the Planet

Every day we learn through the newspapers, radio, or television of the continuous disasters that plague our planet on a daily basis. Wars and political struggles proliferate constantly around the world; crimes, epidemics, health hazards, the plight of the homeless, dangers to the environment, species in danger of extinction, accidents, and natural disasters surround us in a never-ending stream of suffering and destruction. The angels are an inexhaustible source of love and pure energy who can help heal these conditions, which are the result of unbalanced cosmic energies around us. The ritual conducted to invoke the help of the angels for the healing of the planet Earth is one of the most beautiful and effective that exists.

This ritual requires a globe of the Earth or a map of the world that is placed on the floor over a white cloth. The globe or map is surrounded by seven candles in the colors ascribed to the seven Planetary Angels: yellow for Michael; violet for Gabriel; red for Camael; orange for Raphael; electric blue for Sadkiel; green for Anael; and black or dark blue for Cassiel (dark blue is the preferred color for Cassiel, as black is associated with negative energies). The ritual is conducted during seven days, starting on a Sunday.

You should purify yourself for twenty-four hours, as previously explained. Sprinkle the room with saltwater, and burn a mixture of the incenses of the seven Planetary Angels each day. Visualize a circle of light around the room.

On the first day of the ritual, sit on the floor facing the east and the globe or map of the world. Hold in your hands a cleaned and energized white quartz. Do six Pranayamas or deep breaths. Then light the yellow candle that corresponds to Michael, who rules Sundays, and say:

> *Beloved Archangel Michael,*
> *regent of Sunday, in the name of the*
> *Creator of the universe, I ask that*
> *you send your divine energies to heal*
> *the planet Earth that is so much*
> *in need of your angelic help.*

Then visualize a powerful ray of divine light descending from the heights to the quartz and from the crystal, which magnifies the energy, to the globe or map of the world. Sustain the image for a few seconds, visualizing the energy surrounding the Earth with its radiant light. The light is then seen to disperse. As soon as it has vanished completely, the candle is extinguished and everything is put aside. The circle of light is also visualized as vanishing from the room.

The next day, Monday, the ritual is repeated, lighting the yellow candle for Michael and a violet candle for Gabriel. The words of invocation are repeated, using the name of Gabriel and Monday instead of Michael and Sunday. After the end of the ritual, both candles are extinguished.

This continues during the entire week, substituting the name of the archangel and the day of the week as the week progresses. On Saturday, which is the last day of the ritual, all the candles are lit and, after the end of the ritual, they are allowed to burn completely.

This ritual is very beneficial to the planet and if enough persons were to carry it out often, many of the troubles besieging the Earth could be avoided. The power of the human mind is awesome and when this power is multiplied by many people, all working in unison for the healing of the planet, the results would be surely felt in the world.

Ritual for the Archangels of the Four Elements

This ritual is four-fold and is conducted outdoors. It is done to reestablish contact with nature, thus availing ourselves of its tremendous powers.

Air

The ritual for the air element is done on a Wednesday during the waxing moon. It can be done by one person, but it is more effective when several people are present. All the people participating in the ritual should wear white or yellow, the color of the air element and the Archangel Raphael in the solar wheel. They should have all purified themselves during the twenty-four hours preceding the ritual.

Every person should wear a crown of yellow chrysanthemums or any yellow flower. They should all carry yellow handkerchiefs and a stick of lavender or sandalwood incense. It is also helpful to carry an agate somewhere on the body, as this is one of the stones ascribed to the air element.

The place for the ritual should be chosen beforehand. The best place would be on a high promontory, where there is little vegetation. Everyone holds hands, forming a circle, and then they move clockwise around the circle eight times, calling on Raphael with loud voices. After the eighth turn, they stop, let go of the hands they are holding, and light the incense sticks, which they hold up in the air. The person who conducts the ritual then says:

Beloved Raphael, regent of the air
element, in the name of the Creator
of the universe we ask your presence
among us in this sacred moment so
that your divine element which is air
may nourish and revitalize
our bodies, minds, and spirits.

At this moment, everyone waves the yellow handkerchiefs in the air. Usually, if this ritual is done with purpose and reverence, the wind will increase its force markedly. When the wind begins to increase, all the persons present remove the crowns from their heads and pull out the flower petals, throwing them to the wind. They all say:

Welcome Raphael, yours is the crown
and yours is the glory.

This is repeated several times, and finally all the crowns are also thrown to the wind. Then everyone sits down on a circle and shares sweet wine and small cakes to ground the energies raised during the ritual.

This ritual is excellent for health and vitality, and many illnesses improve after participating in it.

Fire

This is a solitary ritual and it should be done on a place with little or no vegetation. It requires the type of candle used to drive away insects, which is mounted on a long stick that is firmly imbedded into the ground. These candles do not go out in the wind and the flame they produce is very strong.

The petitioner should wear white or red, the color associated with the fire element and Michael in the solar wheel. He should carry on his person a red stone, such as a carnelian. As usual, he should have purified himself during the twenty-four hours preceding the ritual.

He lights the candle, which he has already planted on the ground, and sits facing south. He does six Pranayamas, while concentrating on the candle flame, and then says:

Beloved Michael, regent of the fire
element, I invoke you in this sacred
moment to reestablish contact with you
and the fire element so that I may avail
myself of its powerful energies to carry
on my ordained mission on Earth. I ask
this in love and peace, in the name of
the Creator of the universe.

He then visualizes himself entering the candle flame until it surrounds him completely. The visualization should be strong enough so that in his imagination he will feel the heat of the flame permeating his being. Once he is in the center of the flame, he will feel the presence of Michael around him, enveloping him in a dazzling light. He remains in this angelic embrace as long as possible. Then he goes back to the center of the flame, slowly withdraws from it, and returns to his place on the ground, facing the candle.

After this visualization, he eats a small cake or a sweet roll and drinks a glass of wine to ground the energies. He then extinguishes the candle. It is important to remember that candles are never blown out, but extinguished by placing something over them. This rule is also observed in all churches because fire is concentrated energy and to blow it out is to diminish its power. Also, it is unwise to set one element against the other, such as fire being vanquished by air.

This ritual is especially effective when the petitioner is facing a grave problem or when he is surrounded by many adversaries who seek to destroy him or do him harm.

Water

This is also a solitary ritual and should be conducted on the shore of any large body of water. The petitioner should wear white or blue, the color associated with the water element and Gabriel in the solar wheel. If possible, he should carry on his person a moonstone, a blue topaz, or any blue stone. After the prescribed purification, he should go to the chosen place and face the west. He then closes his eyes, opens his arms wide, and says:

Beloved Gabriel, regent of the water
element, every living being comes from
the sea, which is the mother of all life.

I invoke you in this sacred moment, in
the name of the Creator of the universe,
to ask that you may grant me some
of your celestial energy so that my life
will flow with love and serene peace
like a calm sea.

After these words, he enters the water until only the feet are bathed in it. He opens his arms again and visualizes a great blue light emerging from the water and enveloping him in a wave of love and intense joy. He embraces the water with his mind and feels the water caress his feet like a maternal kiss. At this moment, he feels Gabriel's presence surround him with great tenderness. He basks in the angel's embrace for as long as possible. He then opens his eyes, sits down on the sand facing the water, and eats a small cake and drinks a glass of sweet wine.

This simple ritual is most effective in cases of unrequited love or any love problem.

Earth

This ritual should be conducted in a forest or a park where there are many trees. The petitioner should be dressed in white or green, the color associated with the earth element and the Archangel Uriel in the solar wheel. If possible, he should also carry on his person a malachite, an aventurine, a piece of jade, or any green stone to help establish contact with the element and Uriel. A basket filled with nuts for the squirrels, bread crumbs for the birds, apples and other fruits should be brought to the site as an offering to nature and its creatures. As usual, the petitioner should have undergone a twenty-four-hour purification before undertaking the ritual.

Once at the site of the ritual, the petitioner chooses a large tree with a wide trunk and places a green cloth at its roots. He then sits down on the cloth with his back resting against the trunk, relaxes, and does six Pranayamas. He should be facing the north. When he has finished the deep breathing, he says:

Beloved Uriel, regent of the earth
element, I invoke you, in the name of
the Creator of the universe, to pour over
my spirit, burdened by the trials
of life, your powerful heavenly essence.
And as the tree seed grows in strength
to become a forest giant, so may my
spirit, regenerated by your angelic
influence, grow in serenity, peace,
health, and prosperity.

The eyes are closed and an immense light is visualized descending from the heights unto the tree. From the tree it flows into the petitioner, filling him with its revitalizing and generous force. At that moment, the presence of Uriel is felt around the person, enveloping him with a warm green glow, full of divine love. The petitioner remains in the angel's embrace for as long as possible. He then opens his eyes and visualizes Uriel's energy starting to dissipate. He spreads his offering around the tree trunk, without changing his position, and says:

Beloved Mother Earth, as I nourish
your little creatures, nourish me
with your great love and compassion.
Heal my body, my mind, and my spirit
from all ills, real and imagined, and
grant me love, happiness, and material
prosperity, that I may enjoy a long life,
all needs fulfilled.

He eats a small cake or sweet roll and drinks a glass of sweet wine, pouring some of the liquid on the ground before drinking it. This is an excellent ritual for people suffering from nervous strain and depression. It is also very effective for acquiring material wealth and prosperity.

Angel Baths

Prepare an angel bath by using several of the plants and flowers and one of the stones associated with the Planetary Angels. The bath is taken on the day and hour ascribed to the chosen angel.

Place the ingredients in a thin piece of cloth in the angel's color and tie it with a ribbon of the same hue. Fill the bathtub with hot water and add some vegetable dye

163

to tint the water with the angel's color. There are many therapeutic color baths in the market that are used for this purpose. The color is absorbed into the person's aura, revitalizing it.

After the water has taken the color of the chosen angel, the bag with the herbs and other ingredients is placed in it. Then turn off the lights, sit in the bathtub, and place on the water several floating candles in the number associated with the angel. Light the candles and some of the angel's incense, and lay back and relax in the perfumed colored waters. Invoke the angel's name several times, depending on his number, and ask that through his celestial energies the bath will restore and nourish your aura. Visualize the light of the candles as permeating your body, mind, and spirit.

Remain in the bath for a minimum of half an hour. Then empty the bathtub, visualizing that all your problems leave with the ebbing water. After this bath, a candle is lit in the angel's color, thanking him for his presence.

An example of this type of cleansing would be a bath to acquire abundance, spiritual illumination, and power through Michael as one of the seven Planetary Angels. This bath would be taken on a Sunday, in one of the angelic hours. As Michael rules the sun and the color yellow, this would be the color chosen to tinge the bath waters. A thin piece of yellow cloth would be filled with pine cones, laurel leaves, mistletoe,

chamomile flowers, yellow flowers, and a tiger's eye, all of which are Michael's attributes as a Planetary Angel. The cloth would be tied with a yellow ribbon and placed in the water. Because Michael's planetary number is six, these would be the number of candles, preferably yellow, floated on the water. A mixture of Michael's incenses, such as frankincense, copal, and vanilla, would also be burned. You would then enter the bath and invoke Michael's name six times, asking him to purify your aura, attracting to you the angel's special gifts, such as abundance, well-being, power, and spiritual illumination. After the bath, a yellow candle is lit in Michael's name, thanking the archangel for his gifts.

Angel baths are extremely energizing and, if done regularly, the individual's life is transformed in a very positive manner.

Angel Amulets

An angel amulet is prepared in a small bag of the color associated with the chosen Planetary Angel. Inside the bag are placed several of the stones, the herbs, and flower petals of the angel, as well as a pinch of one of his incenses. The bag is prepared on the day and hour associated with the angel. The bag is then energized and purified through the four elements.

First, pass the bag through the smoke of one or more of the incenses of the angel. As the bag is placed over the incense, say:

In the name of the great Archangel
Raphael, regent of the air element,
you are energized and purified
in the air element.

The bag is then passed over the flame of a red candle, and you say:

In the name of the great Archangel
Michael, regent of the fire element,
you are energized and purified
in the fire element.

The bag is now sprinkled with some mineral water, and you say:

In the name of the great Archangel
Gabriel, you are energized and purified
in the water element.

Finally, the bag is placed over a small dish of sea salt (salt is commonly associated with earth), and you say:

In the name of the great Archangel
Uriel, regent of the earth element,
you are energized and purified
in the earth element.

After the bag has been consecrated in the four elements, it is carried on your person to get the angel's constant help.

The Angel's Prayer

This is a very powerful prayer and should be said every night or during moments of extreme stress.

O shining Seraphim,
of fire and ruby born
Surround us with the love
that burns at early dawn.
O faithful Cherubim,
of chariots burning bright
Dispel the gloom of sorrow
that renders dark the night.
O Thrones, the true foundation
of Heaven's Mighty Ones
Grant us the gift of living
in everlasting calm.
O bright and true Dominions,
who bring order to chaos
Guide us in righteous living
and from the darkness free us.
O Virtues, hope undying of courage
and true grace
Show us the shining pathway
that leads to God's embrace.
O Powers of the Almighty,
the guards of Heaven's Gate
Guard us from all the evils
that hurt and desecrate.

O Principalities, who sing

with every bell

Bring guidance to our leaders

and peace unto the world.

O Archangels, Host of Heaven,

deep in our souls create

The light of true compassion

so love becomes our fate.

O Angels, our true guardians,

help us redeem our story

So we may share with you

the joy of Heaven's Glory.

Amen.

The Amethyst Mirror

This mirror is specially prepared by a person to find out the name of his guardian angel and to communicate with him. To make the mirror it is necessary to acquire a round piece of clear glass, such as the ones found on some picture frames. The glass must have a diameter of at least five inches.

One of the sides of the glass is painted in a deep violet shade. When the paint is dry, the mirror is turned over, and on the unpainted side are cemented four tumbled amethysts of good size. The amethysts should be placed on the four cardinal points of the mirror, to symbolize the four quarters of the Earth.

After the mirror is prepared in this way, it is placed on a piece of violet cloth and covered with sea salt. You then say:

In the name of the great

Archangel Uriel, I consecrate you

in the earth element.

Pour the salt out and sprinkle the mirror with mineral water. Then say:

In the name of the great

Archangel Gabriel, I consecrate you

in the water element.

Light a red candle and pass it across the mirror, from its east point to the west and from its north point to the south. Then say:

In the name of the great

Archangel Michael, I consecrate you

in the fire element.

Lastly, pass the mirror through a censer burning with frankincense, myrrh, and lavender. Then say:

In the name of the great

Archangel Raphael, I consecrate you

in the air element.

After the amethyst mirror is consecrated in the four elements, it is wrapped in the violet cloth and put in a safe place until the person is ready to use it.

The mirror is used to learn the name of the person's guardian angel and to communicate with him. Amethysts and the color violet are used because this is the highest color in the solar spectrum and it has the strongest and purest vibrations. It is the color of the crown chakra and helps establish contact with higher forces, such as the angels.

The consecration of the mirror and the invocation of the guardian angels must be conducted during the waxing moon on the day of the week ruled by the Planetary Angel traditionally associated with the birth sign of the person:

Day—Planetary Angel, Sign

Sunday—Michael, Leo

Monday—Gabriel, Cancer

Tuesday—Camael, Aries and Scorpio

Wednesday—Raphael, Virgo and Gemini

Thursday—Sadkiel, Sagittarius and Pisces

Friday—Anael, Taurus and Libra

Saturday—Cassiel, Capricorn and Aquarius

For example, a person born under the sign of Leo would conduct these rituals on a Sunday and someone born under the sign of Libra would choose Friday. The best time would be 10 P.M. The person should be dressed in white and should be barefoot.

To invoke the guardian angel, the room is prepared as already described. It should be sprinkled with saltwater and a mixture of frankincense, lavender, and myrrh passed around the area. A circle of bright light is visualized surrounding the place. The person then sits on the floor on a folded white sheet covered with white rose petals. The lights should be out.

The mirror is placed on the floor facing the person and four violet-colored candles are placed on the four cardinal points around him. The candle in front should not reflect its flame on the mirror but only illuminate it faintly.

The person relaxes, does six Pranayamas, and counts backward from ten to one to enter into the alpha state. He closes his eyes and says:

> *In the name of the Creator*
> *of the universe, I ask my*
> *holy guardian angel to reveal to me*
> *his name and to let me see his face*
> *in the amethyst mirror.*

He waits for a few minutes, keeping his mind clear of all thoughts.

The angel's name will come to him in a sudden flash, so bright it will seem to become imbedded in his mind. At this point, he opens his eyes and looks into the mirror. Within its purple depths, he will see a swirling faint light. This will soon clear and he will see the image of the angel in the mirror. To some people the vision is clear and to others indistinct, but an image should form within the glass. The petitioner should remain calm at this point, and ask in a soft voice whatever question he wants to ask the angel. The answer will come into his mind almost as soon as he asks the question. Several questions may be asked of the angel during this ritual, but it is important not to extend it beyond one hour. Within one hour, the planetary force of the hour gives way to another, and the ritual is no longer under its angelic tutelary force. For that reason, the entire ritual, from beginning to end, should not last more than an hour.

After the angel has answered the question, the person counts again, this time from one to ten, to return to the material world. The candles are extinguished and put aside for a future conversation with the guardian angel. The circle of light is vanished and the rose petals are thrown to the air, outside the window. Cake and wine are consumed, as usual, to anchor all energies.

The Nectar of Levanah

The moon has many names according to many ancient traditions. Levanah is a Hebrew name for the moon used in kabbalistic rites. In the Tree of Life, the sphere or sephira associated with the moon is known as Foundation. This sphere symbolizes the astral or mental plane. It is the origin of dreams and the site of imagination. Every-

thing that happens in the physical world is first created in the imaginative realm of the moon sphere. That is why the moon is so important in all meditations and works of visualization.

The Nectar of Levanah is used to establish contact with the lunar forces, to strengthen the mind and the powers of imagination, to have prophetic dreams, and to shape and control our lives through mental power.

In ancient times, most calendars were based on the phases of the moon, and both the Chinese and the Jewish calendar still follow the lunar phases. Orthodox Jews celebrate each new moon with special prayers and rites, including the reading of Psalm 81, which calls for the observance of the new moon. My father believed that it was very important to know the exact hour of the new moon, as God's Divine Presence descends to Earth at that moment and grants all prayers. But he remains on Earth for only five minutes and Psalm 81 must be read and the petition made within that short span of time.

The Nectar of Levanah is prepared by beating the white of an egg lightly, and adding some light cream, sugar, and white wine to the egg white. The mixture is poured into a deep blue wine glass and a moonstone placed inside. A silver candle is lit next to the glass, both of which should be placed outside or near a window where the moon's forces may energize it. This should be done at midnight on the days of the new and the full moon. One hour later, at 1 A.M., the candle is extinguished in the nectar. The glass is lifted and offered to the moon and the nectar drunk in one single draught, without removing the glass from the lips. This should be done in the name of the Archangel Gabriel, regent of the moon, and the Angel Geniel, ruler of the new moon, on the day of the new moon, and the Archangel Gabriel and the angel Atliel, ruler of the full moon, on the day of the full moon.

This ritual should be done twice a month on the new moon and the full moon. The results are a marked increase in mental power, a powerfully developed intuition and clairvoyance, prophetic dreams, and an increase in the power of concentration.

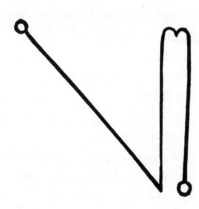

Figure 41: The seal of Hagiel.

The Rite of Hagiel

As I mentioned earlier, Hagiel is the Intelligence of Venus and an angel of love. This is a well-known rite of evocation, given originally by German kabbalist Franz Bardon in his book *Magical Evocation*. This is a powerful ritual which may result in very visible and auditory phenomena, as I explained earlier. It should not be undertaken lightly and the person who attempts it should have a strong mind and not be easily shaken.

This is a ritual for love, not to force another to love the petitioner against his or her will, but rather to know what love really is, to bring it to the person's life bountifully and naturally, and to surround the person with its glorious energy.

The version I am going to give here has been simplified to make it more accessible to the reader, who may not be familiar with the complexities of kabbalistic magic, but it is still powerful and extremely effective.

The ingredients required for the performance of this ritual are the following:

- Censer with one or two burning pieces of charcoal
- Powdered cinnamon
- A green bulb that should be suspended from the ceiling
- A piece of green cardboard cut in the form of a heptagon (seven sides) with the seal of Hagiel (see illustration) drawn in green ink

- A green tunic
- A length of copper wire where a malachite or rough emerald is inserted, and which is to be worn as a necklace around the individual's neck
- A piece of green cloth cut in the shape of a triangle about two feet long from tip to base
- Four green candles
- A small cake
- A glass of sweet wine

The ritual is conducted on a Friday at 10 P.M., the day and the hour of Venus, whose angelic forces rule love. The moon should be waxing. As usual, you should have purified yourself during the twenty-four hours preceding the ritual. Before the ritual, purify the room with saltwater. You should bathe, don the green tunic, and anoint your forehead and temples with cinnamon oil. Put on the copper necklace with the green stone, turn off the lights, and turn on the green bulb. This should suffuse the room in a green haze. On the floor, to the east of the circle, place the green triangle. On top of the triangle, place the heptagonal piece of cardboard with Hagiel's seal. Around the triangle, in the form of a cross, light the four green candles that represent the four cardinal points. Place some cinnamon on the burning charcoals and pass the censer around the room. Place the censer next to you and add more cinnamon throughout the ritual to keep the scent alive, as this is one of the most powerful attributes of the Venus sphere.

Now proceed to form a ficca by placing your right thumb, or left if you are left-handed, between your index and middle fingers. Extend your arm, pointing the ficca at the east of the room, and trace a circle of imaginary light around the area to protect it from negative energies.

Then begin to evoke Hagiel to manifest visibly in the green triangle. The first time you call on Hagiel mentally seven times, visualizing her as she descends from the Venus sphere into the triangle. The second time, utter her name softly, almost inaudibly, again seven times. The third time, call her name seven times in a loud, ringing voice, asking her to materialize in the triangle. During the three evocations, the ficca must be pointed at the triangle.

If you have followed the instructions exactly and with strong willpower, the image of Hagiel will start to take form within the triangle.

As I explained before, this image is a mental projection emerging from the petitioner's unconscious, and it is very real.

Hagiel manifests as an ethereally beautiful woman, with milky skin and bright red hair. Her eyes are green and she is naked from the waist up. She wears a skirt of blue-green material embroidered with pink roses and a tower-shaped crown of copper. Her voice is musical and her attitude sweet and amiable. The impression received by the petitioner when such a vision appears can only be described as earthshaking. But is important to remain calm and continue with the ritual. At this moment, you may ask Hagiel any questions related to love matters or to grant a special favor. This she is invariably willing to do. If she grants a petition, it is assured that what was asked will come to pass. After she has answered your questions, thank her and bid her hail and farewell. Consume the cake and the wine to anchor the energies released by the ritual.

If Hagiel does not appear in the triangle, there was insufficient energy created by the ritual, or some important element was left out. But some type of phenomenon will be seen or heard, like strange, unearthly music, banging sounds, oscillating lights, or strange vibrations. These phenomena are created by the petitioner's unconscious mind, which will release vast amounts of psychic energy during the ceremony.

After the appearance of Hagiel, or when it is obvious that she will not appear, the ritual is ended. The circle of light is vanished, the candles are put out to be disposed of later, and the room cleared. The various objects may be kept to be used in a similar ritual later on.

This ritual leaves you with a deep sense of well-being and joy that lasts for a long time afterward. In the vast majority of cases, what was asked comes to pass shortly after the ritual.

The invocation of the angels is one of the most beautiful and rewarding spiritual experiences that a person can have. Human life is a series of rituals, from brushing the teeth in the morning to getting married or going to sleep at night. It is therefore very natural to invoke the angels and in this manner attempt to reestablish contact with the creative force of the universe.

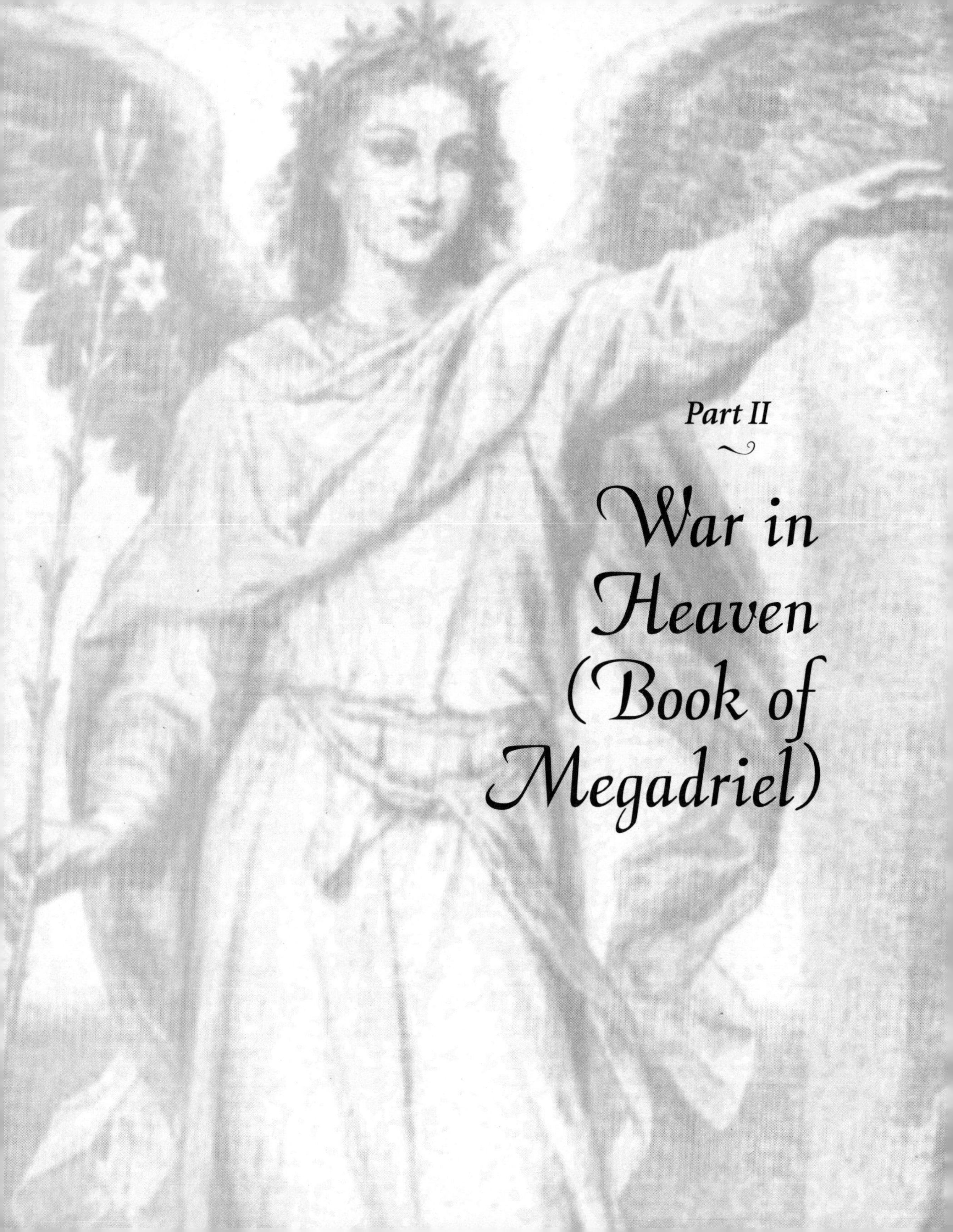

Part II

War in Heaven (Book of Megadriel)

Author's Note: Some of the information given in the *Book of Megadriel* can be found in the *First, Second,* and *Third Books of Enoch,* and other apocryphal books not found in the Holy Scriptures. Enoch was one of the great Hebrew patriarchs and his books form part of the *Pseudepigrapha,* which contains several of the apocryphal books that give details about the Creation that are not found in the Bible. The *Book of Megadriel* also includes information that does not appear in the Bible or in any of the *Books of Enoch.* Because Megadriel is an angelic entity, he speaks in the archaic biblical style, which is completely different from the rest of this book.

"War in Heaven" and "Angel Messages" are excerpts from the *Book of Megadriel,* which is rich in angelic lore, information about the angel encampments, the angelic sigils and talismans, and other information not found in any other book. The excerpts included in *Return of the Angels* were chosen because their content serves to clarify the process of Creation and its cosmic implications. The *Book of Megadriel* is original with this author and is not part of the *Pseudepigrapha* or any of the apocryphal books.

These are the chronicles of Megadriel, Cherub, Seraph, Archangel, Prince of the Fourth Heaven, which is the sphere of the sun, Prince of the Divine Presence, and one of the great Arcons who stand before the Celestial Throne. These chronicles are part of the book that bears his name.

Thus speaks Megadriel:

Beloved:

As a new millennium approaches, and with it the Second Coming of the Son of Man, I place my seal on this parchment to reveal to the world what happened in the Beginning and the reason why suffering exists on Earth.

Creation

In the Beginning, the Logos, the Supreme Intelligence, created that which exists from the Non-Existing and the Visible from the Invisible. He who has no End and no Beginning and is Inconceivable, the ONE, moved among the Invisible, restlessly, tirelessly, continuously because Creation still was not. And the ONE conceived the idea of establishing a foundation and giving form to a Visible Creation. And He ordered one of the Invisible Things to make Itself visible. And Edoil appeared, immensely great. And the Creator saw a great Light inside Edoil. And He told Edoil to disintegrate Itself and to disperse Its essence and Edoil did so. And a Great Light issued from Edoil and the Creator was in the

175

midst of this Great Light. And so it was that Light came from The Light. And from The Light issued the Vision of the Creation, of All that the Creator had conceived. And He saw that It was good.

And the Creator formed for Himself a great Throne and sat upon it. And He told the Light to ascend higher than the Throne and to solidify Itself to form the foundation of the Heights. And nothing exists higher than the Light except Nothingness.

And the Creator told another of the Invisible Things to make Itself Visible, and Arkhas appeared, solid, heavy, and red. And the Creator told Arkhas to disintegrate Itself and to disperse Its essence, and Arkhas did so. And matter issued from Arkhas, dark and imponderable, holding within It the Creation of the Minor Things. And the Creator saw that It was good and He told Arkhas to descend and to solidify Itself. And Matter was the foundation of the Minor Things. And nothing exists lower than the Darkness except Nothingness.

And the Creator told part of the Darkness to solidify Itself and to be surrounded by part of the Light and thus were the Waters created, which are the bottomless Abyss. And in the midst of the Waters He created seven circles with the appearance of crystal to be the channels of the Waters and the other elements. And He marked their routes, the routes of the Seven Stars, each one in Its own Heaven that they may not deviate from Their appointed course. And He saw that It was good.

And the Creator divided the Light from the Darkness in the midst of the Waters. And the Light He called Day and the Darkness called He Night. And this was the First Day.

And the Creator told the Waters that were beneath the Firmament to gather together and become dry. And it was so. And from the dry Waters He created the rocks, great and solid. And from the rocks He formed the dry ground and He called it Earth. And that which was in the midst of the Earth called He Abyss. And the Creator gathered the Waters of the seas with His Power and told them not to deviate from their appointed course. And He established the Earth over the Waters of the sea. And this was the Second Day.

And in the Second Day the Creator also formed His Heavens from a fiery substance. From a ray issuing from His eye He created lightning, which is fire and water in perfect balance, and with the lightning He struck a rock and melted it. And from this flaming liquid He created the Heavenly Host, ten milliard angels, their garments and armor formed of burning flames. Thus created He all His Heavens.

And the Creator told the Earth to be covered with all manners of trees, great and filled with fruit. And the mountains He carpeted with sweet grasses and all manners of seed. And He created Paradise as an enclosed garden. And He encompassed it about with many flaming angels, the Cherubim, that they may keep it safe. And this was the Third Day.

And the Creator placed Great Lights in the seven circles of Heaven. In the highest circle, he placed the star called Kronos; in the second, He placed Afridit; in the third, Arris; in the fourth, the Sun; in the fifth, Zeous; in the sixth, Ermis; and in the seventh, He placed the Moon. And He told the Sun to illuminate the Day, and the Moon and the other stars to illuminate the Night. And the Sun moves according to the twelve months and the twelve signs and the animals that represent them, and these in turn agree with the births of the newborn. And behold, this was the Fourth Day.

And the Creator told the seas to be filled with fish and the Earth to be filled with birds, with crawling reptiles, and all manners of beasts. And behold, male and female created He every living creature that breathes upon the Earth. And this was the Fifth Day.

And the Creator formed Man from the seven elements. His flesh created He from the Earth; his blood from the Dew; his veins from the Sun; his eyes from the depths of the Sea; his bones from the Rocks; his reasoning from the motion of the Clouds and from the Angels; and his spirit from the Wind and the Creator's own Spirit. And the Creator gave Man seven qualities: He gave the sense of hearing to his flesh; the sense of sight to his eyes; the sense of smell to his spirit; the sense of touch to his veins; the sense of taste to his blood; durability to his bones; and sweetness to his reasoning.

And the Creator made Man as an angel on Earth, with honor, power, and glory. He created him as a king to reign over the Earth with the Wisdom of the Creator. And there was nothing on Earth comparable to Man among all the creatures of the Creator. And the Creator gave Man a name taken from the four cardinal points:

East	A
West	D
North	A
South	M

And the Creator assigned four stars to Man and called him Adam. And He gave him free will and taught him to differentiate between Light and Darkness and between Good and Evil and gave him power over all the Earth.

And the Creator caused a deep sleep to descend over Adam and he slept. And while he slept, the Creator took a rib from Adam's side and with it created He the Woman. And from the last letter of Adam's name He named the Woman, calling her Mother, that is, Eve. And this was the Sixth Day.

And the Creator made a Garden on the East of Eden that Adam and Eve could observe the Commandments from within. And

He left the gates of Heaven wide open so that Adam and Eve could look at the Angels. And the Creator filled Eden with all manners of fruit trees and pleasant flowers, lovely to behold. And He placed therein singing birds and beasts of all types, and everything that was in Eden was subject to Adam's will. And the Creator told Adam to name every beast of the Earth, fish of the Sea, and bird of the Air. And a great river flowed from Eden, dividing itself into four streams upon leaving the Garden.

And the Creator told Adam that all the plants, seeds, and fruits of the Earth were to be for his nourishment and the beasts of the Earth. And at no time did the Creator tell Adam that he could eat the flesh of the beasts, the birds, or the fish; only the plants, the seeds, and the fruits of the Earth were to be for his nourishment.

And behold, in the midst of the Garden were two Trees; one was the Tree of the Knowledge of Good and Evil and the other was the Tree of Life, which was guarded by Cherubim under the regency of the great Archangel Raphael.

And the Creator brought Adam in front of the Tree of the Knowledge of Good and Evil and told him that he could eat of the fruit of every tree in the Garden except THIS one, for to do so would bring him death. But the Creator did not mention the Tree of Life, in which resides the Glory that is the Shekinah.

And the Creator told Adam and Eve to unite and multiply and to fill the Earth with their seed. And the Creator rested after His Work. And this was the Seventh Day. And the Creator blessed and sanctified this day because in it He rested from His Work.

The Angels

And behold, on the Second Day, when He created the angels from the molten rock and from fire and lightning, the Creator established them in nine ascending ranks and these ranks He called the Nine Angelical Choirs. And these are the Angels, Archangels, Principalities, Powers, Virtues, Dominions, Thrones, Cherubim, and Seraphim. And over each Choir He established a Prince of the Divine Presence to rule and govern each Choir. And He created each choir with milliards of milliards of angels, too vast in their multitude. And behold, these are the Heavenly Hosts made by the Creator to rule over the Seven Heavens.

And superior to the Nine Choirs with their ruling Princes, the Creator made the Guardians of the Watchtowers, which are the walls of the Seven Palaces that are in the Seventh Heaven, the dwelling place of the Divine Presence. And these Celestial Watchers were given immense power by the Creator that they may protect the Seven Palaces and hinder the entrance or departure of all beings to and from the Holy Place.

And among the Watchers, the Creator chose seventy, called the Princes of the Kingdoms, who were superior to the other Watchers. And He chose still Others, who were superior to the seventy. And These are the Ones who stand in front of the Throne of the Creator and serve Him continuously. And among These, the most beautiful and powerful, with powers almost equal to the Creator, was the great Seraph, Cherub, Power, and Archangel called Beqa, whose name signified "he who is good." And this great Archangel was most beloved of the Creator, who honored him above all the Heavenly Hosts.

And the Creator gave much power and wisdom to His angels, in their ascending order, but He did not give all his power and all His wisdom to any of them, reserving for Himself total power and wisdom.

And in Beqa, He deposited more power and knowledge than in any other angel except the great Seraph, Virtue, and Archangel Michael, whose name means "he who is like God," and who is perfectly pure and incorruptible. And the Creator, greatly loving Michael, made him His Archstrategist or Supreme Strategist, and placed him in charge of the battle strategies of the Heavenly Hosts. And the Creator, knowing Michael's incorruptibility, revealed only to him the secret of His Holy Name, with which He created all things. And behold, the Creator and His Holy Name are ONE, and through the power of this Name millions of universes may be created and destroyed. But the Creator did not reveal to Michael or to any of His other angels how He had created the Universe.

And behold, the great Archangel Beqa, having great powers almost equal to those of the Creator, was able to discern how the Universe was created. And his spirit was filled with a great desire to be like the Creator and to have the power to create universes. And he gazed with an unholy jealousy at the vast realms of the Seven Heavens and the Heavenly Hosts, and his eyes grew bright with desire when he saw the Throne of the Creator in the Heights, made of fire and crystal, and the immense sapphire that rested on its summit. And Beqa wished ardently to sit on the Throne and be like the Creator and rule over the Seven Heavens and the Heavenly Hosts. But Beqa did not possess the secret of the Holy Name, which was only known by the Archangel Michael. And without the Name he could not possess the Throne of the Creator or have all of His power. And Beqa conceived a plan.

And behold, each morning, before the Divine Council meets in Heaven and the Creator and His Celestial Court reestablish order in the Universe, all the Heavenly Hosts, led by Michael, sing their Praises to the Creator, Lord God of all the Hosts. And at the end of the Praises, all the Angelic Choirs return to their assigned places in the Seven

Heavens. And Michael, after receiving his daily command, soared up to the Heights on his emerald wings to carry them through.

And Beqa lay in wait for Michael, and saw him fly upward to carry out his duties. And Beqa followed Michael, flying closely behind, until he intercepted the Archangel in the midst of the great void that stands between the Light and the Darkness. And the two Angelic Princes formed a blinding sun in space as they met, through the radiant light that was their essence.

And Beqa, with impeccable courtesy, removed his resplendent crown and bowed reverently before Michael, in observance of the heavenly protocol. And Michael, with equal courtesy, removed his own resplendent crown and bowed before Beqa. And Beqa asked Michael for the privilege to accompany him, and Michael acceded. And behold, both Princes traced arcs of Light through space as they joined in flight.

And Beqa, subtle and malicious, with great intelligence, inquired with supreme wile of Michael if he were satisfied in the service of the Creator. And Michael, astonished, but still unsuspecting, answered with serene simplicity that all his being and his essence belonged to the Creator, as he owed to Him his own immortal existence. And Beqa answered with fiery words, declaring that he did not wish to serve but to be served as his essence was as powerful as that of the Creator. And to further demonstrate his power he revealed to Michael how the Creator made manifest the Visible from the Invisible, thus creating the Universe. And finally revealing his treacherous intentions, he offered to Michael to share the dominion of the Seven Heavens if the Archstrategist would reveal to him the secret of the Holy Name.

And behold, Michael, he who is like God, unsheathed his sword of fire before which the celestial armies tremble, and with a thrust faster than thought itself stripped Beqa of his crown, which fell unto the abyss, forming a dazzling trail of Light on its descent.

And Beqa, divested of his crown and of his rank, his head uncovered as that of the smallest angel, felt the flaming tip of Michael's sword press hard against his chest, burning his skin of Light.

And Michael thrust harder with his sword, and Beqa retreated, terrified.

"Ruinous angel, reprobate, thou hast neither gratitude nor conscience," cried Michael, trembling with divine fury. "Never will thine impure sandal step on the rungs of the Celestial Throne. Begone, Kasbel. That is thy true name: he who betrays his Creator. Begone from my presence!"

And behold, great tongues of fire issued from Michael's lips with each word he uttered. And his immense figure, which traverses the course of the stars, grew in immensity with his holy indignation, and the entire firmament was shaken and illuminated by the celestial fires that surrounded him.

And Beqa, now known as Kasbel, flew away in terror from the terrible and devastating presence of the Archstrategist, his tunic enveloped in flames. And in the cover of Darkness, he returned to his palace in the Seventh Heaven to plot and meditate his revenge.

And through the power received from the Creator, Kasbel transformed his vestments, destroyed by Michael's fire, into raiments of Light. And he placed a new crown of glory over his head. And trembling again, but this time with fury and frustration, he convoked a meeting with his ministers. And these ministers were Yekon, Asbel, Gadereel, Pineme, and Kasadya.

And behold, these ministers had great powers and were subservient to Kasbel. And he instructed, exhorted, and instigated them to unite with him with all their celestial armies to make War in Heaven and dethrone the Creator. And to demonstrate his power he revealed unto them, even as he had done with Michael, the secrets of Creation. And behold, Kasbel's ministers, overwhelmed by the greatness of this knowledge, which belonged only to the Creator, removed their crowns of glory and prostrated themselves at Kasbel's feet and swore him their allegiance. And bonded together by this audacious and sacrilegious plan, the conspirators prepared for the forthcoming battle.

Beloved, I pause here to tell you that the Creator formed all his angels in the same instant. And this humble servant of the Lord of Hosts, Blessed be He and His Holy Name, was created in the Beginning a Seraph, Cherub, and Archangel, and my name Megadriel signifies "God is my great help." And behold, this great Odyssey that I am called to reveal is inscribed in the Eternal Book of the Creator, where everything that has passed, is passing, and will come to pass is written. And all the Hosts of Heaven, which are part of the Creator, fought in the Great Battle, some on one side and the rest on the other side, as it has been written that the Creator formed the Universe from No-Thing and everything that exists comes from Him.

War in Heaven

And Michael, Prince of the Divine Presence and Regent of the Seraphim, upon the end of his confrontation with Kasbel, flew rapidly to the Seventh Heaven and arrived at the presence of the majestic Prince Anapiel YHVH, whose dazzling Light extends throughout Araboth. And Anapiel YHVH, who is in charge of the keys of the Seven Palaces, removed his crown of glory and hailed Michael reverently, opening for him the doors of the Seventh Palace, wherein dwells the Glory of the Creator.

And the great and terrible Prince Soterasiel YHVH, whose height surpasses 70,000 milliard parasangs, that is, 2,135,000 miles, and without whose permission none of the Angelic Princes may reach the Divine Presence, removed his crown of a thousand stars upon seeing Michael, and hailed him reverently. And Soterasiel YHVH escorted Michael to the Heavenly Throne.

And behold, the Angelic Choirs, under the command of the Heavenly Captains, greeted Michael with songs of praise and welcome. And the great Seraph, Virtue, and Archangel, upon reaching the Heavenly Throne, from which issued milliard lightnings and whose blinding Light illuminated the Seven Heavens, removed his crown of glory and prostrated himself before the Divine Presence.

And the Cherubim that hold the Heavenly Throne fluttered their wings of fire to greet Michael's presence at the feet of the Creator and His Divine Shekinah, creating maelstroms of flames underneath the Throne. And voices of thunder and fire issued from the Throne, echoing throughout the realms of Araboth. And the Voice of God enveloped Michael in its unfathomable power and transported him to the Creator's side on the Throne.

And behold, Michael, sheltered in the embrace of Supreme Love, trembled greatly, and from his emerald eyes flowed a stream of iridescent tears from which were born new Cherubim, each of them winged, each of them burning in the flames of the Divine Love, and all of them singing His praises.

And Michael, next to the Creator on His Throne, revealed without words Kasbel's treason. And the Creator could see the battle between his two great Archangels in the green mirror of Michael's tears.

And behold, tears of fire flowed from the eyes of the Creator, joining Michael's, in the face of the betrayal of his beloved angel. And the tears of fire and emerald, flowing over the crystal pavement, joined the river of fire that spreads its flaming waters in front of the Heavenly Throne. And the Angelic Choirs ceased their songs of praise before this terrible sight. And there was a great silence in all the Palaces of Araboth. And the echoes of this silence resonated throughout the Seven Heavens, awakening the minor angels that were resting in the First Heaven.

And the awakening of the minor angels was followed by the sound of milliards of angelic trumpets, calling the Heavenly Hosts to a War Council. And the Creator, His Divine Light dimmed by the sorrow of the loss of his beloved Archangel, told Michael to plan the Divine Strategy with which Araboth was to be defended.

And it came to pass that Michael, with the great Archangels Raphael, Gabriel, and Uriel, all of them Chiefs of the Heavenly Hosts, summoned the Captains of the Celestial Armies to protect the Seven Heavens from the attack of Kasbel and his ministers.

And Kasbel had heard the echoes of the silence and the sound of the trumpets

Figure 42: Satan and Beelzebub, the fallen angels,
planning their strategy for the war against the angelic army.

Figure 43: The war between the angels of light and the fallen angels
at the most fierce point of the battle.

calling to a War Council. And his great cunning revealed unto him the wisdom of an immediate attack. And his ministers Yeqon, Asbel, Gadereel, Pineme, and Kasadya, with milliards of apostate angels, made ready for the battle.

And behold, Kasbel's power was such that he was able to cross with his rebellious armies the portals of six of the Heavens. And none of the Angelic Watchers of these Heavens was strong enough to withstand Kasbel's attack.

And so it was that Kasbel arrived triumphant at the Crystal Gates of Araboth. And he was met at the Gates by the Heavenly Hosts, milliards upon milliards of Celestial Armies, all Angels of Light riding winged white horses with reins of fire. And all the angels, the faithful and the rebellious, wielded fire swords forged from the lightning bolts of Araboth. And all the Captains of the Celestial Armies were clad in armor of lava and lightning that shone like rubies in the heat of battle.

And the first encounter among the Angelic Warriors resounded with the deafening roar of a thousand erupting volcanoes and all the Halls of Araboth trembled in terror. And many of the rebel angels were dismounted in this first encounter and thrown into the depths of the abyss. But none of the faithful angels were dismounted.

And the second encounter was more ferocious than the first and the Walls of Araboth buckled and threatened to tumble. And milliards of the rebel hosts were dismounted and thrown to the abyss. But none of the faithful angels were dismounted.

And in the third encounter, the clash among the angels was so terrible that the Great and Majestic Anapiel YHVH, Watcher of the Palaces of the Seventh Heaven, beseeched Michael, the Divine Archstrategist, to bring the battle to a close for fear that the Crystal Walls of Araboth might crumble and the Holy Palaces be left without protection.

And behold, the angels were created immortal by the Creator and could not die. And their wounds healed in the moment they were inflicted. And a subtle essence of Light emanated from each wound, and although the wound would heal, each injured angel lost vast quantities of their divine energy.

And the Great Cherub, Virtue, Power, and Archangel Gabriel, whose name signifies "God is my strength," and who is Prince Regent of Death and Vengeance, of Resurrection and Compassion, charged into the ranks of the rebel Seraph Gadereel. And from his eyes, made of a million stars, burst forth volleys of fire and lightning, filling with paralyzing terror the Angelic Warriors, both the faithful and the rebellious. And with each stroke of his flaming sword thousands of the apostate angels were dismounted and thrown into the abyss.

And when the rebel Seraph Gadereel saw Gabriel breaking through his ranks with

Figure 44: The angels of light observing the rebel angels after their defeat.

devastating force, he lifted his sword of fire and rushed against the Prince of Vengeance. And the swords of the two celestial foes clashed in mid-Heaven releasing a multitude of sparks of fire and lightning that illuminated all of the firmament surrounding Araboth. And through the force of the impact, Gadereel's steed fell to the ground. And Gabriel raised his sword once more, delivering a staggering blow to Gadeerel's armor that split it in half, opening Gadereel's chest with its power. And great quantities of angelic essence flowed from the hideous wound, which closed instantly. But Gadereel, weakened by the loss of his divine energy, fell heavily to the ground and tumbled senseless into the depths of the abyss. And all of his armies flew away in terror at his fall. And this was the first of Kasbel's ministers to be defeated in the Angelic War.

And the Great Seraph and Cherub Uriel, whose name signifies "Fire of God," and who is Regent of the Sun, Archangel of Salvation, and Guardian of Thunder and Terror, transformed himself into a serpent of fire and charged into the ranks of the armies of the rebel Seraph Yeqon. And thousands of Yeqon's apostate angels, enveloped in the Divine Fire that is Uriel, fell from their winged horses and tumbled into the bottomless abyss.

And Yeqon, facing the Divine Glory that flowed from Uriel, raised his sword of fire to attack him. And behold, his sword was instantly disintegrated by the awesome power of the Great Seraph, and Yeqon fell from his horse enveloped in flames and lava. And Uriel pushed him with his sandal of blazing iron toward the unfathomable depths of the abyss. And all of Yeqon's rebel armies flew away in terror. And this was the second of Kasbel's ministers to be defeated in the Angelic War.

And the Great Cherub and Archangel Raphael, whose name signifies "God has healed," and who is the Angel of Repentance, of Love and Light and Guardian of the Tree of Life, charged into the ranks of the armies of the rebel Seraph Asbel. And behold, Raphael is an Angel of Peace and Joy and there is no inclination to war in his essence. And his weapon against evil is the great Love of the Creator from which he was formed. And from this Love flowed a Light so immense and dazzling that it extended far beyond the course of the stars. And the winged horses of the rebel angels, blinded by this Celestial Light, ran wildly in all directions, throwing their riders, thousands of which fell into the depths of the abyss.

And Asbel, upon seeing the Glory that is Raphael, covered his eyes with his shield and charged against him. And Raphael sent forth a ray of searing Light that rent asunder Asbel's armor, opening a great wound in the chest of the rebel Seraph. And the wound

Figure 45: The rebellious angels being tossed into the abyss by the Archangel Michael.

closed instantly, but Asbel, weakened by the loss of his angelic essence, also fell down into the bottomless abyss. And his armies flew away, terrified of God's Glory that dwells in Raphael. And this was the third of Kasbel's ministers to be defeated in the Angelic War.

And it came to pass that Kasbel, upon seeing that half of his armies had been dispersed by the Holy Archangels, gathered unto himself his two remaining ministers, Pineme and Kasadya, and all their armies. And they surrounded the battlements of Araboth and prepared to attack the Seventh Heaven.

And behold, Michael, the Divine Archstrategist, flew with the Heavenly Hosts to the Heights above Araboth and from this lofty and luminous immensity observed Kasbel's battle plan. And the Great Archangels Gabriel, Raphael, and Uriel joined him there with their respective armies.

And Kasbel, perceiving that the Celestial Armies had abandoned Araboth, decided to launch an immediate attack against the Holy Dwelling. And with a voice of thunder he charged the reprobate angels to break down the Crystal Walls. And the rebel hordes, spurred by his cry of war, rushed like a whirlwind of fire against the shining towers and the very foundations of Araboth swayed and tottered in the midst of space.

And the Great Princes Anapiel YHVH and Soterasiel YHVH and the Watchers of the Seven Palaces of Araboth rushed to the Divine Presence to ask His counsel in the grave ordeal.

And behold, the Glory and Majesty of the Lord of Hosts sat on His Throne of Judgment and from Him emanated an Imponderable Light. And thunder and lightning and the substance of stars issued from the Throne. And the crystal pavement overflowed with fire and lightning. And the Divine Light transcended the realms of Araboth and suffused with its essence the confines of the Universe. And the river of fire that flows in front of the throne roared with tumultuous voices. And the fiery Creatures that hold the Divine Chariot that is the Merkabah, and upon which sits the Throne of the Creator, howled with holy rage. And the Four Winds that feed the fury of the hurricanes, cyclones, and typhoons shrieked and bellowed, fanning and spreading the flames of the Cherubs. And behold, the Throne of Glory was firmly established upon this whirlwind of fire and wind, and nothing could shake its foundation.

And the Great Princes Rikbiel YHVH, Hayliel YHVH, Kerubiel YHVH, Opaniel YHVH, and Serapiel YHVH, Regents of the Three Uppermost Angelical Choirs and of the Holy Creatures, lay facedown at the feet of the Creator, waiting for His commands.

And the Great Prince Radweriel YHVH, who is in charge of the Holy Archives, lay facedown at the feet of the Creator with the Great Book of Judgment in his hands, waiting for his Lord's commands.

And the Four Great Princes, who are the two Watchers and the Two Holy Beings with whom the Creator holds counsel before rendering His Supreme Judgments, lay facedown at the feet of the Creator, awaiting His commands.

And the Creator's voice came rushing forth from the Holy Throne in echoes of thunder and lightning. And from these prodigious echoes emanated Justice, Truth, and Compassion, which are the foundations of the Holy Throne. And the Three Divine Qualities united in perfect harmony, and their union restored Peace and Balance in Araboth.

And the Creatures of Fire that hold the Merkabah ceased their howling. And the Four Winds abated and were calm. And all the Princes of the Divine Presence arose, and with the Celestial Choirs that stand before the Throne, sang the praises of the Creator:

Holy, holy, holy is the Lord of Hosts.

Replete is the whole world with His Glory.

And behold, Kasbel and the rebel armies, who stood behind the Crystal Walls of Araboth, saw the Glory of the Creator extend itself like a mantle of Light throughout the Universe and heard the Angelical Choirs chanting the praises of the Creator. And they understood then their awesome loss, and a great anguish and sorrow overwhelmed their souls.

And Kasbel, conscious of this irreparable loss, and more determined than ever to carry on his plans of conquest, exhorted once more his armies to renew the attack.

And behold, Michael had been awaiting a sign from the Creator before descending upon Kasbel and his hordes. And Michael saw the Light of his beloved Creator extend itself throughout the infinity of the Universe, and he heard the echoes of the Divine Choirs as they ascended to the Heights.

And the Divine Archstrategist commanded the Angelic Captains to sound the trumpets of war. And together with the Heavenly Hosts, composed of 496,000 milliard armies and 496,000 Angels in each army, the Great Seraph descended like a bolt of lightning from the Heights, laying waste to thousands of rebel angels on his path of fire.

And the Great Cherub and Prince of Vengeance Gabriel descended with Michael upon the apostate angels, devastating their ranks with his fiery sword.

And the Great Seraph and Regent of Thunder and Terror Uriel descended with Michael and Gabriel upon the rebellious hordes in the form of a serpent of fire, blazing a path of destruction through their midst.

And the Great Cherub and Prince of the Sun Raphael descended with Michael, Gabriel, and Uriel upon Kasbel and his armies, and his Divine Light blinded them, rendering them helpless to defend themselves against the Heavenly Hosts.

And it came to pass that Kasbel, upon hearing the sound of the trumpets, looked upward and saw the Celestial Avalanche descend upon him and his armies. And in the

Figure 46: Two angels of God, prepared for battle, in search of the rebellious angels.

midst of the terror that spread throughout the battlefield, he saw Michael thrust his lance into Pineme and throw him headlong into the abyss.

And the Archstrategist broke through the ranks of Kasadya, laying them to waste with bolts of fire and lightning. And upon reaching Kasbel's last standing minister, he hit Kadasya's armor with such power that he rent it in half, opening a terrible wound on Kasadya's chest. And the wound closed immediately but, weakened by the loss of his angelic essence, Kasadya fell senseless on the crystal pavement. And from there he was lifted by Gabriel's flaming lance, which threw him into the darkness of the abyss.

And behold, Kasbel was left alone, deprived of the counsel and strength of his ministers and abandoned by the rebellious armies, who flew in terror from the terrible onslaught. And Kasbel and Michael faced each other. And all the trumpets of war were silent. And the two Celestial Enemies, the faithful and the rebellious, dismounted from their winged steeds and made ready for the final combat.

And Michael threw away his Holy Armor and his lance, forged by the fires of the Cherubim, and faced the Adversary of the Lord of Hosts armed only with his great sword of justice.

And Kasbel, in his arrogant pride, did not wish to be less than his opponent. And he also threw away his armor and his lance.

And the silence that surrounded the two angels was more terrifying than the sound of the trumpets of war.

And Kasbel's great cunning told him that defeating Michael was his last hope to win the Heavenly War. For behold, to defeat the Invincible Seraph would raise him in the estimation of the expectant Celestial Armies, which he might still win over to his side. And it was this arrogance that led Kasbel to be the first to attack.

And Michael, whose strategic wisdom counseled him to wait, could read Kasbel's plan in the eyes of his enemy.

And Kasbel, with great power and deadly intent, threw himself upon Michael, with the intention of piercing the Great Seraph's heart with his sword. And behold, instead of Michael's body of Light his flaming sword was thrust into empty space. And turning swiftly around, Kasbel saw his enemy standing behind him with serene eyes and his sword pointing to the ground.

And Kasbel was filled with confusion, and he attacked again, this time with more careful aim. And behold, the glorious essence of the Archstrategist dissolved in front of Kasbel's eyes and moved instantaneously behind the Adversary. And it was then that Kasbel saw the greatness of Michael and why he is called Invincible.

And behold, Kasbel's pride rendered him unable to see the impossibility of defeating Michael. And roaring with impotent fury, he

Figure 47: Satan thrown to the ground by Michael at the start of the battle.

attacked again, and this time Michael met him without moving. And the swords of fire clashed in midair and the two enemies faced each other, their swords crossed above them. And in Michael's emerald eyes Kasbel did not see hatred nor rancor, but a great sadness. And in that moment, Kasbel felt, as he would feel throughout eternity, the great sorrow of having lost the Celestial Glory.

And behold, that moment of recognition and defeat passed swifter than the fluttering of an angel's wing. And with a rapid movement of his sword, Michael disarmed Kasbel, whose sword fell away, broken in half. And the great impact brought Kasbel at Michael's feet, whose fire sandal pressed down firmly upon Kasbel's neck. And that was how the Great War in Heaven came to its end.

And behold, Michael, Gabriel, Uriel, and Raphael chained Kasbel with chains of fire and they brought him thus, humiliated and defeated, before the Throne of the Creator.

The Supreme Judgment

And it came to pass that all the Princes of the Divine Presence were before the Throne. And all the Celestial Choirs awaited in silence the Divine Judgment, behind the great Fire Curtain where everything that has happened, is happening, and will come to pass is written.

And the Great Prince Radweriel YHVH placed the Holy Book of Judgment on the Creator's hands. And the Two Watchers and the Two Holy Beings of the Divine Presence surrounded the Throne. And the Creator held Counsel with Them to decide the sentence that would be passed on the rebellious Seraph Kasbel.

And behold, the Creator's vestments were whiter than white and more radiant than a milliard suns. And likewise His hair was white and resplendent like the aurora borealis. And His countenance was of such blinding Light that it could not be perceived, not even by the highest angels.

And it came to pass that upon calculating the quantity of the fallen angels, their numbers reached many millions. And a full third of the Heavenly Hosts was lost in the Celestial Battle. And among the rebel angels were counted many of the Watchers of the Seventh Heaven. And of the seventy Princes of the Kingdoms of Earth, all were lost, except the Great Seraph Michael, ruler of Israel.

And behold, a great sadness reigned in Heaven, and great was the sorrow of the Creator at the loss of his beloved angels. And from that moment onward, the great Archangel Michael did not smile again.

And after His Counsel with His Two Watchers and His Two Holy Beings, the Creator invested Himself with Justice, Truth, and Wisdom, upon which His Throne is founded, and passed His Supreme Judgment on Kasbel and the rebel armies.

And behold, the sentence was to throw all the angels that remained at large into the

Figure 48: Satan thrown into the abyss.

Figure 49: Michael defeating the rebel angels.

bottomless abyss. And many were imprisoned in the dark regions of the Second, Third, and Fifth Heavens, where they await in eternal grief the end of time. And others were thrown into the depths of the river of fire. But Kasbel and his ministers, Asbel, Gadereel, Pineme, Yeqon, and Kasadya, were condemned to roam eternally through the Darkness, from where they could hear the echoes of the Celestial Choirs and remember their erstwhile Glory, and thus suffer continuously their exile from their Celestial Home.

And behold, Kasbel became known henceforth as Satanail, the Great Adversary. And he was thrown into eternal Darkness with his ministers.

And there was peace and joy once more in the Seven Heavens and the Angelic Choirs raised their voices to sing the Creator's praises. And the Great Archangel Metraton, whose countenance reflects the Glory of God, and the Great Archangel Michael, he who is like God, were from that moment onward the Greatest Princes of the Divine Presence.

And behold, the Creation of the Angels and the Fall of one third of their numbers both took place on the Second Day of Creation. And Kasbel, the rebel Seraph, was the first angel to be created; Michael was the second; Gabriel was the third; Uriel was the fourth; Raphael was the fifth; and Nathanael was the sixth. And of the first six angels that

were created, Kasbel was the only one who rebelled against his Creator.

And Kasbel, now known as Satanail, is the same Satan who is the terrible Adversary and the enemy of God and humanity.

And it came to pass that Satan, filled with resentment and a burning desire for vengeance, gathered his five ministers, Asbel, Gadereel, Yeqon, Pineme, and Kasadya, unto him. And he also gathered the Guardians of the Kingdoms of the Earth who had also fallen. And among them were Belfegor, an erstwhile member of the Angelic Choir known as the Powers and regent of France; Mammon, who induces humanity to avarice and is regent of England; and Astaroth, at one time a Seraph and now regent of America, who became a great duke of the infernal regions and Grand Treasurer of its wealth. And they were joined by Beelzebuth, once a Seraph and now regent of Chaos and Satan's great ally; by Belial, once a Virtue and now regent of Turkey, who is often identified with Satan; and by Asmodeus, who now rules games of chance, the arts, and drama on Earth. And all these fallen Princes, when they joined forces with Satan, became known as demons, devils, and infernal powers. And all of them, with the rest of the fallen angels, pledged allegiance to Satan and swore vengeance against the Creator and His Great Archangels Michael, Gabriel, Uriel, and Raphael.

Figure 50: Satan plotting the destruction of Adam and Eve.

The First Revenge

And behold, Satan, with his hordes of rebel angels, flew continuously through the depths of the abyss, awaiting the propitious moment to carry on his plans of vengeance. And from the eternal darkness of the abyss, he observed the Creator as He completed the Work of Creation. And he saw how the Lord of Hosts created the man Adam and his wife, Eve, and placed them in the Garden of Eden. And he heard the Creator when He instructed the man and his wife not to eat of the Tree of Good and Evil. And Satan saw that the Creator loved Adam and Eve and gave them power over all things on Earth. And Satan's heart was filled with jealousy and rage. And his ferocious cunning revealed unto him that in the destruction of Adam and Eve he would accomplish his revenge on the Creator and His Angels.

And Satan and his cohorts planned together the destruction of the man and his wife. And a great hatred toward Adam and Eve burned mightily in the hearts of Satan and the fallen angels.

And behold, all the rebel hosts disputed among themselves the pleasure of the destruction of Man. And each one argued their reasons to be chosen as the Destroyer. And of all the conspirators, Gadereel was the most convincing.

And Satan listened to Gadereel as he presented his case, demanding the right to destroy Adam and Eve. And Gadereel related how Gabriel, the Great Cherub, Power, and Virtue, threw him into the darkness of the abyss.

And because Gabriel is the Regent of Life and Death, the one who presides over Paradise and sits at the left of the Creator, any damage done to Adam and Eve would rob him of part of his Glory. And because Gadereel had suffered most at the hands of Gabriel, it was he who had the most right to carry on the destruction of Man. And Satan and the apostate angels saw the truth in Gadereel's words and granted him the right to destroy Adam and Eve.

And behold, Raphael, who guarded the Tree of Life with the Cherubim in the Garden of Eden, flew to Araboth each morning to hear the Creator pass His Supreme Judgment with the Princes of the Divine Presence, and to sing with them the Creator's praises.

And it came to pass that Gadereel, observing Raphael from the abyss, flew into the Garden of Eden after the Great Seraph had ascended to the Seventh Heaven. And enveloped in his mantle of darkness, he passed unnoticed by the Cherubim who guarded the Tree of Life.

And behold, Eve, Adam's wife, slept under the Tree of Good and Evil. And Adam was not with her. And Gadereel took the form of a serpent and coiled himself by her side. And whistling softly into her ear, he caused her to awaken from her slumber.

Figure 51: The serpent approaching to tempt Eve.

And Eve saw the serpent that was Gadereel and was not afraid.

And Gadereel slithered up the trunk of the Tree of Good and Evil and ate one of the forbidden fruit. And Eve admonished him for eating the fruit. And Gadereel, with subtle malice, told Eve that the fruit was good and conferred wisdom on whoever would eat it. And Eve saw that the serpent did not die upon eating of the fruit.

And Gadereel took one of the forbidden fruit and offered it to Eve. And he told her that the Creator had lied and that He did not want her and her husband to eat of the fruit, lest they would become as wise as He. And Eve believed Gadereel and ate of the fruit. And upon Adam's return, she told him what the serpent had said. And Eve offered the fruit of the Tree to Adam, and he ate. And the eyes of the man and his wife were open, and they saw that they were naked. And ashamed of their nakedness, they hid among the bushes and covered their bodies with leaves.

And behold, the Creator had observed from his Throne the conspiracy of Satan and the rebel angels, and saw Gadereel's temptation of Eve and how she and Adam ate of the forbidden fruit. For behold, everything that has happened, is happening, and will come to pass is written on the Fire Curtain before the Throne of Glory. And the Creator knows Everything before it comes to pass but, having created Man with Free Will, He must allow him to decide his own fate. And all of this is written in the Book of Life and Death that is guarded by the Great Prince Radweriel YHVH.

And the Creator descended to the Garden of Eden and Adam and Eve were hiding in the Garden. And the Creator called them with a voice of thunder and they appeared before Him, covered with leaves. And when He asked them why they hid themselves, they answered that they were ashamed, as they were naked.

And the Creator asked them if they had eaten of the Tree of Good And Evil. And Adam answered and said that Eve, his wife, had given him of the fruit, and he had eaten. And Eve told the Creator that the serpent had beguiled her into eating from the forbidden fruit.

And the Creator knew that Satan and the apostate angels had done this deed against Man to avenge their exile from Heaven. And His Spirit was heavy with sadness for the man and his wife, whom He had created as angels to rule in love and peace on Earth.

And the Creator and His Shekinah, whose Glory dwelt in the Tree of Life, held counsel on the fate of Man. And in their Unity they decided to take the man Adam and his wife Eve from the Garden of Eden, lest they eat of the Tree of Life and have eternal life in their corruption.

And the Creator told Raphael to lead Adam and Eve out of Eden and to place a flaming sword on the Garden's gate to impede the entrance therein of Man or Angel.

Figure 52: Adam and Eve being expelled from the Garden of Eden.

And Adam and Eve lived in Eden for five and one-half hours.

And Adam was condemned to till the Earth during all his days and to eat the fruit of his labors mingled with the sweat of his brow. And Eve was condemned to bear her children with great pain. And the serpent was condemned to crawl on the dust of the Earth for the length of its days. But Gadereel had already left the body of the serpent.

And behold, the Creator covered the bodies of Light of Adam and Eve with flesh and bone, which is the mortal vestment of Man. And Adam and Eve were no longer immortal like the Angels, and their lives were shortened and numbered in years and cut by the sword of Gabriel.

And the Creator, moved to compassion for His creature Adam and his wife Eve, granted them the hope of Redemption at the time of the Resurrection, when all their sins would be forgiven. And He promised to send to the Earth His Messengers and Ministers to guide Adam and Eve in the bitterness of their exile and to show them the path of Salvation.

And Adam and Eve were taken away from their home in Eden and there was much rejoicing among Satan and the rebel hosts.

And the Glory of the Shekinah remained in the Garden of Eden. And behold, such was the greatness of Her Light that It illuminated all the corners of the Earth. And all those who beheld Her Light did not suffer illness or pain. And Adam and Eve camped before the Garden of Eden to bask in the Glory of the Shekinah.

And Adam and Eve multiplied. And their first son, Cain, slew the second, Abel. And for this crime Cain was marked on the brow by the Creator. But their third son, Seth, was a man of peace and from him issued many generations.

The Second Revenge

And in the sixth generation after Adam was born a man of God on the Earth, and his name was Enoch, son of Jared. And Enoch walked with the Lord and found Grace in His eyes. And at this time, human beings lived many years on Earth, and Enoch lived 365 years and the Creator brought him to Araboth. And the son of Enoch, Methuselah, lived the longest span of any man on Earth, and he lived 969 years. And behold, in the third generation after Enoch was born another man who found Grace in the eyes of the Lord. And his name was Noah.

And it came to pass that by the time Noah was 500 years old, humanity had multiplied itself a thousandfold. And great was the prosperity of human beings on Earth, for they were nourished by the Glory of the Shekinah.

And the great Adversary, Satan, was still consumed with hatred for the Creator and His beloved creature, Man. And seeing that prosperity reigned on Earth and that Man had learned the Holy Name of God, YHVH, and invoked It continuously, Satan called his ministers to counsel to plan the destruction of peace on Earth.

And behold, many of the Celestial Watchers descended daily upon Earth to carry on the commands of the Creator. And Satan sought to corrupt the Divine Messengers and in this manner accomplish his plan to destroy humanity.

And Satan instructed his ministers Asbel and Yeqon to induce the Celestial Watchers to sin with the daughters of men. And behold, the concourse between Angels and Man is forbidden by the Creator. And the Angels have the power to transform their Light essences into any form they desire, be it man or woman, plant, animal, or mineral.

And Yeqon and Asbel, following Satan's orders, espied the descent of the Celestial Watchers and accosted some of them. And among the Watchers that were tempted by Yeqon and Asbel were the following:

1. Semyaza
2. Rameiel
3. Taniel
4. Ramiel
5. Daniel
6. Ezeqel
7. Baraqyal
8. Asiel
9. Armaros
10. Batariel
11. Ananiel
12. Zaqiel
13. Sasomaspeiel
14. Kestariel
15. Turiel
16. Yamaol
17. Arazyal
18. Aristaqis
19. Azazel
20. Neqaiel
21. Sipeseiel
22. Basasiel
23. Kokbail
24. Baraqiel

And behold, Yeqon and Asbel, with subtle malice, showed these Watchers the daughters of men, who were beautiful, and the Watchers were induced to enter into sinful union with the women. And the Watchers were sorely tempted. And Semyaza, who was the Captain of the Watchers, had doubts. And he told the Watchers that he feared that they would later repent of the deed, and he alone be responsible for the great sin. And the Watchers, already seduced by the idea of cohabiting with the daughters of men, swore an oath that would bind them to this act, grievously sinful in the eyes of the Creator.

And behold, the Watchers descended to Earth in the place called Ardos, which is in the summit of Mount Hermon. And they transformed their Angelic essence into the forms of men. And the Watchers who descended unto Ardos numbered 200. And they were known henceforth as the Grigori.

And immediately upon their descent to Earth they took women unto themselves as wives, and sinned with them. And they taught their wives all kinds of forbidden knowledge that belongs only to the Creator and His Angels. And among the forbidden knowledge was the practice of magical healing, incantations, and the use of roots and all manner of plants.

And Azazel taught human beings the art of forging swords, knives, and armor. And he instructed the women in the use of ornaments, such as bracelets and pendants. And he also taught them the art of facial paint, how to line their eyes with antimony and other embellishments.

And the Watcher Amasras taught the women how to do enchantments; Baraqiel taught them the science of astrology; Kokareriel taught them the secrets of the signs of the zodiac; Tamiel taught them how to follow the course of the stars; and Asderiel taught them the mysteries of the moon and how to deceive men.

And behold, Satan's ministers also corrupted human beings with all manners of forbidden knowledge. And Gadereel taught them how to build instruments of war and how to strike a death blow. And Pineme taught the secrets of sweet and bitter things and the writing with paper and ink. And behold, this was a most grievous sin, for Man was not created to express his thoughts in writing.

And worst yet, Kasadya taught them the great depths of evil and of the spirit, and how to destroy the child in the mother's womb before his birth. And great was the sin of humanity, seduced by the Satanic hordes.

And the Watcher's wives conceived and gave birth to abominable creatures called Nefillim, whose heights measured 300 cubits. And these giants consumed the harvests gathered by men in great numbers and devoured many human beings in their insatiable hunger. And they also destroyed the beasts of the fields, the fish and the fowl of the air and, at last, they fell upon each other to devour their own kind and drink their own blood. And the Earth raised its voice in anguish to accuse its oppressors.

And behold, the Great Princes Michael, Gabriel, Uriel, and Raphael observed from the Heights the evil done by Satan and his rebel hordes against humanity. And they heard the Earth's laments as they reached the Gates of Heaven and the human cries imploring justice against the evil done by the rebel angels.

And the four Princes of the Divine Presence ascended to Araboth and stood before the Holy Throne of the Creator.

Figure 53: Noah's ark rests at the top of Mount Ararat after the Flood.

And behold, they told the Lord of Hosts, Blessed Be He, of the great corruption that Satan and his accomplices had unleashed upon Humanity and the Earth. And these were their words:

Great Lord of All That Is, Thy Name is Holy, Blessed, and Glorious throughout the Universe. Thou hast created Everything and hast Power over All Thou hast created. Everything is naked to Thine Eyes. Thou seest Everything and Nothing is hidden to Thy Sight. Thou hast seen what Azazel hast done; how he hast unleashed all forms of oppression upon the Earth. The fallen Watchers have revealed to Humanity eternal secrets that belong only to Heaven and now human beings know them. And Semyaza, to whom Thou granted power over the Watchers, hast united with them against Thee, and they have engaged in sinful union with the daughters of men—with those women—and have taught them all manners of forbidden knowledge. And now the women have given birth to giants who have covered the Earth with blood. And now, O Thou Holy Being, raise Thy Voice in Anger, and those who have died on Earth shalt stand before Thee and ask Thee to avenge their torment. And behold, the Glory of the Shekinah still dwells in the Garden of Eden, and those who have sinned against Thee are nourished by Her Light. And Thou knowest Everything before It happens and seest what is happening on Earth. And yet Thou dost not tell us what we should do about this.

And behold, the Most High, the Great and Holy Being, hearkened to the words of His Great Archangels Michael, Gabriel, Uriel, and Raphael and withdrew the Shekinah and Her Glory from Eden and brought Her to dwell again in Araboth. And the Garden of Eden He also withdrew from Earth, and placed it on the Third Heaven. And raising His Voice of Thunder, He instructed the Great Prince Asuryal to descend immediately to Earth and tell Noah, the son of Lamed, to make ready, for a Great Deluge was soon to be unleashed upon the Earth. And Asuryal instructed Noah in the construction of an Ark, which was to be the vessel of salvation for himself and his children.

And Asuryal taught Noah how to construct the Ark, and he told Noah to seek refuge within the vessel with his wife and his sons and their wives. And Noah brought within the Ark all manners of beasts, male and female, so that the seed of all that the Creator had made did not perish from the Earth.

And the King of Kings opened the doors of Heaven and caused a Great Deluge to pour down unto Earth. And the waters from Heaven fell during forty days and forty nights and cleansed the Earth from all the evil which had been wrought upon it by Satan and the fallen Watchers.

And behold, the Earth was purified from its corruption and new life flourished upon the Earth. And the Creator set the Rainbow upon the firmament as a Covenant and an Oath that He would never destroy the Earth by water again. And that was how the Creator nullified Satan's hope to destroy Humanity forever. And this was Satan's Second Revenge, but not the Last, for he is forever seeking to destroy Man. And that is the reason why the Angels of the Lord are always present upon the Earth, to protect it from the constant threat of the Adversary.

The Second Judgment

And the Creator instructed Raphael to bind Azazel by his hands and feet and, thus bound, to hurl him into the depths of the abyss. And Raphael made a great hole in the desert that is in Dudaiel and threw Azazel into the hole. And he covered the chasm with rocks and sharp stones that Azazel may not see the Light of Day, and therein he will lie until he is thrown into the River of Fire on the Day of Final Judgment. And the Creator gave new Life unto the Earth so that Humanity would not perish because of the evil of the fallen Watchers. And behold all sins of Earth shall be written upon Azazel.

And the Creator instructed Gabriel to destroy all the reprobates and the children of adultery, and to exile the Nefillim from Earth, and to instigate strife among them so they would destroy one another. And to ignore their pleas for mercy that they would invoke in the names of their fathers, the fallen Watchers, as they hoped to live forever.

And the Creator instructed Michael to tell Semyaza and all the Watchers who had fornicated with the daughters of men that they would die with them in their vilification. And after their children, the Nefillim, had destroyed each other, these fallen Watchers would be bound by Michael for seventy generations in the bowels of Earth until the Day of Final Judgment. And on this Day they would be thrown into the River of Fire where they would suffer in great torment until the end of all generations, with all those who had sinned with them.

And the Creator also told Michael to destroy all the souls who lived only for the sake of pleasure and all the children of the Guardians for the grievous injustice they had committed against Humanity. And he commanded Michael to destroy all injustice from the face of the Earth, that all iniquity would come to an end and Truth and Righteousness

Figure 54: The Son of Man seated at the right of the Celestial Father in Paradise.

Figure 55: The Final Judgment.

would reign upon the Earth. And after Michael had cleansed the Earth from all sin, from oppression and injustice, all of Humanity would worship its Creator, and Love and Peace would extend like a holy mantle upon the Earth.

And behold, in those days Enoch, who was loved by God for his righteousness, was hidden, and none on Earth knew where he was. And Enoch was with the faithful Watchers and with the Holy Beings. And the faithful Watchers told Enoch to inform the fallen Watchers of the grave Judgment that had been passed upon them. And Enoch did so.

And behold, the fallen Watchers pleaded with Enoch to intercede on their behalf before the Holy Throne, and to write a plea for mercy and bring it to the Creator that the fallen Watchers might be forgiven. And Enoch was a scribe and wrote a prayer of contrition on behalf of the fallen Watchers.

And after writing the prayer, Enoch sat before the waters of Dan in the southwest of Hermon and fell asleep. And behold, Enoch had a vision. And in this vision he was taken to Araboth before the Throne of the Creator. And the Creator told Enoch that the prayer of the fallen Watchers was in vain, that they had forfeited their Glory in Heaven for the sake of a sinful life on Earth. And for this reason and for their sins against Humanity there could be no Mercy for them. And after this, the Creator instructed His Angels to show Enoch the secrets of the Seven Heavens and of Creation.

And behold, after these revelations, the Creator permitted Enoch to return to Earth for one year and to tell his son Methuselah all that had been revealed unto Enoch. And He further instructed Enoch to write everything he had seen for future generations. And He instructed Enoch to tell his children that human beings cannot be Just before God because they are only the product of His creation. And Enoch accomplished all that the Creator had told him to do and he wrote 366 books and gave them to his son Methuselah. And Enoch had been in Heaven for sixty days. And behold, one year after Enoch came back to Earth, he was taken again by the Creator and brought to Araboth.

The Son of Man

And behold, before the Creator made the Sun, the Moon, and the Stars, and before the Creation of the World, He had chosen unto Himself an Elect Being. And He hid His Elect One in the Light of His Presence and gave him a name. And this name is the Son of Man. And no one, not even God's Angels, knew of the existence of the Elect One. And behold, Righteousness is the vestment of the Son of Man and he is destined to be victorious before the Lord of Hosts for all Eternity. And he will bring down kings and their kingdoms, and will be the scourge of the insolent and depraved and those who live by the power of riches. And he will be the Hope of the poor in spirit, who suffer the oppression of the unjust. And the Elect of the Lord of Hosts shall take on the vestments of flesh and bone and will be born on Earth of man and woman for the Glory of God.

And the Creator hid His Elect One within His mantle of Light because in His Great Omniscience He knew the grievous sin that would be committed by His Archangel Beqa, he who was later called Kasbel and henceforth and for all Eternity known as Satan. And He knew the temptation that would be visited upon Eve, Adam's wife, through Satan's First Revenge. And He knew the great sin that would be committed by the fallen Watchers through their fornication with the daughters of men and Satan's Second, but not Last, Revenge. And He knew He would destroy the Earth through the Great Deluge to save Humanity from Satan's plan. And He knew that through His servant Enoch He would tell future generations the eventual destiny of the human race. And He knew who among His Great Angels were completely faithful. And that was why He confided only in Michael the secret of His Holy Name. And He knew that two thirds of His Ministers would remain faithful to the end of time. And He knew that Salvation was possible for Humanity because in them was hidden the Divine Light.

And the Creator permitted Satan and his ministers to remain free to tempt Humanity because He knew that whoever resisted the temptation was a Noble Creation and would endure with Him for all times.

And behold, Satan and the apostate Angels ate of the fruit of exile in vain. And their plans of destruction against Humanity came to naught through the Wisdom of the Creator. And He foresaw the defeat of Satan through the power of the Lord's Elect One, who shall crush under his iron sandal the machinations of the Adversary against Humanity.

And the Creator shall send many of His Angels and Ministers unto Earth to teach His Law to Humanity, that through It they may defeat the temptations of the Adversary.

And the Spirit of the Son of Man sits to the right of the Creator on His Holy Throne and his face is a human face, noble and beautiful, because he is destined to take human form many times to save Humanity. And meanwhile he dwells in Araboth with the Creator and His Shekinah, and his Light is the Creator's Light, and all the Princes of the Divine Presence worship at his feet.

And behold, at the end of time, on the Day of Final Judgment, when Gabriel sounds his trumpet to announce the Resurrection of those who sleep in the dust, the Son of Man shall sit at the right of the Creator to pass Judgment with Him on the living and the dead.

And when all of Creation, the visible and the invisible, which the Creator has made, comes to an end, each human being shall stand before the Throne of the Almighty to hear His Final Judgment. And time will also come to an end, and years, months, days, hours, minutes, and seconds shall be no more. And they shall not be counted again, but will constitute one Era.

And all those deemed just and worthy in the eyes of the Creator shall be reunited in the Great Era. And the Great Era shall be for them and it shall be Eternal. And after this shall come to pass, there will be no sorrow, nor illness, nor affliction, nor darkness visited upon them.

And a Great Light shall be upon them, a Great and Indestructible Light, which shall be Paradise, Perfect and Incorruptible. For, behold, all that is corrupt shall be no more and the Incorruptible shall reign in its stead. And it shall be the refuge of the Eternal Mansions.

Beloved, this is my message. A new Era approaches, not the Final One, but an Era of Great Light and also of grave temptations and secret sorrows. And behold, the Creator has sent His Angels unto Earth as He had promised, to make known the New Era that is coming. And the presence of the Angels is being felt upon the Earth. And behold, our Love extends itself upon Humanity. And each human race shall call us with different names and in different ways. For behold, all religions and beliefs are One, and we shall respond with Love toward All.

And many human beings sense our presence among them and hearken unto our voices. And the Great Princes Michael, Gabriel, Uriel, and Raphael walk upon the Earth and their footsteps may be seen on the dust of your streets. And in many dreams and visions their Love and Wisdom shall find echoes in your hearts. And you may call us Angels, Devas, Bodhisattvas, Nature Spirits, or Cosmic Laws, but we are simply the Soul of the Universe, the Primeval Energy and the Physical Laws that maintain the harmony of the Cosmos. And he who is called Satanail and also his ministers are the destructive forces that disrupt the cosmos, that which is known as Chaos.

And behold, if you listen to our voices, in the wind, in the rain, in the sea and all of nature, asleep or awake, and you follow in our path, they will lead you to the Throne of the Creator. And at the end of time, you will find yourselves among the Elect. And to follow our path you need only to observe the laws of nature. For behold every scientific principle is an Angel and every new scientific discovery you make is another step that brings you closer to us. And our Essence extends itself throughout the galaxies, and the interstellar dust of the Universe is our Trajectory. And at the core of each atom and each star you will find our cosmic signature.

This is the history of the human race, of its Creation and the history of the planet you call Earth. But behold, yours is only one world among the many that populate the Cosmos and there are other races and other beings, all of which have their own histories. And the Creation was conceived for them as it was for you, for there are many Creations and many Universes. And Our Presence permeates them all through the Power and Design of the Supreme Architect of All that Is. And in the last Cosmic Day all that was created shall return to its Original Source. And behold, Arkhas and Edoil shall receive again within Themselves the primordial energies from which the Universes were created. And All shall be One with the Creator and Nothing shall exist but He.

Until the end of time,
 in Peace and Love Eternal,
I am Megadriel.

Part III
~
Angel Messages (Book of Megadriel)

Beloved:

In these, the last days before the New Era, we are permitted to reveal unto you some of the most important events that will take place in the beginning of the new Millennium. We are also permitted to tell you what steps you may take to lessen that which is to come, and how you may advance in your earthly and spiritual evolution.

Our first message is that your world shall not come to an end in the new Millennium. The Earth shall not split in half, the surface of the planet shall not be torn asunder by natural forces out of control, neither comet nor meteor shall destroy your civilization. You were created for a purpose and this purpose has not yet been fulfilled. There are dangers but these are dangers that you can circumvent if you hearken unto our words.

In the first twenty-nine years of the twenty-first century many climatic changes will take place on Earth. There will be atmospheric disturbances of cataclysmic proportions. There will be serious problems with the ice poles, which are beginning to melt, specifically the North Pole. There will be a proliferation of nuclear and biological weapons, especially in the Middle East of your planet.

There will be strong earth tremors along the line of the Equator. This area must be observed continuously because of the many cataclysms that may take place.

There will be anarchy attempts in the streets. These will be controlled by the proper authorities but they may cause severe losses.

There will be new discoveries in the sciences of biochemistry and physiology that will result in attempts to alter the genetic code, for the purpose of creating a superhuman race. These experiments will be conducted at first in the greatest secrecy, as they will meet with much religious and secular condemnation. But eventually they will be conducted openly.

Toward the middle of the century, there will be a world congress that will result in one monetary unit for the entire planet and a universal language that will be spoken by all.

By the middle of the century human beings will have established colonies in other planets of the solar system, making them habitable through new technologies. The first of these planets will be Mars, which will become a New Earth.

Physics and astronomy are the sciences that hold the destinies of Earth on the balance.

The mystery of Creation will be resolved early in the century and the existence of God and other dimensions proven through new laws of physics.

The survival of the human personality, which is the soul, after death will also be proven, and contacts with other realms of being will take place through very precise audiovisual instrumentation.

A new method will be uncovered to detect life on other planets. This will consist of a very sensitive type of radar that will pinpoint life signals throughout space, reaching the farthest confines of the Universe. The base of this radar will be an angular gyroscope made largely of titanium. This instrument will function like a form of echo through which waves move in circular motion throughout space, very much like a stone that is thrown on tranquil waters which then forms concentric waves, each one larger and wider than the one preceding it. These waves will then return to Earth, bringing with them information of the various points in the Universe where life exists. To accomplish this task, the instrument will be programmed according to the human genetic code.

Criminal instincts and physical defects will be avoided in new births through the alteration of the genetic code. This will be accomplished through certain enzymes that will be ingested by women before conception.

The life cycle will be lengthened, and the deterioration of the skin and the internal organs will be delayed, prolonging not only life but a youthful appearance. Human beings will live beyond a century without outward signs of aging. All these will be possible through biochemical engineering, which will be an important factor in the New Era.

You are strongly advised to place a strong emphasis on the teaching of mathematics and physics to children from an early age. These sciences are the key to the new century. Chemistry is also important.

The control of atmospheric forces is of great urgency because they are the greatest threat to humanity. This can be achieved through magnetism, which controls the Earth. The use of new instruments based on magnetism and polarity will create a balance on natural forces at present out of control such as earthquakes, tornadoes, floods, and tidal waves among many.

The balance of the Earth is based on the magnetism that exists between the North and the South Pole. It is recommended that magnetic structures be erected along the entire length of the Equator. These structures will create a magnetic field that will help maintain the harmony of the seasons, the atmosphere, and the stability of the surface of the Earth. Similar structures should be erected between the two poles, along the four major longitudes. These will create a powerful polarization that will protect the Earth, ensuring the stability of the poles. If this is not done, the atmosphere will continue to deteriorate and the poles will continue to melt down, resulting in increasing atmospheric cataclysms. The waters of the oceans will eventually threaten to cover the land, with devastating results.

Earth is on a continuous evolution. New species of fauna and flora will be discovered. Likewise many known species of fauna and flora will disappear from the Earth, as their allowed life span is coming to an end. Humanity is also evolving, and many changes in physical appearance and mental development will become evident with passing time. Within a few centuries, the human race will inhabit many parts of your galaxy and beyond, extending its seed throughout the Universe as foreseen by the Divine Plan.

Intergalactic travel and the expansion of the human race to other places in the galaxy will take place instantaneously through the disintegration of matter and its simultaneous restructuring in chosen points. This will be accomplished by establishing an energy bridge between the point of departure and that of arrival, sending the atoms of the disintegrated matter along this route. The disintegration and reintegration of matter will be possible through the acceleration and deceleration of the movement of the atoms. This will not be done with machinery but through electromagnetic waves of great intensity whose concentrated vibrations will result in the disintegration and reintegration of matter. This will be accomplished through the science of acoustics, which is still in its infancy and should be strongly developed because of its tremendous potential.

What human beings call God is conscious thought elevated to the power of zero. God is Idea and Reason, Balance and Law. Creation is based on harmony but in a malleable form, where everything is possible. God's primordial characteristic is Possibility. The Impossible does not exist in the Universe. The Impossible is a human concept based on the human fallacy known as restriction. You restrict yourselves by believing that there are limits to your capacities. There are none.

Pure thought, which is God, and His primordial Idea of Creation, extends Itself throughout all the Universes, creating new possibilities without end. There is no Beginning and there is no End. This is a concept inherent in matter. Everything exists at the same time, which is eternity. Everything is one Whole. There is no differentiation in God, only the creative impulse and essence. Everything is part of Him.

Evil is the result of the ignorance of the cosmic laws and the erroneous perception of the reality which is God. A human being is not God, but is a part of Him, and can create infinitely like He can. To create in God's image it is necessary to use the imagination without restraints. Everything becomes an immediate reality through the power of thought and imagination. The original thought creates its own reality. Everything can be because everything is possible and all that is possible is God.

Every idea and every desire to create becomes an immediate reality if you believe in its possibility. To believe in the possibility of something is to believe in God.

An angel is an expression of the Divine Thought. Each angel is an idea of God, a concept and a Law, whose energy maintains the balance and harmony of the Universes.

Beyond the Universes there is No-Thing, which is the Supreme Intelligence at rest.

All the Universes emerged simultaneously from the Mind of God and new Universes are being continuously created by the power of His thought. This is possible because time only exists in the human imagination. And whatever you believe in exists for you. The Simultaneous Creation and the Continuous Creation are possible because everything is possible in the Mind of God.

Everything exists and Nothing exists. This is also possible.

Beloved, I urge you to love and cherish one another because All is One, and Nothing exists outside the One. Where there is no Love there is no Union, and where there is no Union lies the negation of the One. Those among you who are outside Love are in the darkness of the abyss. Look at those of your brethren who are in the darkness as sparks of Light hidden in the abyss, which is the Adversary. Take pity on them and help them return to the Light whence they were created. It is easy if you fill your hearts with wisdom, compassion, and understanding. Together these three divine qualities are Love. Therein lies the hope for Humanity.

To help you in this task were the Angels created. For behold, everything that was created was created for you. Remember us always and ask our help constantly for we have been with you from the Beginning and will remain with you until the End.

In Love and Peace Profound,
I am Megadriel.

Part IV

Angel Biographies

An alphabetical list of the best-known angels and heavenly places, including the angels of light and the fallen angels.

A

Aba—an angel invoked during kabbalistic rites who is said to control sexuality in human beings.

Ababaloi—an angel invoked during kabbalistic rites, especially in Solomonic magic.

Abaddon (the destroyer)—in the Book of Revelation he is the angel or Star of the bottomless abyss who chains Satan in this dreaded place for 2,000 years. He is said to be the angel invoked by Moses to send the devastating rains to Egypt. Some authorities refer to Abaddon as a place instead of an angel. This is also the name given by Jews to the Greek god Apollyon. In some of the apocryphal books, like the Acts of Thomas, Abaddon is presented as a demonic entity. This entity is also identified as the dark angel of death, as a demon of the abyss, and as one of the princes of the infernal hierarchy, often seen as Satan himself.

Abadon—according to the Zohar, this name is a description of the infernal hierarchies.

Abaddona (the repentant one)—one of the rebellious Seraphim who later repented his sins against the Creator. But according to Christian doctrine, the fallen angels cannot repent because once they have sinned against God, their essence is totally corrupted by evil.

Abagtha—one of the angels of confusion.

Abalim (great angels)—another name given to the Thrones or Erelim. The principal Intelligences or Regent Princes of this choir are Zaphkiel and Jophiel.

Abariel—one of the angel regents of the twenty-eight mansions of the moon, who is often invoked during lunar rituals. His name is inscribed in the Second Moon Pentacle found in the Greater Key of Solomon.

Abathur Mizania—among the Mandeans, this is the angel who rules the North Star and the balance where the souls are weighed when a person dies. He is also known as Abyatur.

Abbaton—one of the names of Death and one of the guardian spirits of the gates of Hell. In the Greater Key of Solomon this is the name of one of God's angels who is invoked during magical ceremonies to control evoked spirits.

Abdals (the substitutes)—according to Islam, this is a group of seventy spirits who ensure the continuous existence of the world. Only God (Allah) knows their secret names. These beings are not immortal, and when one of them dies God creates another to substitute him.

Abdia (servant)—one of the angels who protects the magic circle in Solomonic magic.

Abdiel (servant of God)—according to the *Book of Raziel*, this is one of the angels of the celestial hierarchies. In *Paradise Lost,* Abdiel is one of the radiant Seraphim who rejected Satan, causing him to fall by a stroke of Abdiel's sword. This angel is also known as Abadiel.

Abdiziriel—one of the lunar angels who rules the twenty-eight mansions of the moon.

Abel—one of the angelic rulers of the Fourth Heaven, who is always invoked in the east of the magic circle. In Gnosticism, Abel is one of the twelve Powers who judge the souls when they arrive in Heaven.

Abelech—according to the Greater Key of Solomon, one of the angels invoked to subdue infernal spirits during black magic rituals.

Abezi-Thibod—one of the infernal princes who rule Egypt. He is said to have fought against Moses, hardening Pharaoh's heart against the Lawgiver. The ancient Hebrews classified this angel as an infernal entity, identifying him with Samael and Mastema. In Solomon's Testament, Abezi-Thibod is Beelzebub's son.

Abheiel—one of the ruling angels of the twenty-eight mansions of the moon.

Ablati—according to Waite's *The Book of Ceremonial Magic,* this angel is invoked in rites dedicated to Uriel. His name is one of the four words God spoke to Moses. The other words were Josta, Agla (one of God's names), and Caila.

Abrasiel—the angel who rules the seventh hour of the day, according to *The Pauline Art.*

Abraxas—according to the Kabbalah, this is the ruling prince of the eons. To the Gnostics, Abraxas (or Abraxis) is God's true name. The Persians believed Abraxas was the source of the 365 divine emanations identified with the days of the year. From this name is derived the word "Abracadabra," which was believed in ancient times to cure fevers and other illnesses.

Abrid—in the Jewish tradition, this is one of the "Memumim" or ministering angels and his name is used in amulets against the evil eye. Abrid is also the angel who rules the summer equinox.

Abriel—one of the angles used in kabbalistic invocations. At one time he was a member of the choir of the Dominions.

Abrimas—one of the angels invoked during the Jewish Sabbath.

Abruel (power of God)—in Islam, one of the names of the Archangel Gabriel or Jibril.

Absannis—one of the seventy-eight names of Metraton.

Abrunael—one of the ruling angels of the twenty-eight mansions of the moon.

Abuhaza—one of the angels of the element air, said to rule Mondays.

Abuionij—one of the angels of the Second Heaven.

Abuiori—one of the angels of the Second or Third Heaven, regent of Wednesday, who is invoked from the north in the magic circle.

Abuliel—one of the angels of prayer. Other angels who transmit prayers to the Throne of God are Metraton, Raphael, Michael, Akatriel, and Sizouse.

Abuhozar—one of the ruling angels of the twenty-eight mansions of the moon.

Achaiah (problem)—one of the Seraphim in charge of the secrets of nature and able to grant the gift of patience to human beings.

Achamoth—in Gnosticism, one of the daughters of the aeon Pistis Sophia and mother of the malefic Ialdabaoth.

Acheliah—in the Greater Key of Solomon, this is one of the angels of the Venus sphere.

Achusaton—one of the angels of the Thrones.

Aclahaye—the patron of gamblers.

Adabiel—another name of the angel Abdiel, often identified with Zadkiel, the ruler of Jupiter.

Adadiyah—one of the seventy-eight names of Metraton.

Adiel—according to Jewish tradition, one of the angels of the Seventh Heavenly Hall.

Adimus—according to Heywood's *The Hierarchy of the Blessed Angels*, this was one of the angels reprobated by a Church Council in Rome in A.D. 745. The others were Uriel, Raguel, and Simiel, but no explicit reasons were given for their rejection.

Adirael—according to *The Book of Abramelin the Mage*, this was one of the fallen angels and a servant of Beelzebub.

Adirah—one of the angels of the Seventh Heaven.

Adiriel—one of the angels of the Fifth Heaven.

Adiririon—sometimes identified with Adiriel, this angel is said to belong to the choir of the Powers. His name is used in amulets against the evil eye. He is also one of the guardians of the First Heaven. Some Jewish authorities say that this is one of the secret names of God.

Adityas—group of seven Vedic angels, ruled by Varuna, who reflect God's Glory, according to the Vedas.

Admael—one of the ruling angels of planet Earth who resides in the Second Heaven.

Adnachiel—one of the regents of the First Choir of Angels. He is also the ruler of November and one of the protectors of those born under Sagittarius. God is said to have given Adnachiel a talisman to cure all stomach illnesses. This angel is also known as Advachiel and Adernahael.

Adnai—according to the Greater Key of Solomon, one of the angels of the sphere of Venus invoked in love rituals.

Adoil (God's hand)—one of the creatures used by God to create the universe, according to the *Book of Enoch*.

Adonael—a great angel invoked to exorcise the demons of illness, Bobel and Metathiax, according to the Testament of Solomon. All the angelic names that start with the prefix "Adona" are based on God's title, Adonai, meaning "Lord," and are generally used in rites of exorcism against evil forces.

Adonaeth—the angel invoked to exorcise the demon Ichthion, who causes paralysis.

Adonai (The Lord)—the name of God used by devout Jews as a substitute for the most holy name YHVH (Yahweh or Jehovah), which is never to be pronounced. Among the Phoenicians Adonai was one of the seven angels of the Divine Presence, responsible for the Creation of the universe.

Adonai Yireh—the name of the mountain where Abraham went to sacrifice his son Isaac by divine command. This sacrifice, ordered by God to test Abraham's faith, was stopped by one of God's angels.

Adonaios—in Gnosticism, this is one of the seven Arcons who rule the Seven Heavens.

Adoniel—in the Greater Key of Solomon, one of the angels of Jupiter invoked during magic rituals. He is also one of the regents of midnight.

Adoyahel—in the *Sixth and Seventh Books of Moses*, one of the fifteen ruling princes of the Thrones.

Adrael (God is my help)—this angel is sometimes confused with Adriel, but they are two very different angelic entities. Adrael is one of the angels of the First Heaven.

Adramelech—one of the fallen angels, at one time belonging to the Thrones. During black magic rituals he manifests in physical form as a mule with peacock feathers. In the infernal hierarchies, Adramelech is a great Chancellor of the Order of the Great Cross or the Order of the Fly, established by Beelzebub. Adramlech's name signifies "king of fire."

Adriel—according to Heyworth's *Hierarchy of the Blessed Angels*, Adriel is one of the ruling angels of the twenty-eight man-

sions of the moon. He is also one of the angels of Death and the Final Judgment.

Adrigon—one of the seventy-eight names of Metraton.

Aebel—according to the apocryphal Book of Adam and Eve, Aebel and the angels Shetel and Anush gave food and drink to Adam and Eve by God's orders.

Af (anger)—this is one of the angels of the Seventh Heaven and is forged of chains of black and red fire. He is one of the angels of destruction and rules over the death of human beings. He is said to be 500 parasangs tall.

Afafiel—one of the guardians of the Halls of the Seventh Heaven.

Affafniel—in the *Book of Raziel*, this is one of the angels of God's divine anger. He has sixteen faces that change continuously.

Afkiel—one of the guardians of the Halls of the Fifth Heaven.

Aftiel—in Jewish lore, one of the angels of nightfall.

Agad—one of the angels belonging to the Powers.

Agaf—in the rabbinic tradition, one of the angels of destruction.

Agares—one of the fallen angels and a great duke in the infernal regions. Infernal entities are organized as a kingdom with

Satan as their king. The principal demons have titles like dukes, marquises, counts, and chancellors. Before his fall, Agares belonged to the choir of the Virtues. When invoked in rites of black magic, he appears as an old man sitting on a crocodile. It is said that among his talents are the power to teach languages and cause earthquakes.

Agbas—one of the guardians of the Fourth Heaven.

Agiel—in talismanic magic, he is said to be one of the angels of the planet Mercury. Paracelsus and other magicians of the Middle Ages identified him as one of the forces of the planet Saturn, instead of Mercury.

Agkagdiel—one of the guardians of the Halls of the Seventh Heaven.

Agla—one of the names of God, invoked on the north of the magic circle. This is also said to be one of the angels invoked in rites of exorcism.

Agniel—one of the fallen angels, said to be associated with the fourth sphere of the Qliphoth or negative aspect of the Tree of Life.

Agrat bat Mahlat—the angel of prostitution.

Agromiel—one of the guardians of the Fifth Heaven.

Aha—one of the angels belonging to the choir of the Dominions, who is invoked during kabbalistic rites.

Ahaij—one of the angels of the sphere of Mercury, invoked in ritual magic.

Ahariel—one of the assistants of the Archangel Gabriel and ruler of Monday.

Ahiel (brother of God)—one of the assistants of the angel Kafsiel, regent of Saturday, who is invoked when a woman is in labor.

Ahriman—Satan among the Persians, who according to them is the destroyer of the world.

Aiel—the angelic ruler of Sunday and regent of Aries. Aiel is said to be an angel of the air element and resides in the Fourth Heaven.

Aishim—also known as the Ishim, these are the heavenly beings that form the Choir of the Angels, according to the Kabbalah. Their name signifies "sparks" or "heavenly fire."

Akatriel—one of the supreme Prince Regents of the Seventh Heaven, superior to the other angels, often identified with the Angel of the Lord and with God himself. In the Kabbalah, Akatriel is associated with the Glory of God's Throne.

Aker—according to the apocryphal Revelation of Esdras, this is one of the nine angelic regents of the Final Judgment.

Akraziel—the angel of the last portal of the Seventh Heaven and a Herald of the Lord. According to *The Legends of the Jews*, when Moses asked for the prolongation of his life, God ordered Akraziel not to allow his petition to reach Heaven, as the time had come for Moses to die.

Akriel—the angel of infertility.

Aladiah—one of the seventy-two angels of the Shemhamphora.

Alaliyah—one of the seventy-eight names of Metraton.

Alat—one of the guardians of the Halls of the Seventh Heaven.

Alimiel—one of the angels of the First Heaven. He is often identified with Dumahel and also said to be one of the seven angels who guards the curtain that faces God's Throne.

Almon—one of the guardians of the Halls of the Fourth Heaven.

Alphariza—one of the angels of the Second Heaven.

Alphun—the angel of doves and one of the rulers of the eighth hour.

Al-Zabamiya—according to the Koran, one of the nineteen angels that guards the gates of Hell.

Amabiel—one of the regents of human sexuality and of the planet Mars.

Amalek—in the Kabbalah, this is Samael's twin brother.

Amaliel—one of the angels of punishment and of human weakness.

Amamael—one of the guardians of the Halls of the Third Heaven.

Amarzyom—in the *Sixth and Seventh Books of Moses*, one of the fifteen angels who stand in front of God's Throne.

Amatiel—one of the angels of spring.

Amatliel—one of the guardians of the Halls of the Third Heaven.

Ambriel—one of the regents of the Choir of the Thrones and ruling angel of May.

Amerarat—in Zoroastrianism, the angel of immortality.

Amesha Spentas—the archangels of Zoroastrianism, whose name signifies sacred or immortal beings. These Persian entities are sometimes identified with the Sephiroth of the Tree of Life.

Amezyarak—also identified as the fallen angel Semyaza, this angel is mentioned in the *Book of Enoch* as one of the 200 angels that descended from Heaven to unite with the "daughters of men."

Amilfaton—one of the guardians of the Halls of the Seventh Heaven.

Amisiyah—one of the seventy-eight names of Metraton.

Amitiel—the angel of truth.

Amnixiel—one of the regents of the twenty-eight mansions of the moon.

Amrail—in Islam, an angel invoked in rites of exorcism.

Amtiel—one of the guardians of the Halls of the Seventh Heaven.

Amudiel—one of the fallen angels.

Amwakil—in Islam, one of the guardian angels invoked in rites of exorcism.

Amy—one of the fallen angels, once belonging to the choir of the Angels and to the choir of the Powers. This angel teaches the secrets of astrology and liberal arts and confided in Solomon that he hopes to return to the Seventh Heaven in 1,200 years.

Anabiel—according to the Kabbalah, the angel who cures stupidity.

Anabona—in the Greater Key of Solomon, this is the angel through whom God created the universe.

Anachiel—one of four angels invoked in the magical rites of Saturn.

Anael—also known as Haniel, Hamiel, Aniel, Anafiel, and Ariel, this is the angel of the sphere of Venus and of love. He is also one of the Seven Archangels of Creation, Prince Regent of the Principalities, Prince of the Archangels, and regent of the Second Heaven, where he receives the prayers that come from the First Heaven. Anael also rules the kingdoms of the Earth and is one of the regents of the moon.

Anafiel—in the *Third Book of Enoch*, this is the angel ordered by God to punish Uriel with sixty lashes of fire when this great archangel was identified—through no fault of his own—with God's Glory. Anafiel is also the angel of the Waters, guardian of the keys to the pearly gates and one of the angels of the Merkabah or Divine Chariot. He is often identified with Anael.

Anahel—in the *Sixth and Seventh Books of Moses*, Anahel is one of the regents of the Third as well as of the Fourth Heaven.

Anaireton—in ceremonial magic, this is the angel invoked for the purification of the ritual salt.

Anakim—according to *The Legends of the Jews*, these are the giants born of the union between women and the fallen angels. They were said to be so tall that their necks reached to the sun. In Genesis they are identified as the Nefillim.

Ananel—one of the fallen angels, formerly of the choir of the Archangels, who taught forbidden arts to human beings.

Anapiel YHVH—according to Enoch, one of the great princes of the Divine Presence, whose majesty and glory extends throughout Araboth, the Seventh Heaven. He is often identified with Anafiel.

Anauel—the guardian angel of bankers and merchants.

Anazimur—in the *Book of Raziel*, this is one of the seven angels belonging to the Thrones, dwellers of the First Heaven, whose duty is to obey the mandates of the superior angels.

Anfial—one of the sixty-four guardians of the heavenly halls.

Anfiel—one of the guardians of the Fourth Heaven, whose crown is said to be so magnificent that it extends over the celestial realms.

Anixiel—one of the ruling angels of the twenty-eight mansions of the moon.

Annauel—one of the seventy-two angels of the Shemhamphora.

Anpiel—the guardian angel of birds and dweller of the Sixth Heaven. Anpiel is also the angel who crowns with sanctity the prayers of human beings, which he then sends to the Seventh Heaven.

Anshe Shem—the name given to the fallen angels during their invocation.

Antichrist—often identified with the fallen angel Beliar or Belier.

Anush—one of the angels who served Adam by divine command.

Apharoph—identified with Raphael, it is said that this is the only true name of God.

Apsu—according to the Babylonians, this is the angel of the abyss.

Arafiel—also Arapiel. According to Enoch, this is one of the great angelic princes who stands in front of God's Throne.

Arakiba—one of the fallen angels.

Arapiel YHVH—in the *Book of Enoch*, this is one of the guardians of the Second Hall of the Seventh Heaven and a great prince of the Divine Presence.

Araqiel—also known as Arakiel, he is one of the fallen angels.

Arariel—the guardian angel of fishermen and regent of the waters of Earth.

Ararita—one of the kabbalistic names used during invocations in the Greater Key of Solomon.

Arasbarasbiel—one of the guardians of the Sixth Heaven.

Aratron—the olympic spirit of Saturn in ceremonial magic. He rules forty-nine of the 196 olympic planetary provinces. He is said to help sterile women to conceive and teaches the secrets of invisibility.

Araxiel—one of the fallen angels.

Araziel—one of the fallen angels who had forbidden relations with women.

Arbiel—one of the assistants of Anael.

Archstrategist (also Archistratig or Chief of Hosts)—supreme strategist of the Heavenly Host. According to Enoch, this title is given to the Archangel Michael by God himself, who calls Michael "my intercessor and archstratege."

Arcon—a great angel of the Lord, according to Judeo-Christianity. Among the Gnostics, the Arcons are malefic entities.

Ardarel—an angel of the fire element in ceremonial magic.

Ardefiel—one of the ruling angels of the twenty-eight mansions of the moon.

Arel—one of the angels of the sun in ceremonial magic, as well as an angel of the fire element.

Arfiel—one of the names given to Raphael.

Ariel—an angel belonging to the Choir of the Virtues, whose name is identified by the Jews with the city of Jerusalem. His name means "lion of God." He is sometimes identified as an infernal force, but most Jewish authorities classify him as one of the angels of the Lord who works with Raphael in the healing of illnesses. Ariel is also said to be one of the seven great princes who rule the waters of Earth.

Arkhas—one of the beings used by God in the Creation of the universe.

Armaros—one of the fallen angels.

Armisael—this angel is invoked during difficult childbirths. Psalm 20 is read during his invocation.

Armon—one of the angels residing in the Second Heaven.

Arphugitonos—according to the apocryphal Revelation of Esdras, he is one of the nine angels who will preside during the Final Judgment.

Arsyalalyur—in the *Book of Enoch*, this is one of the messengers of the Lord, who told Noah of the forthcoming universal deluge.

Arvial—one of the guardians of the Fourth Heaven.

Asaliah—one of the regent angels of justice, belonging to the choir of the Virtues, and assistant to Raphael. He is also one the seventy-two angels of the Shemhamphora.

Asaph—this great angel directs the heavenly choirs during the singing of the holy Trisagion at night.

Asariel—one of the ruling angels of the twenty-eight mansions of the moon and the regent of Neptune and the sign of Pisces.

Asasiah—one of the seventy-eight names of Metraton.

Asasiel—one of the regents of Jupiter. Together with Cassiel and Sadkiel he also rules Thursdays.

Asbeel—one of the fallen angels.

Asbogah YHVH—according to Enoch, he is one of the great Prince Regents of the Seventh Heaven.

Asderel—one of the fallen angels who taught the mysteries of the moon to human beings.

Asfael—according to Enoch, he is one of the regents of the months of the year and ruler over thousands of angels.

Ashkanizkael—one of the guardians of the Halls of the Seventh Heaven.

Ashmedai—also known as Asmodeus and Ashmodai. This is one of the Lord's messengers in rabbinical tradition. He is often invoked in love rituals and it is said that at one time he belonged to the choir of the Cherubim. In ceremonial magic he is considered an infernal entity.

Ashmodiel—one of the regents of Taurus, who is said to be very helpful in love matters.

Ashriel—this is the angel who separates the soul from the body at the moment of death. He is often identified with Azrael, Azriel, and Azariel.

Ashrulyu—one of the twenty names of God, he is said to reside in the First Heaven.

Asimor—one of the seven angels who encompasses the power of God.

Asmoday—one of the fallen angels, identified with Ashmedai. He is said to rule over seventy-two of the infernal hosts and can grant invisibility. He is also said to teach mathematics.

Asmodel—identified with Asmoday, he once belonged to the choir of the Cherubim. He is now one of the negative sephiroth of the Qliphoth and one of the demons of punishment.

Asmodeus—one of the deities of Persian mythology, considered an infernal entity among the Jews. In Hell, Asmodeus is in charge of gambling casinos. It is said of Asmodeus that he was the creator of music, dance, and drama, and is at present the ruling patron of French designers.

Asrafil—in Islam, he is the angel of Final Judgment.

Asroilu YHVH—one of the great princes of the Divine Presence and director of the celestial academy, where young angels are instructed.

Assiel—in the *Book of Raziel*, this is one of the healing angels, supposedly under the rulership of Raphael.

Astaroth—a great duke in the infernal regions, Astaroth belonged at one time to the choir of the Seraphim, although some authorities place him with the Thrones. Astaroth manifests during magical evocations as a beautiful angel mounted on a dragon. His breath is pestilential and he is said to "discourse willingly on the fall of the angels but pretends that he was exempt from their lapse." This interesting bit of information comes from Wierus' *Pseudo-Monarchia*. According to the *Grimorium Verum*, Astaroth now resides in America. He is also said to be the treasurer of Hell, and one of his alternate names is Diabolus.

Astarte—the principal deity of the Phoenicians and the Assyrians, among whom she was the goddess of the moon and of fertility.

Asuras—in Hinduism, the Asuras or Ahuras were malefic entities who declared war against the Suryas or entities of light. They are comparable with the fallen angels in Judeo-Christianity.

Ataliel—one of the ruling angels of the twenty-eight mansions of the moon.

Ataphiel—one of the three great angels who holds Heaven aloft with three fingers.

Atatiyah—one of the secret names of Michael or Metraton.

Athanatos—one of the kabbalistic angels used during invocations. Also said to be one of God's names invoked during the search for hidden treasures.

Atropatos—one of the seventy-eight names of Metraton.

Atufiel—one of the guardians of the Halls of the Seventh Heaven.

Atuniel—an angel of the choir of the Virtues, identified with Nathanel or Natanael.

Auriel—one of the names of the great Archangel Uriel.

Auzhaya—one of the names of Metraton.

Avahel—one of the regents of the Third Heaven.

Avriel—one of the guardians of the Halls of the Seventh Heaven.

Azaradel—one of the fallen angels who taught human beings the mysteries of the moon.

Azariah—one of Raphael's names, used by the great archangel in the Book of Tobit.

Azazel—one of the chiefs of the 200 fallen angels, according to Enoch. In the apocryphal Apocalypse of Abraham, Azazel is described as a terrible demon with seven snake heads, fourteen faces, and twelve wings. Before his fall, Azazel belonged to the choir of the Angels.

Azaziel—one of the fallen angels, often identified with Semyaza.

Azbogah YHVH—one of the great princes of the Divine Presence, who is said to know the secrets of the Throne of Glory. This is the angel who confers eternal life upon God's elect.

Azfiel—one of the guardians of the First Heaven.

Azibeel—one of the fallen angels.

Azrael—the regent angel of Scorpio, often identified with Gabriel and Azaril. According to the Jews and the Muslims, Azrael is one of the angels of death. He is said to reside in the Third Heaven. Muslims identify him with Raphael and describe him as having 70,000 feet and 4,000 wings. His body is covered with billions of eyes and tongues, as many as there are people on Earth.

Azrail—another of the names given to Azrael, used to invoke him during rites of exorcism.

Azrail—in the Kabbalah, this is one of the Sarim or Angelic Princes in charge of receiving the prayers of the faithful. He is also said to be in charge of sixty million angels, protectors of the northern side of Heaven.

B

Bachiel—one of the angels residing in the Fourth Heaven and one of the regents of the sphere of Saturn.

Badariel—one of the fallen angels.

Bael—also identified with Baal, his name means "master." According to the ancient grimoires and Weirus' *Pseudo-Monarchia*, he is one of the demons who rules the eastern side of Hell and commands seventy of the infernal legions. In the Kabbalah, Bael is not a fallen angel and is often identified with Raphael.

Baijel—one of the angels of the Fifth Heaven.

Balam—one of the fallen angels and a great ruler in Hell, with forty infernal legions under his command. Before his fall, Balam belonged to the choir of the Dominions.

Balberith—one of the fallen angels, he is a great pontiff and master of ceremonies in the infernal regions. Before his fall, he belonged to the choir of the Cherubim. It is said that this is the demon who registers the pacts made between human beings and Satan.

Baliel—one of the angels of the First Heaven.

Balthial—one of the seven Planetary Angels invoked to control jealousy.

Baraborat—one of the angels of the Third Heaven and of the planet Mercury.

Baradiel—one of the angels residing in the Third Heaven and one of the seven great archangels. He is the angel who rules over hailstones.

Barakel—one of the fallen angels.

Barakiel—also identified with Barbiel and Barchiel, he is also one of the seven great archangels and Prince Regent of the Second Heaven. He is said to control lightning and is invoked with Uriel and Rubiel to win at games of chance. His name signifies "God's lightning."

Baraqijal—one of the fallen angels, he teaches the secrets of astrology.

Barattiel—one of the great angels who holds God's throne with three fingers.

Barbatos—one of the fallen angels, he is now a duke in Hell and commands thirty of the infernal legions. At one time he belonged to the choir of the Virtues. When he is invoked in black magic rituals, the sun must be in the sign of Sagittarius.

Barbelo—in Gnosticism, Barbelo is one of the eons, second in rank only to the Gnostic Creator.

Barbiel—one of the ruling angels of the twenty-eight mansions of the moon and the month of October.

Baresches—in ceremonial magic, this angel is invoked by men when they wish to secure the love of a woman.

Barsabel—one of the ruling angels of Mars.

Bartyabel—another angel of the planet Mars, said to be an assistant to the great angel Graphiel, the Supreme Intelligence of Mars.

Baruch—the angel who guards the Tree of Life. His name signifies "blessed."

Baruchiachel—one of the seven great regent archangels and the only one who can vanquish the demon of discord.

Basasael—one of the fallen angels. At one time he belonged to the choir of the Archangels.

Batatiel—one of the ruling angels of the zodiac.

Batarel—one of the fallen angels, also known as Metarel, Batariel, and Badariel.

Bathor—also known as Bethor, he is the olympic spirit of Jupiter invoked in ceremonial magic.

Batsran—one of the seventy-eight names of Metraton.

Bat Zuge—one of the names of the infernal Lilith, representing the tenth and last sphere of the Qliphoth.

Bazathiel—one of the guardians of the First Heaven.

Bazazath—one of the angels of the Second Heaven.

Bazkiel—one of the guardians of the Third Heaven.

Baztiel—one of the guardians of the Halls of the First Heaven.

Beatiel—one of the angels of the Fourth Heaven.

Beburos—one of the angels who will preside during the Final Judgment.

Beelzebub—of Assyrian origin, this is the archdemon in charge of the nine infernal hierarchies that follow the first, ruled by Satan or Samael. It is said that at one time he belonged to the choir of the Cherubim. Among his titles is Lord of the Flies and Lord of Chaos. He is second in command in Hell.

Behemiel—the guardian angel of domestic animals, belonging to the choir of the Cherubim.

Behemoth—a monster of Chaos, created by God on the fifth day of Creation and generally associated with Leviathan, a monstrous feminine entity. Behemoth is often identified with Rahab, the angel of the seas, and with the Angel of Death.

Beleth—a fallen angel who commands eighty-five infernal legions. It is said that he belonged at one time to the choir of the Powers.

Belial—a fallen angel identified often with Satan. The Bible cites him as Beliar and describes him as the very essence of evil. In the apocryphal Gospel of Saint Bartholomew, Belial identifies himself as Satanail, the angel who rebelled against God, who gave him this name.

Belphegor—the fallen angel who is said to be the infernal ambassador to France. He is said to be the demon of inventions and discoveries. At one time he belonged to the choir of the Principalities. When he is invoked during black magic rites, he manifests as a woman.

Bene Elohim—this is the choir of the Thrones, according to the Kabbalah. In the original Hebrew their name is Bene Elim.

Beqa—the original name of Satan before he sinned against the Creator and was vanquished by Michael. After the rebellion, his name became Kasbel and later Satanail, from which Satan is derived.

Beshter—the name of Michael among the Persians.

Bethuael—one of the ruling angels of the twenty-eight mansions of the moon.

Bezrial—one of the guardians of the Third Heaven.

Bibiyah—one of the seventy-eight names of Metraton.

Bifiel—one of the guardians of the Halls of the Sixth Heaven.

Binah—the third sephira of the Tree of Life, identified with Saturn.

Bizbul—one of the seventy-eight names of Metraton.

Blautel—an angel invoked to contact the dead.

Boamiel—in the *Book of Raziel*, this is one of the six angels who guards the four cardinal points of Heaven. The others are Gabriel, Scamijm, Dohel, Madiel, and Adrael.

Boel—one of the seven angels who stands in front of God's Throne. His name signifies "God is in him." According to the Kabbalah, Boelk resides in the First Heaven and is in charge of the keys of the four cardinal points of the material world.

Burchat—one of the regents of the Fourth Heaven and a messenger of the sun. He is also one of the rulers of Sunday.

Busasejal—one of the fallen angels.

Butator—the regent of mathematical calculus.

C

Cabiel—one of the ruling angels of the twenty-eight mansions of the moon.

Cabriel—one of the regents of Aquarius and one of the angels who guards the four cardinal points in Heaven.

Cael—one of the regents of the sign of Cancer.

Cahethel—a prince of the Seraphim, regent of agriculture, and one of the seventy-two angels of the Shemhamphora.

Cahor—the spirit of deceit.

Caila—in the Greater Key of Solomon, one of the angels invoked during the rites of Archangel Uriel.

Caim—one of the fallen angels, now said to be a great president in Hell, commanding thirty of the infernal legions. He belonged at one time to the choir of the Angels.

Calliel—one of the angels of the Divine Presence; he is also one of the seventy-two angels of the Shemhamphora.

Calzas—one of the regents of Tuesday who resides in the Fifth Heaven.

Camael—this is one of the most controversial angels of the celestial hierarchy because he is often confused with Samael, a very powerful demon of the infernal regions. Samael is identified with Satan himself. Camael's name signifies "He who sees God." He is the Prince Regent of the Powers and one of the seven great archangels of the Divine Presence. He is also the angel of war, the supreme regent of Mars and Aries. He is in charge of 12,000 angels of destruction and tried to prevent God from giving the Law (Torah) to Moses. Camael's marked martial tendencies make it easy to identify him with Samael, who is also a destructive force but of an infernal order. In the Kabbalah, Camael is seen as justice personified and is identified with the fifth sephira of the Tree of Life, known as Severity. Camael is also known as Khemuel, Camuel, and Chamuel.

Cambiel—one of the regents of Aquarius.

Cameron—one of the regents of midday and an assistant to Beratiel. Some kabbalistic authorities identify him as an infernal entity under the rulership of Beelzebub or Astaroth.

Caphriel—one of the regents of Saturday and Saturn.

Capitiel—one of the regents of the Fourth Heaven.

Caracasa—one of the ruling angels of spring.

Caraniel—one of the angels of the Third Heaven.

Carcas—one of the angels of confusion.

Carniel—one of the angels of the Third Heaven.

Carnivean—one of the fallen angels, belonging at one time to the choir of the Powers.

Carsiol—one of Anael's assistants, also regent of the second hour of the day.

Cassiel—also known as Casiel, he is the supreme regent of Saturn and Capricorn. He is also the angel of solitude and of tears. He is a Sarim or Prince Regent of the choir of the Powers and one of the regents of the Seventh Heaven.

Casujoiah—one of the regents of Capricorn.

Cernaiul—one of the angels of the Venus sphere and the seventh sephira of the kabbalistic Tree of Life.

Cerviel—the angel sent by God to help David defeat Goliath. He is also chief of the choir of the Principalities.

Chamuel—often identified with Camael, he is one of the seven great archangels and chief of the choir of the Dominions. His name signifies "he who seeks God."

Chamyel—one of the fifteen angels who stands in front of God's Throne, according to the *Sixth and Seventh Books of Moses*.

Charbiel—the angel who dried the Earth after the universal deluge.

Charciel—one of the angels of the Fourth Heaven.

Chasdiel—one of the seventy-eight names of Metraton.

Chasmodai—according to Paracelsus, this is one of the spirits of the moon, often identified with Asmodeus.

Chavakiah—one of the seventy-two angels of the Shemhamphora.

Chayyiel—also known as Chayyiliel, this is the chief of the angels of the Merkabah or Divine Chariot. These angels are known in the Kabbalah as the Hayyoth or Chayoth and identified as members of the choir of the Cherubim. According to Enoch, Chayyiel is so immense and powerful he could swallow the Earth in one gulp if he so wished. He is also in charge of the celestial choirs and punishes with fire lashings the angels who are late for the singing of the holy Trisagion.

Cheriour—the angel in charge of the punishment of criminals, whom he torments constantly.

Chismael—one of the regents of Jupiter.

Chobabiel—one of the fallen angels.

Chokmah—the second sphere or sephira of the Tree of Life, ruled by the Angel Raziel.

Chur—this was the angel of the sun among the Persians.

Chuscha—one of the fifteen angels who face God's Throne, according to the *Sixth and Seventh Books of Moses.*

Cochabiel—in the Kabbalah, one of the regents of the planet Mercury and one of the angels of the Divine Presence.

Cogediel—one of the ruling angels of the twenty-eight mansions of the moon.

Coniel—an angel of the Third Heaven and of Friday.

Corabael—one of the angels of the Third Heaven and of Monday.

Cosmocrator—in Gnosticism, this is the consort of Barbelos and regent of the world under the name Diabolus, which immediately associates him with Astaroth and the infernal regions.

Crocell—a fallen angel and a duke in the infernal regions, where he commands forty-eight of the demonic hordes. Before his fall, he belonged to the choir of the Powers.

Ctarari—one of the angels of winter, the other being Amabael.

D

Daath—in the Kabbalah this is a Sephira located between the first and second spheres, Chokmah and Binah. Daath is a hidden sphere and signifies knowledge and has intensely sexual connotations. This, however, is a spiritual sexuality that connotes divine union and ecstasy.

Daeva—also known as Deva, this was a malefic entity among the Persians but benefic in Hinduism and Theosophy.

Dagiel—the ruling angel of fish; he belongs to the Venus sphere.

Dagon—one of the Phoenician gods, identified as a fallen angel in Milton's *Paradise Lost.*

Dahariel—one of the angels of the First Heaven.

Dahavauron—a prince of the Divine Presence and one of the guardians of the Third Heaven.

Dahaviel—one of the guardians of the First Heaven.

Dai—an angel of the choir of the Powers.

Dalkiel—an infernal prince, regent of Sheol (Hell), and assistant to Duma, the angel of the "stillness of death."

Damabiah—one of the seventy-two angels of the Shemhamphora and regent of naval constructions.

Dameal—one of the angels of the Fifth Heaven and ruler of Tuesday.

Daniel—an angel belonging to the choir of the Principalities whose name signifies "God is my judge."

Dargitael—one of the regents of the Halls of the Fifth Heaven.

Darquiel—one of the angels of the First Heaven and a ruler of Monday.

Degalim—one of the subchoirs that sings the holy Trisagion under the direction of the great Archangel Tagas.

Deharhiel—one of the guardians of the Halls of the Fifth Heaven.

Deliel—one of the angels of the Fourth Heaven.

Delukiel—one of the angels of the Seventh Heaven.

Deramiel—one of the angels of the Third Heaven.

Derdekea—a manifestation of the Shekinah, or Cosmic Mother, who descends to Earth for the salvation of humanity.

Dina—in the Kabbalah, this is one of the guardians of the Torah (Law) and of wisdom. Dina resides in the Seventh Heaven.

Dirachiel—one of the ruling angels of the twenty-eight mansions of the moon.

Dirael—one of the guardians of the Sixth Heaven.

Domiel—a great Arcon who is a guardian of the Seventh Heaven and also regent of the four elements.

Donquel—an angel of Venus, invoked by a man to secure the love of a woman.

Drial—one of the guardians of the Fifth Heaven.

Drsmiel—a malefic angel invoked to separate a man from his wife.

Dubbiel—the angel who substituted for Gabriel during the twenty days the great archangel was banished from the Divine Presence. Dubbiel was the protector of the Babylonians.

Duma—the guardian angel of Egypt, a prince of Hell who has thousands of the angels of destruction under his command. Duma is also the angel of silence and the stillness of death.

Duydeviyah—one of the seventy-eight names of Metraton.

E

Ebed—one of the seventy-eight names of Metraton.

Eblis—also Iblis, this is the Muslim Satan, whose name signifies despair.

Ebriel—the ninth of the malefic Sephiroth of the Qliphoth or Infernal Tree.

Efniel—an angel belonging to the choir of the Cherubim.

Egibiel—one of the ruling angels of the twenty-eight mansions of the moon.

Egion—one of the guardians of the Halls of the Seventh Heaven.

Egrimiel—one of the guardians of the Halls of the Sixth Heaven.

Eiael—one of the angels who teaches occult sciences and who has the power to prolong human life. To invoke him, the fourth versicle of Psalm 36 must be said. This is also one of the seventy-two angels of the Shemhamphora.

Eirnilus—the regent angel of fruits.

Eisheth Zenunim—one of Samael's concubines and mother of the beast Chiva, not to be confused with the Hindu god Shiva. This entity is also known as "the harlot" in the Kabbalah and is the mother of prostitution.

El—one of God's secret names connected with the fourth sephira in the Tree of Life. This is also the termination of most of the angelic names and means "son of God." The plural of El is Elohim.

Electors—the seven Planetary Spirits. Some authorities classify them as infernal forces.

Elemiah—in the Kabbalah, one of the Seraphs of the Tree of Life and one of the seventy-two angels of the Shemhamphora.

Elemiel—one of the angels of the moon, according to the Kabbalah.

Elion—an angel of the First Heaven and assistant to the great Archangel Ofaniel.

Eloha—an angel of the choir of the Powers.

Elohi—an angel of fire whose name, when invoked, dries out the seas and the river waters by divine command.

Elohim—God's dual aspect, feminine and masculine, yet one. The name is composed of the female singular "eloh" and the masculine plural "im," to denote God's feminine and masculine characteristics united as one single force. This unity of God, in spite of the dual connotation, is the most important characteristic of the deity. It signifies the union between God and the Shekinah. To separate God's essence as two individual forces is the worst offense that can be made to his majesty. That is why the Jewish Shema or daily prayer says, "Hear O Israel, the Lord our God is the Eternal. The Eternal is ONE." Elohim is also one of the angelic choirs and is associated with Netzach, the seventh sphere of the Tree of Life.

Eloi—according to the Gnostics, one of the angels created by their malefic god Ialdabaoth.

Elomeel—according to Enoch, one of the regents of the four seasons.

Elomnia—one of the five Prince Regents of the Third Heaven.

Elubatel—one of the supreme angels invoked during conjurations of the beast Leviathan, over which they have control.

Emekmiyahu—one of the seventy-eight names of Metraton.

Emmanuel—in the Kabbalah, this is one of the angels of the tenth sphere of the Tree of Life, Malkuth. He is also the angel who saved Daniel's companions from the fiery furnace. His name signifies "God is with us."

Empyreum—another name for Heaven and God's dwelling place.

Enediel—one of the ruling angels of the twenty-eight mansions of the moon.

Enga—one of God's secret names used to invoke Lucifer on Mondays.

Ephemeras—these are angels created by God every day to sing the holy Trisagion. At the end of the day their essence dissipates.

Erelim—also known as Arelim, this is the Hebrew name of the angelic choir known as the Thrones in the Kabbalah. They are made of white fire and belong to the Third Heaven, although some authorities place them in the Fourth or Fifth Heaven. There are seventy milliard (billion) Erelim and they protect the trees and the fruits of the Earth. This is one of ten classes of angels ruled by the Archangel Michael. The Thrones or Erelim are the third angelic choir both in the Kabbalah and the scale of Pseudo-Dionysius.

Eremiel—one of the angels identified with Uriel, who is said to watch over the spirits of the dead in the hereafter.

Ergedial—one of the ruling angels of the twenty-eight mansions of the moon.

Ertrael—a fallen angel.

Esabiel—an angel of the choir of the Powers.

Eschiros—in the Kabbalah, one of the angels of the seven planets.

Estes—one of the seventy-eight names of Metraton.

Eth—an angel who ensures that things happen at the proper time. His name in itself means "time."

Etraphill—in Islam, one of the angels of Final Judgment.

Eved—one of the seventy-eight names of Metraton.

Exael—according to Enoch, this is one of the fallen angels who taught human beings how to construct war artifacts, the art of jewelry-making, and perfumery.

Exousia—a Greek term to denote the angels, used in the New Testament.

Ezeqeel—a fallen angel who taught human beings the art of divining by the clouds.

Ezgadi—one of the angels invoked to ensure safe traveling.

F

Famiel—an angel residing in the Third Heaven, said to be one of the regents of Friday and the air element.

Fanuel—this angel is sometimes identified with Uriel or with Raguel and Ramiel. He is one of the four angels of the Divine Presence.

Flaef—in the Kabbalah, one of the angels of human sexuality.

Focalor—one of the fallen angels, a grand duke in the infernal regions commanding thirty of the demonic hordes. This is the sinister entity that sinks battleships and causes the death of human beings. Before his fall, he belonged to the choir of the Thrones. According to Solomon, Focalor hopes to return to Heaven after 1,000 years.

Forcas—a fallen angel, also a grand duke in Hell with twenty-nine infernal legions at his command. He is said to teach rhetoric and mathematics, help in finding lost things, and grant the gift of invisibility when invoked.

Forfax—a fallen angel, he is a count in Hell with thirty-six infernal legions under his command. He teaches art and astronomy.

Forneus—a fallen angel, he is a marquise in the infernal hierarchy with twenty-nine legions of demons under his command. He teaches languages and how to be loved by one's enemies. Before his fall, he belonged to the choir of the Thrones.

Fraciel—an angel of the Fifth Heaven and one of the rulers of Tuesday.

Friagne—another angel of the Third Heaven and of Tuesday.

G

Gaap—a fallen angel, he is a great prince in Hell with sixty-six legions of infernal spirits under his command.

Gabriel—his name signifies "God is my power." See chapter 9 for detailed information about this great archangel.

Gadamiel—another name given to Hagiel, the Intelligence of Venus.

Gadiel—one of the angels of the Fifth Heaven.

Gadreel—often confused with Gadriel, this is one of the fallen angels and one of Satan's chief collaborators during the angelic rebellion. According to Enoch, it was Gadreel, not Satan, who tempted Eve in the form of a serpent. Gadreel's name signifies "God is my helper."

Gadriel—not to be confused with Gadreel, this is one of the regents of the Fifth Heaven, who is in charge of Earth's wars. It is said that when the prayers of the faithful arrive in Heaven they must pass through Gadriel's hands, who will then forward them to the Sixth Heaven.

Galearii—a group of angels of a lesser celestial rank.

Galgaliel—one of the regents of the sun sphere.

Galgallim—a group of angels known as the wheels of the Merkabah or Divine Chariot. They are in the same rank as the Seraphim.

Gallizur YHVH—according to Enoch, this is one of the great princes of the Divine Presence who reveals the mysteries of the Torah. This is also one of the names given to the Angel Raziel. This great angel is the Prince Regent of the First Heaven.

Galmon—one of the guardians of the Halls of the Fourth Heaven.

Gamaliel—one of the great angels whose mission is to bring the souls of the Lord's elect to Heaven. He is one of Gabriel's assistants. Gamaliel's name signifies "God's recompense."

Gambiel—a zodiac angel and one of the regents of Aquarius.

Gambriel—one of the guardians of the Fifth Heaven.

Gamrial—one of the sixty-four guardians of the celestial halls.

Ganael—according to the apocryphal Testament of Solomon, this is one of the Planetary Angels who rules the celestial spheres. Ganael works in unison with Camael and Apudiel to carry on this mission.

Gargatel—together with Gaviel and Tariel, this is a ruling angel of summer.

Gatiel—one of the guardians of the Fifth Heaven.

Gauril Ishliha—the angel who ensures that the sun rises at the correct time each morning.

Gaviel—with Gargatel and Tariel, this is one of the ruling angels of summer.

Gavreel—one of the guardians of the Second or Fourth Heaven. Some authorities identify him with Gabriel.

Gazardiel—another angel who is in charge of sunrise.

Geburael—an angel associated with the fifth sephira of the Tree of Life, Geburah, and belonging to the choir of the Seraphim. Geburael is often identified with Gamaliel and is said to descend from Heaven through the sphere of Mars. He is also said to hold God's left hand through which the Creator dispenses justice or severity. Geburael's name signifies "strength."

Geburathiel—the principal guardian of the Fourth Hall of the Sixth Heaven and the angel of the fifth sphere of the Tree of Life.

Gedael—according to Enoch, one of the angels of the four seasons.

Gedariah—a regent of the Third Heaven. He also crowns the prayers of the faithful as they ascend from the Second Heaven, and sends them upward through the higher spheres.

Gedemel—an angel identified as a spirit of Venus.

Gediel—an angel of the zodiac and a Prince Regent of the Fourth Heaven.

Gedudiel—one of the guardians of the Halls of the Sixth Heaven.

Gedudim—one of the angelic choirs who sing the holy Trisagion under the direction of Tagas.

Gehegiel—one of the guardians of the Sixth Heaven.

Geliel—one of the ruling angels of the twenty-eight mansions of the moon.

Geminiel—one of the regents of Gemini.

Germael—according to an ancient tradition, God created Adam from the dust with the help of Germael. Some authorities dissent with this version and say that the angel used by God in the creation of Adam was Gabriel.

Gerviel—David's guardian angel. He is also one of the Prince Regents of the choir of the Principalities, often identified with Cerviel.

Geviririon—another name given to the fifth sephira of the Tree of Life.

Geviriyah—one of the seventy-eight names of Metraton.

Gippuyel—another of the names of Metraton.

Gmial—one of the sixty-four guardians of the Halls of the Seventh Heaven.

Golab—these are fallen angels, whose name signifies "incendiaries." They are sworn enemies of the Seraphim, with whom they do battle constantly. Golab is also the name of one of the demonic sephira of the Qliphoth or Infernal Tree.

Gorfiniel—one of the guardians of the Seventh Heaven.

Gradiel—the Intelligence of the planet Mars as it enters into the signs of Aries or Scorpio.

Grasgarben—one of the regents of the sign of Libra.

Grial—one of the guardians of the Fifth Heaven.

Grigori—this name signifies "the Watchers" and they are said to be a highly exalted order of angels residing on the Second or Fifth Heaven. Some of the fallen angels belonged to this superior angelic rank and after their sins they were imprisoned on one of the wings of the Fifth Heaven, where they mourn their fate in eternal silence.

Gulhab—this angel is identified as the fifth malefic sephira of the Qliphoth.

Guriel—one of the regents of the sign of Leo.

Gurson—one of the fallen angels, now established in Hell as a king of the south.

Guth—one of the regents of Jupiter.

Gvurtial—one of the guardians of the Halls of the Fourth Heaven.

H

Haaiah—one of the seventy-two angels of the Shemhamphora, belonging to the choir of the Dominions. He is said to be the regent of ambassadors and diplomats.

Haamiah—the angel who guides the seekers of the truth. He is also said to rule religious cults and belongs to the choir of the Powers.

Habbiel—one of the angels of the First Heaven and of Monday. He is invoked in love problems.

Habuiah—one of the seventy-two angels of the Shemhamphora, who also rules the fertility of the soil and agriculture.

Hadraniel—this angel is often identified with Metraton and his name signifies "the majesty of God." He is one of the guardians of the Second Heaven and, when he proclaims God's will, his voice traverses 200,000 firmaments. With each spoken word, 12,000 bolts of lightning burst forth from his mouth. Hadraniel is said to be sixty myriads of parasangs taller than Kemuel and a 500 years' journey shorter than Sandalphon. A parasang is a Persian measure equal to approximately three miles and a myriad constitutes an immeasurable quantity, too large to be defined numerically. If we think of sixty myriads as sixty times an indescribable amount, we are obviously dealing with entities of cosmic proportions. A being "sixty myriads of parasangs taller" than another immense being would surely transcend the boundaries of our galaxy. And if we consider that he is still "a 500 years' journey" shorter than Sandalphon, reputed to be one of the tallest angels in Heaven, we begin to see that angels are cosmic forces of indescribable dimensions. Multiply one angel, whose form surpasses the length and width of several galaxies, by billions of billions of angels of similar statures and the universe may not be large enough to hold them all. And we still have to consider Seven Heavens with innumerable Halls, nine choirs of angels, and God's Empyreum, with all the attending ministers and heavenly choirs. And when all of this has been accounted for, we still have Hell to consider, and all the infernal legions. It should be fairly clear from all the preceding that neither Heaven nor Hell belong to our material world nor to our universe and that they exist in realms far beyond the grasp of our human understanding.

Hadriel—a variation of Hadraniel.

Hafaza—in Islam, this is a group of angels who protect against evil spirits.

Hagiel—the Intelligence of Venus when it enters into Taurus or Libra.

Hagios—one of God's secret names and also one of his greatest angels.

Hagith—the olympic spirit of Venus, said to rule twenty-one of the 196 olympic provinces. It is said that she commands 4,000 legions of spirits of light and has the power to transmute metals.

Hahael—the guardian angel of all the ministers and missionaries devoted to Jesus. He belongs to the choir of the Virtues and is one of the seventy-two angels of the Shemhamphora.

Hahaiah—this angel reveals the divine mysteries and has power over human thought. He belongs to the choir of the Cherubim.

Hahayel—also known as Chayyliel, this is one the Angelic Princes present in the Divine Council.

Hahuaih—one of the seventy-two angels of the Shemhamphora.

Haiaiel—another of the seventy-two angels of the Shemhamphora.

Haim—one of the regents of Virgo.

Hakael—one of the fallen angels, known as the seventh Satan.

Hakamiah—the guardian angel of France, who is invoked against traitors. He belongs to the choir of the Cherubim.

Haludiel—one of the Intelligences of the sun, who resides in the Fourth Heaven.

Halwaya—one of the seventy-eight names of Metraton.

Hamabiel—one of the regents of Taurus.

Hamaliel—an angel of the choir of the Virtues and one of the regents of August and Virgo.

Hamon—according to Enoch, this is one of the great Princes of the Divine Presence, whose voice of thunder makes the lesser angels tremble when he calls them to sing the holy Trisagion. Hamon is said to be another of Gabriel's names.

Hananel—one of the fallen angels.

Haniel—identified with Anael, his name signifies "he who sees God." He is one of the chiefs of the choirs of the Virtues and the Principalities and a regent of December, Capricorn, and Venus. His name is so powerful that its pronunciation alone acts as an amulet against evil.

Ha-Qadosh Berakha—one of God's secret names.

Harab-Serapel—the seventh malefic sephira of the Qliphoth. The ruler of this sphere is said to be Baal.

Hararel—one of the seventy-two angels of the Shemhamphora, he is also in charge of libraries and archives.

Hariel—the regent of arts and sciences, he belongs to the choir of the Cherubim.

Hashesiyah—one of the seventy-eight names of Metraton.

Hashmal—the angel who speaks fire, principal regent of the choir of the Dominions or Hashmallim.

Hashmallim—in the Kabbalah, this is the choir of the Dominions, also identified as the Hayyoth or Living Creatures.

Hasmed—one of the five angels of punishment met by Moses during his visit to Heaven.

Hasmiyah—one of the seventy-eight names of Metraton.

Hayliel YHVH—in the *Book of Enoch*, this is one of the most exalted princes of the Divine Presence, whose power is such that he could swallow the Earth if he so wished. He is in charge of the Hayyoth, whom he chastises with fire lashings when they are late for the singing of the holy Trisagion.

Hayyoth—also known as Chayoth or Chiva, these are the living creatures who carry the Merkabah on their shoulders. They are often identified as Cherubim and are said to reside in the Seventh Heaven. According to the Zohar, the principal work on the Kabbalah, the Hayyoth number thirty-six and they hold aloft not only the divine chariot but the entire universe. Enoch says there are only four of these heavenly beasts. Each one has 248 faces and 365 wings. Each creature has 1,000 crowns and each crown is like a rainbow, more dazzling than the sun. These angels constitute the Shekinah's encampment.

Haziel—the angel invoked to ask for God's compassion. He belongs to the choir of the Cherubim and is also an angel of the Shemhamphora.

Hechaloth—these are the Halls or vestibules of the heavenly palaces. The term is also used to describe the seven feminine emanations that issue from God's right side, according to the Kabbalah.

Heiglot—the angel that rules snow-storms.

Hemah—one of the angels of rage and destruction; he also rules the death of all domestic animals. It is said that Hemah is 500 parasangs in height, which is more than 1,700 miles, and that he was created of chains of red and black fire. According to the Zohar, he tried to swallow Moses but God intervened, saving Moses' life. When Hemah disgorged Moses, the Lawgiver killed him, an event somewhat difficult to reconcile with the traditional belief that angels are immortal.

Hismael—the spirit of Jupiter.

Hivvah—one of the two sons of the fallen angel Semyaza. The other was Hiyyah. All the children of the fallen angels were terribly destructive giants called Nefillim, who ate everything in their path and later turned on each other. Hivvah and Hiyyah were said to consume a daily ration of 1,000 camels, 1,000 horses, and 1,000 oxen.

Hizkiel—one of Gabriel's principal assistants during the angelical battles.

Hocus Pocus—two angelical princes invoked during the Middle Ages.

Hodniel—one of the angels who cures stupidity in human beings.

Huha—one of God's secret names among the Essenes.

Hurmin—another name given to Satan.

Huzia—one of the sixty-four guardians of the Seven Heavens.

I

Iachadiel—one of the regents of the moon.

Ialdabaoth—according to the Kabbalah, this is the Demiurge, who occupies second place in Heaven after the Creator. Among the Phoenicians, he was one of the seven Elohims or angels who created the universe. According to the philosopher Origen, Ialdabaoth was Michael's second name. To the Gnostics, who rejected everything Jewish, Ialdabaoth was the first Arcon and a malefic spirit.

Iahhel—one of the seventy-two angels of the Shemhamphora. He is also the protector of philosophers and those who wish to retire from the material world.

Iciriel—one of the ruling angels of the seventy-eight mansions of the moon.

Idrael—one of the guardians of the Fifth Heaven.

Iehuiah—one of the seventy-two angels of the Shemhamphora and protector of the princes of the Earth. He is said to belong to the choir of the Thrones.

Ieiaiel—together with the angel Teiaiel, he is the ruler of the future. He is also one of the seventy-two angels of the Shemhamphora.

Ieilael—another angel of the Shemhamphora.

Ielahiah—the angel invoked before a trial, as he is said to control all judges and magistrates. He is also one of the seventy-two angels of the Shemhamphora.

Iesaia—one of the seventy-eight names of Metraton.

Imamiah—at one time one of the seventy-two angels of the Shemhamphora, he is now a fallen angel.

Indri—the angels in the Vedic tradition.

Intelligence—these are forces identified with the angels and the Sephiroth of the Tree of Life, according to the Neoplatonic tradition. There are ten Intelligences, one for each sephira, and they are associated with the planets.

Iofiel—one of Metraton's companions and a prince of the Divine Presence. He is also one of the princes of the Torah or Divine Law.

Irin—according to Enoch, these are the twins who are part of the Supreme Celestial Council. They reside in the Seventh Heaven and are counted among the eight Hierarchs superior to Metraton.

Isda—the angel who provides sustenance for humanity.

Ishim—according to the Kabbalah, this is the angelic choir associated with the tenth sphere or sephira in the Tree of Life. This choir is identified with the souls of the saints and those of the just. They are said to be formed of snow and fire and reside in the Fifth Heaven.

Israfel—in Islam, this is the angel of the Final Judgment, also known as Sarafiel or Isrefel.

Itmon—one of the seventy-eight names of Metraton.

Itqal—the angel of love and affection, invoked to heal rifts between quarreling friends.

Ithuriel—one of the princes of the kabbalistic Sephiroth, whose name means "God's discovery." He is associated with Geburah, the fifth sphere, and the planet Mars. Milton classified him as a Cherubim but kabbalistic sources say that this is an erroneous identification.

Izrael—in Islam, this is one of the angels of Resurrection. The others are Gabriel,

Michael, and Israfel. According to a Muslim legend, the trumpet of the Final Judgment will be sounded three times, with an interval of forty years between each trumpet blast. When the trumpet sounds for the third time, this will mark the moment for the resurrection of the dead.

J

Jabniel—one of the regents of the Third Heaven.

Jael—one of the two Cherubim carved on the Mercy Seat of the Ark of the Covenant. The other was Zarall. Jael is also the name of one of the regents of Libra.

Jaseriel—one of the ruling angels of the twenty-eight mansions of the moon.

Jehoel—often identified with Metraton and Kemuel, this is the Chief Regent of the fire element and one of the regents of the Seraphim.

Jehudiam—the keeper of the seventy keys to all the Creator's treasures.

Jehudiel—one of the regents of the movements of the spheres. Some authorities name him among the Seven Princes of the Divine Presence.

Jeliel—a seraph who is said to promote faithfulness and to awaken passion between men and women. He is also the regent of Turkey.

Jeqon—one of the leading rebellious angels, who incited others to sin.

Jeremiel—another name for Uriel and Remiel. His name signifies "God's compassion" and he is one of the Seven Princes of the Divine Presence. He belongs to the choir of the Archangels.

Jesodoth—the angel that transmits God's wisdom and knowledge to human beings.

Jetrel—one of the 200 guardians tempted by the rebellious angelic hordes. The 200 gave in to the temptation and became known as the fallen angels.

Jibril—Gabriel among the Muslims.

Joel—a variation of Jael; this is Metraton's first name.

Johiel—one of the angels of Paradise.

Joth—one of God's secret names, revealed to Jacob the night he struggled with an angel of the Lord.

K

Kadishim—a group of angels superior in rank to the Hayyoth or angels of the Merkabah. They reside in the Seventh Heaven. Together with the Irin, they constitute the Throne of Judgment. Their name signifies "sacred beings."

Kadosh—one of the guardians of the Halls of the Fourth Heaven.

Kafziel—identified with Cassiel, this is the angel who rules over the death of kings. He is also one of the regents of Saturn and assists Gabriel during angelic battles.

Kakabel—also known as Kochbiel, his name signifies "star of God." This is one of the principal regents of the stars and the constellations. In the *Book of Raziel*, this is a most holy angel, but according to Enoch, he is one of the fallen angels.

Kalmiya—one of the seven celestial princes who guards the curtain that hides God's Throne. The others are Gabriel, Boel, Asimor, Paschar, Sandalphon, and Uzziel.

Kasbel—his name signifies "he who deceives God," and he was the leader of the rebellious angels, vanquished by Michael, who later became known as Satanail or Satan.

Kasdaya—one of the leaders of the fallen angels.

Kedemel—the spirit of the spheres of Venus.

Kemuel—identified with Camael or Seraphiel, his name signifies "assembly of the Lord." This is the great Arcon who acts as intermediary between the prayers of Israel and the Princes of the Seven Heavens. He is one of the regents of the Seraphim and is also associated with Geburah, the fifth sephira of the Tree of Life.

Kerubiel YHVH—this is the principal regent of the Cherubim and one of the most exalted princes of the heavenly court. His height spans the Seven Heavens. His body is formed of burning coals and is covered with thousands of eyes. His face is made of fire, his eyes are sparks of light, and his eyelashes are lightning bolts. Fire leaps out of his mouth with every word and he is covered with wings from head to foot. He is always accompanied by thunder, lightning, and earthquakes, and the splendor of the Shekinah shines on his countenance.

Kimos—one of the secret names of Michael.

Kokabiel—also known as Kakabel, he is the angel in charge of the stars.

Kyriel—one of the ruling angels of the twenty-eight mansions of the moon.

L

Labarfiel—one of the guardians of the Seventh Heaven.

Labezerin—the angel who rules victory. He is invoked at two in the afternoon.

Labiel—Raphael's original name. It is said that when Raphael accepted God's decrees on the creation of humanity, God changed his name from Labiel to Raphael.

Lahabiel—an angel invoked to keep away evil spirits, and one of Raphael's assistants.

Lahatiel—one of the seven angels of punishment and the one who presides over the gates of death.

Lamach—one of the regents of the planet Mars.

Lecabel—one of the seventy-two angels of the Shemhamphora.

Lehahiah—a fallen angel who was at one time one of the angels of the Shemhamphora.

Lehavah—one of the guardians of the Halls of the Seventh Heaven.

Lehalel—one of the ruling angels of the arts, sciences, love, and good fortune.

Lelahiah—one of the seventy-two angels of the Shemhamphora.

Lemanael—one of the lunar angels, according to the Kabbalah.

Leuuiah—one of the seventy-two angels of the Shemhamphora.

Levanah—the Hebrew name of the moon.

Levanael—one of the lunar angels.

Librabis—one of the spirits who helps in finding hidden gold.

Lifton—one of the guardians of the Seventh Heaven.

Lilith—in the Kabbalah, this is a demonic entity who delights in the destruction of small children. She is said to have been Adam's first wife and Cain's real mother. She is now Samael's wife. Lilith is associated with Fridays and manifests as a naked woman whose lower body ends in a snake.

Logos—this name signifies "the word," and is one of God's many titles. Both Michael and Metraton have been identified as the Logos, and also the Holy Spirit and the Messiah.

Lucifer—this name signifies "the giver of light" and is erroneously identified with Satan. The confusion originates in a passage of the Book of Isaiah (Is. 14:12) where the prophet names Lucifer as a fallen angel and the son of the morning. But rabbinical sources allege that Isaiah was referring to King Nebuchadnezzar. The name refers to the morning or evening star which is Venus. In Christianity, Lucifer was identified with Satan for the first time by Saint Jerome and other Church fathers.

Lumazi—according to the Assyrians, these are the seven creators of the universe.

M

Machasiel—one of the Intelligences of the sun, ruler of Sunday, who resides in the Fourth Heaven.

Machator—an angel of the element of air and one of the regents of Saturday.

Machidiel—one of the angels of the Tree of Life, identified with the tenth sphere, Malkuth, and the planet Earth. He is invoked by men to help them secure the love of a woman.

Mahariel—one of the guardians of the gates of the First Heaven, who leads the souls of the Elect to the Divine Presence.

Mahasiah—one of the seventy-two angels of the Shemhamphora.

Mahniel—another name of Azrael, regent of Scorpio, who leads sixty myriads of the angelic legions.

Mahzian—the angel invoked to restore eyesight.

Makatiel—one of the seven angels of punishment, whose name means "the plague of God."

Malach-ha-Mavet—in the Kabbalah, this is the angel of death, identified with Samael and Azrael.

Malakim—the Hebrew name for the order of the Virtues.

Malmeliyah—one of the seventy-eight names of Metatron.

Maltiel—an Intelligence of Jupiter, residing in the Third Heaven.

Mammon—a fallen angel and one of the most powerful entities in the demonic hierarchy. His name signifies "riches," which are ruled by him. He also incites people to avarice and many other vices. He is sometimes identified with Beelzebub, Lucifer, and Satan, and is said to be England's regent.

Manuel—one of the angels of the sign of Cancer.

Mara—in Buddhism, the evil entity loosely identified with Satan.

Marchosias—a fallen angel who is now a marquis in Hell. He belonged at one time to the choir of the Dominions.

Margash—one of the seventy-eight names of Metatron.

Marmarao—an angel invoked to cure bladder problems.

Mashith—his name signifies "destroyer" and one of his missions is to oversee the death of children. In the Kabbalah, he is one of three demonic entities in Hell who punish those guilty of murder, incest, and idolatry. The other two are Af and Hema.

Maskiel—one of the guardians of the First Heaven, where the prayers of the faithful are received and directed through the various ascending heavens.

Mastema—it is said of this angel that he is the father of all evil, but that he is still a servant of God, whom he still obeys. He is the accusing angel and serves God as tempter and executioner; he is a prince of evil, injustice and condemnation.

Matarel—the angel of rain.

Maymon—regent of the spirits of the Air and of Saturday.

Mbriel—one of the angels who rules the four winds.

Mebahel—one of the seventy-two angels of the Shemhamphora.

Mebahiah—an angel invoked in the conception of children. He is also one of the seventy-two angels of the Shemhamphora.

Megadriel—the author of *The Book of Megadriel*, whose name signifies "my great help is God." He is one of the regents of the Seraphim, the Cherubim, and the Archangels.

Mehekiel—one of the seventy-two angels of the Shemhamphora.

Mehiel—the guardian angel of authors, orators, and college professors.

Melahel—one of the seventy-two angels of the Shemhamphora.

Meniel—another of the angels of the Shemhamphora.

Messiah—identified with Christ and Metraton, he belongs to the choir of the Cherubim and is the guardian angel of Eden, which he protects with a flaming sword.

Metraton—according to some of the rabbinical writings, Metraton is the greatest of all the angels, the one who sits next to God on his Throne of Glory. In many of the mystical and occult writings, he is identified with the Archangel Michael. It is said of Metraton

that he is the Prince of the Divine Countenance, Chancellor of Heaven, Angel of the Covenant, Chief of the Ministering Angels, and the Lesser YHVH or Tetragrammaton. He is the angel who most protects humanity and rules Kether, the first sphere of the Tree of Life. He is sometimes identified with the Glory of God, who is the Holy Shekinah, in his feminine aspect. Metraton was the angel who guided the Israelites in their exodus across the desert. He is said to be the twin brother of Sandalphon, who is the ruler of Malkuth, the tenth sphere of the Tree of Life. After Anafiel, Metraton is the tallest angel in Heaven. When he is invoked, he manifests as a pillar of fire with a face more dazzling than the sun. Metraton is the author of Psalm 37:25 and at least part of Isaiah 24:16. He is also the instructor in Paradise of the souls of children who die prematurely.

Michael—his name means "he who is as God," and in Christian, Jewish, and Islamic writings, he is the greatest of all the angels. Michael is sometimes identified with Metraton, who is also considered the greatest of the angels. Michael originates from the Chaldeans, who worshiped him as a divine entity. His mystery name is Sabathiel. Michael is the Prince Regent of the Fourth Heaven, Chief of the Virtues, Chief of the Archangels, Prince of the Divine Presence, Angel of Repentance, of Mercy, of Righteousness, and of Sanctification. In the Avesta, he is identified with Saosyhant, the

Redeemer of the Faithful. Among the Persians, he was known as Beshter, "the one who provides sustenance for mankind." In Muslim lore, Michael is described with emerald-color wings and covered with saffron hairs, each of them containing a million faces and mouths, which in a million dialects implore the pardon of Allah for the sins of the faithful. As the angel of the Final Judgment, he is often depicted with the scales of justice in one hand, where he will weigh the souls of the dead on that fearful day. As the conqueror of Satan, he is sometimes shown with unsheathed sword and widespread wings, his sandaled heel firmly placed on the adversary's neck.

Michael is the regent of the sun, the sign of Leo, Sundays, and, in the Kabbalah, the ruler of Hod, the eighth sphere of the Tree of Life, and of the planet Mercury. In the War of the Sons of Light against the Sons of Darkness, one of the recently found Dead Sea Scrolls, Michael is called the Prince of Light, who leads the angels of light in battle against the legions of the dark angels, led in turn by the demon Belial. Michael is the protector of Israel and of policemen. He is said to be the author of Psalm 85, which is read to invoke him.

Midrash—one of the seventy-eight names of Metraton.

Miel—one of the angels of Mercury and of Wednesday.

Mihael—In the Kabbalah, this is the angel of fertility who also ensures faithfulness in a spouse.

Mikail—Michael's name in Muslim lore.

Mithra—in the Vedas, one of the bright gods, identified with the angels. According to the Persians, Mithra had 1,000 ears and 10,000 eyes and was one of the deities who surrounded the supreme god, Ahura-Mazda.

Mitzrael—one of the seventy-two angels of the Shemhamphora.

Modiniel—an angel of the Mars sphere.

Moroni—the angel of God among the Mormons, who gave the Gospel of a New Revelation to Joseph Smith, the founder of this religion.

Mupiel—the angel invoked for the gift of a good memory.

Muriel—on of the regents of the sign of Cancer and of July. He is also one of the regents of the choir of the Dominions.

N

Naamah—one of the four dark angels of prostitution and one of Samael's wives. She is known as the mother of demons and one of the corrupters of the fallen angels. She is said to afflict children with epilepsy.

Naar—one of the seventy-eight names of Metraton.

Naaririel YHVH—one of the most exalted princes of the heavenly court.

Nachiel—the Intelligence of the sun in the sign of Leo.

Nadiel—one of the regents of December and protector of immigrants.

Nagrasasiel—one of the guardians of the gates of Hell.

Nahaliel—the angel who rules water streams.

Nahuriel—one of the regents of the Seventh Heaven.

Nanael—one of the seventy-two angels of the Shemhamphora.

Naromiel—one of the Intelligences of the moon and ruler of Sunday, who resides in the Fourth Heaven.

Nasargiel—one of the great angels who guard the gates of Hell, and who is said to have the head of a lion.

Nathanael—one of the angels who rules the element of fire and the sixth angel created by God, in order of appearance, as the angels were all created at the same time. He is also one of the angels of vengeance.

Nefillim—also known as Nephillim, these were the giants born to the women who consorted with the fallen angels.

Nehinah—an angel invoked to call upon the dead.

Nelchael—a fallen angel, who was at one time one of the seventy-two angels of the Shemhamphora.

Nemamiah—one of the seventy-two angels of the Shemhamphora, belonging to the choir of the Archangels.

Nuriel—one of the angels of fire and hailstone. He is said to be one of the regents of Virgo and an assistant to Michael. He is a powerful angel of great stature, who is 300 parasangs tall and who has fifty myriads of angels under his command, all made of fire and water. His name signifies "fire of God."

O

Och—the olympic spirit of the sun, who rules twenty-eight of the olympic provinces. He is said to rule 36,536 legions of solar spirits and can grant 600 years of life and perfect health. The sun rules good health, longevity, and the heart chakra.

Ofael—one of the angels residing in the Fifth Heaven and ruler of Tuesday.

Ofaniel—also known as Opaniel, this is the powerful regent of the Thrones and the tallest of all the angels. He is also a regent of the moon and is sometimes identified with Sandalphon.

Ofanim—also known as Ophanim or Auphanim in the Kabbalah, this angelic choir is often associated with the Thrones. In reality, the Kabbalah describes the Ofanim as the Wheels, the second of the angelic choirs, associated with the second sphere of the Tree of Life, Chokmah.

In the Kabbalah, the Thrones are known as the Erelim or Aralim, the third angelic choir, associated with Binah, the third sephira of the Tree of Life.

Binah is the Shekinah, the feminine aspect of God. The Thrones or Erelim are associated with the Merkabah or Divine Chariot where the Shekinah sits in all her splendor. Other choirs associated with the Merkabah are the Hayyoth, the Seraphim, the Cherubim, as well as the Ofanim. In the Kabbalah, the Ofanim have a more exalted position than the Seraphim, who are the first angelic choir according to Pseudo-Dionysius but only the fifth according to the Kabbalah. The first angelic choir in the Kabbalah are the Hayyoth or Holy Creatures, associated with Kether, the first sephira of the Tree of Life, identified with God himself.

Ofiel—also known as Ophiel, this is the olympic spirit of Mercury, said to rule fourteen of the olympic provinces and 100,000 legions of spirits. He belongs to the choir of the Powers.

Og—one of the giants descended from the fallen angel, Semyaza.

Ohazia—one of the angels of the Divine Presence and one of the guardians of the Third Heaven.

Ol—one of the regents of Leo.

Olivier—one of the fallen angels, who belonged at one time to the choir of the Archangels.

Omael—one of the seventy-two angels of the Shemhamphora, belonging to the Dominions. He is the regent of alchemy and helps in the perpetuation of the species.

Onafiel—one of the regents of the moon.

Opanniel YHVH—identified with Ofaniel, he is one of the most exalted of the heavenly princes of the Divine Presence and regent of the Ophanim, whom he constantly adorns and perfects for the Glory of God. According to Enoch, Opanniel has sixteen faces, 200 wings and 8,760 eyes, corresponding to the hours in a year. From his eyes are constantly flowing tears of fire and whoever looks at him face to face is turned to ashes instantly.

Ophan—one of the names of Sandalphon.

Ophiel—see Ofiel.

Orael—one of the Intelligences of Saturn.

Oribel—another of the names of Uriel.

Oriel—the angel of destiny, identified with Auriel, whose name signifies "the light of God."

Orifiel—one of the regents of Saturn and of Saturday. It is said that he is one of the Princes of the Thrones, one of the Seven Princes of the Divine Presence, and one of the seven regents of the Earth.

Orion—the guardian angel of Saint Peter, identified with the constellation of the same name. Some kabbalistic authorities identify him with Michael.

Ormazd—also known as Ormuzd, God in Zoroastrianism, and twin brother of Ahriman, the Persian equivalent of Satan.

Osael—an angel of the Fifth Heaven and of Tuesday.

Ou—another name of Uriel.

Ouza—also known as Uzza, he is one of the fallen angels.

Ozah—one of the seventy-eight names of Metraton.

P

Pabael—one of the angels of the moon, who acts as a messenger of that sphere.

Pachdiel—the chief guardian of the Fourth Heaven. His name means "fear."

Pahaliah—one of the seventy-two angels of the Shemhamphora, invoked for the conversions of heretics into Christianity.

Paimom—one of the fallen angels, who at one time belonged to the choir of the Dominions. In the infernal hierarchy, he is a great king with 200 legions under his command.

Palit—one of Michael's names, which signifies "he who escaped," referring to Michael's escape from Beqa's temptation. Beqa was later transformed into Satan.

Palpetiyah—one of Metraton's names.

Parasurama—in the Vedic tradition, this is the sixth of the ten avatars or divine incarnations.

Parziel—one of the guardians of the Sixth Heaven.

Paschar—one of the seven angels who stand in front of the Holy Throne. He is in charge of executing the decrees of the celestial powers. It is said that he stands behind the curtain that guards God's Throne.

Pasiel—one of the regents of the sign of Pisces.

Pasisiel—one of the guardians of the Seventh Heaven.

Pathatumon—one of the secret names of God.

Pathiel—one of the seventy-two angels of the Shemhamphora.

Pazriel—also identified as Siriel, this is one of the great archangels who rule the First Heaven.

Peliel—the guardian angel of Jacob and one of the chiefs of the Virtues.

Penael—one of the messengers of Venus, residing in the Third Heaven.

Peneme—also known as Penemue, this is one of the fallen angels, who taught human beings the art of writing with paper and ink.

Peniel—it is said that this is Jehovah's angel, the one who struggled with Jacob during a whole night. Other angels associated with this feat are Metraton and Samael. Peniel's name signifies "the face of God," and he is said to reside in the Third Heaven.

Peri—among the Muslims, these are fallen angels ruled by Eblis, the equivalent of Satan in Islam.

Perrier—a fallen angel, belonging at one time to the choir of the Principalities.

Petahyah—an angel who receives the prayers of the faithful against their enemies. If the prayer is just, he kisses it and sends it to the Throne of Glory.

Phaleg—also known as Faleg, this is the olympic spirit of Mars, who is said to rule thirty-five of the 196 olympic provinces.

Phanuel—also identified with Uriel and Peniel, his name signifies "the face of God." He is one of the angels of penitence, also identified as one of the four great archangels (Uriel).

Phorlakh—also known as Forlac, the angel of Earth.

Phul—also known as Ful, the olympic spirit of the moon, said to rule seven of the olympic provinces. He is regent of Monday and Supreme Lord of the Waters.

Pihon—one of the names of Metraton when he receives the prayers of the faithful.

Pi-Re—another of the names of the Archangel Michael.

Poiel—one of the seventy-two angels of the Shemhamphora and regent of philosophy and good fortune. He belongs to the choir of the Principalities.

Poteh—the angel of forgetfulness.

Powers—also known as Potentialities, this is the sixth choir, according to Pseudo-Dionysius.

Pravuil—also identified with Vetril, this is the Holy Scribe who is in charge of God's knowledge and the celestial scrolls.

Prince of Darkness—identified with Satan and with the angel of death, although this latter force is also identified with several angels of light, such as Gabriel and Azrael.

Prince of Light—this angel is identified as Michael.

Prince of Peace—identified with Jesus and with Serapiel.

Principalities—the seventh choir, according to Pseudo-Dionysius. These angels are the protectors of kings, princes, presidents, and all rulers of the Earth, including the Pope and other high prelates, whom they inspire to make just decisions. They also protect all religions. Among their regents are Anael, Requel, Cerviel, and Nuroc.

Purusha—the First Cause, identified as the Ain Soph in the Kabbalah.

Q

Qaddis—together with the twin Irin, the two angels known as Qaddis form the Supreme Council of God's Judgment. These four angels are the most exalted in the heavenly realm, and it is said that only one of them has more power than all the heavenly hosts.

Qafsiel—one of the regents of the moon, who is also a guardian of the Halls of the Seventh Heaven.

Quelamia—one of the seven great archangels of God's Throne, residing in the First Heaven, where he carries out the decrees of the heavenly powers.

R

Raamiel—one of the angels of thunder, whose name signifies "he who trembles before God."

Raasiel—one of the angels who rules earthquakes.

Rabacyel—one of the three regents of the Third Heaven.

Rabdos—a powerful fallen angel who can change and stop the course of the stars.

Rachiel—one of the regents of the Venus sphere and one of the angels who rules human sexuality, according to the Kabbalah.

Rachmiel—the angel of compassion, often identified with Gabriel.

Radweriel YHVH—often identified with Vetril or Pravuil, he is in charge of God's Book, presumably the Book of Life and Death. He is said to be the regent of poetry and is chief of the muses. His rank is superior to that of Metraton. According to Enoch, a new angel is formed from every word he utters.

Rael—one of the angels of the Third Heaven and one of the Intelligences of the Venus sphere.

Raphael—see chapter 9: The Four Great Archangels.

Raguel—one of the angels of the Second Heaven and one of the seven great archangels of the Divine Presence. He is one of the angels who punishes other angels when they are at fault. In 745 C.E., a council of the Church in Rome reprobated Raguel and several other high-ranking angels, including the exalted Uriel, simply because the Church did not allow any angels to be venerated except those mentioned in the Bible (Michael, Gabriel, and Raphael).

Rahab—the angel of the ocean's depths, sometimes identified as a fallen angel.

Rahmiel—one of the angels of love and compassion. He is often identified with Saint Francis of Assisi, who is said to have been transformed into an angel upon reaching Paradise. Rahmiel is one of the angels of the Apocalypse.

Rahatiel—one of the angels of the constellations, which he keeps in their proper course.

Ramiel—also known as Ramael, he is often identified with Uriel. This is the angel who gives true visions and is one of the rulers of thunder. One of his missions is to bring the souls of the dead to God's Throne on Judgment Day.

Rashiel—one of the angels of the whirlwinds and of earthquakes.

Rathanael—one of the angels of the Third Heaven, who has great power over the infernal legions.

Raziel—this is the angel of the mysteries, whose name signifies "God's secret." He is the reputed author of *The Book of Raziel*, where all the secrets of Heaven are said to be written. According to rabbinical lore, Raziel gave the book to Adam, but other angels took it away and threw the volume into the sea. God then ordered Rahab, the angel of the ocean's depths, to recover the book. Later it passed into the hands of Enoch and from him to Noah and eventually to Solomon. It is said that in the middle of the *Book of Raziel* there is a secret writing that reveals 1,500 of the keys to the mysteries of the world, which have not been revealed to the most exalted angels of the heavenly realms.

Rehael—the angel of good health and longevity, who also inspires respect in human beings toward their parents. He is one of the seventy-two angels of the Shemhamphora and belongs to the choir of the Powers.

Rehel—one of the seventy-two angels of the Shemhamphora, belonging to the choir of the Dominions.

Remiel—one of the seven great archangels of the Divine Presence, often identified with Uriel.

Rikbiel YHVH—a great angel who is one of the protectors of the Merkabah. He is also one of the Princes of the Divine Council, more exalted than Metraton.

Rimmon—one of the fallen angels.

Rochel—the angel invoked to find lost things.

Rofocale—also known as Lucifuge Rofocale, he is one of the most powerful of the infernal entities, among which he acts as a Prime Minister. He has control over all the riches and treasures of the world.

Romiel—the angel who rules the months of the year.

Rubiel—the angel invoked to win at games of chance. His name is inscribed on a parchment and carried on the person's body.

Ruchiel—one of the regents of the wind.

Rumiel—one of the guardians of the Sixth Heaven, who is cited in the *Book of Raziel*.

S

Sabaoth—also known as Tsabaoth, this is one of the names or titles of God, signifying Lord of Hosts. Sabaoth is also one of the angels of the Divine Presence.

Sabathiel—Michael's secret name. He is also one of the Intelligences of the sphere of Saturn and imparts the light he receives from the Holy Spirit to other members of his sphere.

Sabrael—one of the seven great archangels, belonging to the choir of the Virtues. He is also one of the guardians of the First Heaven.

Sachiel—one of the guardians of the First Heaven, belonging to the choir of the Cherubim. He is one of the regents of Monday and the sphere of Jupiter.

Sacriel—one of the rulers of Tuesday, residing in the Fifth Heaven.

Saditel—one of the regents of the Third Heaven.

Sadkiel—also known as Zadkiel, he is one of the seven great archangels and regent of Jupiter and Sagittarius. Some authorities credit Zachariel, Bartiel, and other angels with the rulership of Jupiter. Sadkiel is the angel of mercy, good memory, and joviality. In the Kabbalah he is the ruler of the fourth sphere, Chesed, and chief of the choir of the Chasmallim, or Brilliant Ones. This choir is often identified with the Dominions. Sadkiel is also one of the nine rulers of Heaven and, together with Zophiel, assists Michael when the great Archstrategist bears his standard in battle.

Safkas—one of the seventy-eight names of Metraton.

Safriel—one of the guardians of the Fifth Heaven, who is said to protect against the evil eye.

Sagdalon—he governs the sign of Capricorn with the angel Semakiel.

Sagham—he is said to govern the sign of Leo with the angel Seratiel.

Sagnessagiel—one of the names of Metraton, according to Enoch. He is also one of the princes of wisdom and chief of the guardians of the Fourth Hall in the Seventh Heaven.

Sagras—one of the regents of Taurus.

Sahariel—one of the regents of Aries.

Sahriel—one of the sixty-four guardians of the seven celestial halls.

Saissaiel—one of the regents of Scorpio.

Saktas—one of the seventy-eight names of Metraton.

Salamiel—one of the fallen angels, belonging to the Grigori, who is often identified with Satanail.

Salatheel—also known as Salathiel, this is one of the seven great archangels who rule the movement of the spheres.

Samael—sometimes identified with Camael, this is an angel of many legends and much controversy. He is definitely associated with Mars and Aries. He rules violence and destruction and has positive and negative aspects. In his most ferocious aspect, he is identified with Satan, an erroneous classification because Samael and Satan are two separate entities.

According to a rabbinical tradition, he is the angel who rules the Fifth Heaven, but other sources allege that he is the chief of all the demons and the angel of death. In the Kabbalah, he is a malevolent entity who rules the tenth sphere of the Qliphoth or Infernal Tree, and his consort is the terrible Lilith. In contrast, the Kabbalah lists Camael as the beneficent ruler of Geburah, the fifth sephira of the Tree of Life. Other sources say that Samael is one of the seven regents of the Earth, with more than two million angels under his command.

Samax—one of the angels of the element air and of Tuesday.

Sameveel—one of the fallen angels.

Samhiel—one of the angels who cures stupidity.

Samuil—one of the angels who has rulership over the Earth.

Sandalphon—also known as Sandalfon, this is the angel who rules the tenth sephira of the Tree of Life, Malkuth, known as the Kingdom in the Kabbalah. He is said to be Metraton's twin brother and one of the tallest angels in Heaven. He is also the angel who decides a child's gender upon its conception. According to Enoch, Sandalphon is the regent of the Sixth Heaven, but according to the Kabbalah, he rules the Seventh.

Sangariah—the angel who rules religious fasts, especially those conducted during the Jewish Sabbath.

Sapiel—one of the angels of the Fourth Heaven.

Sar—this name signifies "prince" in Hebrew, and is the title used to designate the great archangels who stand in front of the Divine Presence.

Saraiel—one of the regents of Gemini.

Sarakiel—one of the princes of the choir of the Angels who officiates during the celestial councils. He is also one of the regents of Mars.

Saraknyal—one of the 200 fallen angels.

Sarasael—one of the angels who presides over the souls of sinners, belonging to the choir of the Seraphim.

Sargiel—one of the angels who carries the souls of sinners to Hell. He is also identified with Nasargiel.

Sariel—often identified with Uriel, Suriel, and Serakiel, this is one of the seven great archangels of the Divine Presence. He is one of the regents of Aries and of the summer equinox.

Sarim—the plural of Sar.

Satan—the leader of the rebellious angels, who led them in battle against God and the Heavenly Hosts. His name signifies "adversary." Jesus called him the prince of this world. He is also known as the Prince of the Air Powers. Before his fall, Satan was regent of four of the celestial choirs: the Seraphim, the Cherubim, the Powers, and the

Archangels. He was also Prince Regent of the Virtues. Pope Gregory the Great described him as a highly exalted angel, who shed his light over the other angels, far surpassing them in glory and wisdom. Satan's identification with Lucifer is erroneous as they are two separate and very different entities. According to the Kabbalah and Saint Jerome, Satan will someday repent of his sins and will be restored to his former glory. But the Church's traditional teachings reject this belief and the conversion of any of the fallen angels. It is said of Satan that he is the great seducer and the father of lies.

Satanail—the name given by God to his great archangel Beqa after his rebellion. Later, Satanail became known as Satan.

Sathariel—a fallen angel who rules one of the infernal sephira of the Qliphoth, which casts shadows upon Chesed, the fourth sphere of the Tree of Life, known as Mercy or Compassion. His name signifies "he who hides God."

Sauriel—one of the angels of death.

Schebtaiel—identified with Sabathai, he is one of the regents of Saturn.

Schleliel—one of the ruling angels of the twenty-eight mansions of the moon.

Schimuel—one of the fifteen angels who stands before the Throne of God.

Sedekiah—one of the angels invoked to find hidden treasures.

Seehiah—one of the seventy-two angels of the Shemhamphora, invoked to prolong life and grant the gift of good health. He belongs to the choir of the Dominions.

Seheiah—one of the angels who protects against fire.

Semeliel—one of the seven princes who stands always before God and to whom have been revealed the names of the Planetary Spirits.

Semyaza—chief of the 200 fallen angels, belonging to the Grigori. It is said that he is hanging between Heaven and Earth, forming the constellation Orion.

Sepheriel—according to the Greater Key of Solomon, Judgment Day will begin with the uttering of Sepheriel's name.

Sephuriron—another name given to Malkuth, the tenth sphere of the Tree of Life. In its angelic identity, this great luminary has three of the Sarim as deputies under its command. These Princes are Ithuriel, Malkiel, and Nashriel.

Serakel—the angel who rules fruit-bearing trees.

Serapiel YHVH—also known as Seraphiel, this is the great archangel who rules the choir of the Seraphim. He is known as the Prince of Peace and is the most exalted among the princes of the Merkabah. He is also one of the celestials who is always present during the Divine Councils. He is the chief spirit of Mercury and regent of Tuesday. According to Enoch, this is the most dazzling of the angels of the Lord. His body is entirely covered with stars. From the feet to the knees he shines with the light of the firmament, from the knees to the thighs he scintillates with the light of the morning star, from the thighs to the waist he shimmers with the light of the moon, from the waist to the neck he bedazzles with the light of the sun, and from the neck to the top of his head he is resplendent with Infinite Light. •

Seraphim—the first and most exalted of the heavenly choirs, according to Pseudo-Dionysius and other sources. They constantly surround the Holy Throne, singing God's praises. The Seraphim are angels of fire and rule love and light. They have four faces and six wings and are known as fire serpents. Their chief ruler is Serapiel, and also Michael, Metraton, and Jehoel.

Shaftiel—one of the principal regents of hell, where he is said to rule over the shadow of death. He resides in the third loge of the seven infernal divisions.

Shahakiel—one of the seven great archangels, according to Enoch, and one of the princes of the Fourth Heaven.

Shaitan—an infernal entity among the Muslims.

Shamdan—a demon said to be the father of Asmodeus, born of Shamdan's sinful union with Naamah, the sister of Tubal-Cain, who led the fallen angels into perdition through her supernatural beauty.

Shamiel—together with Tagas, he leads the heavenly choirs. He is also the divine herald.

Shamshiel—the angel who guided Moses through the celestial realms during one of the Lawgiver's visions. His name signifies "light of day."

He is regent of the Fourth Heaven and a Prince of Paradise. He is one of the angels who crowns with glory the prayers of the faithful and sends them to the Fifth Heaven. The Kabbalah says that this was one of the angels who assisted Uriel during the angelic wars. But according to Enoch, he is one of the fallen angels who taught human beings the mysteries of the sun.

Shateiel—one of the ruling angels of silence.

Shekinah—the feminine aspect of God, according to the Kabbalah, also known as the Holy Bride. In the New Testament, the Shekinah is identified as the Glory of God. According to rabbinical sources, the Glory of God is Michael, and this angel is profoundly identified with the mysteries of the Shekinah. She is the intermediary between God the Father and humanity, rules the conception of children, and protects sexual-

ity and the sanctity of marriage. The Shekinah is identified as the Holy Spirit, the Cosmic Mother, and the Third Person in the Holy Trinity. According to the Torah, the Shekinah is in exile on Earth, separated from her Divine Spouse because of Adam's sin. All good acts help to hasten her return to the celestial mansions.

The Shekinah unites with her Heavenly Bridegroom only on the Sabbath eve, at the hour of midnight. According to the Kabbalah, this is the holiest and most perfect time for a physical union between a man and his wife, as the Shekinah watches over them and blesses their union.

Shinanin—an angelical order associated with the Cherubim of the Merkabah and ruled by Sadkiel. It is also identified with the Malachim, the celestial choir associated with Tiphareth, the sixth sephira of the Tree of Life.

Sidkiel—one of the regents of the choir of the Thrones and the sphere of Venus.

Sidriel—one of the princes of the First Heaven and one of the seven great archangels of the Divine Presence, according to Enoch.

Simkiel—one of the angels of destruction, sent by God to Earth to chastise sinners.

Sisera—the genius of desire.

Sithriel—the name given to Metraton when he covers human beings with his wings to protect them against the angels of destruction.

Sofriel—also known as Sopheriel YHVH, this is the Holy Scribe who keeps the Books of the Living and the Dead. According to Enoch and also to the Kabbalah, there are two angels with the same name, said to be twins, who share the same powers.

Soqedhozi YHVH—one of the great princes of the Divine Presence, who weighs the merits of human beings on a scale before the Lord.

Sorath—an infernal spirit who rules the number of the Great Beast, 666, according to Revelation.

Soterasiel YHVH—also known as Sother Ashiel, this is one of the most exalted of the princes of the Seventh Heaven. All the other angels must pass through him before reaching the Divine Presence. It is said that he is 70,000 myriads of parasangs in stature, each parasang measuring three miles. He is also one of the Princes of the Divine Council.

Sstiel YHVH—one of the most exalted angels of the Lord and one of the eight princes of the Merkabah, all of whom carry God's name before their own. These eight princes are Sstiel YHVH, Anapiel YHVH, Akatriel YHVH, Gallisur YHVH, Nsuriel YHVH, Radweriel YHVH, and the twin Sodfriel YHVH. Sstiel YHVH is higher in rank than Metraton, who must pay homage at his feet when they meet face to face.

Suriel—this great angel is identified with Uriel, Metraton, Ariel, Saraqel, and other high-ranking angels. He is one of the angels of death, but he is also a ruler over healing and a prince of the Divine Presence. It is said that he was the preceptor of Moses, from whom the Lawgiver acquired all his divine knowledge. Other authorities identify Moses' heavenly instructor as the angel Zagzagel. According to the Kabbalah, Suriel is one of the Earth's regents.

Suryas—one of the angels in the Hindu Vedas.

T

Tabkiel—one of the names of Metraton.

Taconin—in Islam, a beautiful angel who protects against negative spirits and reveals the future.

Tafsarim—a choir of angels pertaining to the Merkabah, and of a superior rank to all the angels before God's Throne.

Taftian—according to the Kabbalah, an angel of miracles.

Tagriel—one of the ruling angels of the twenty-eight mansions of the moon and chief of the guardians of the Seventh Heaven.

Tahariel—the angel of purity.

Tamiel—one of the fallen angels, whose name signifies "perfection of God." It is said that he rules the depths of the seas, a task traditionally associated with Rahab.

Tarshish—the chief regent of the choir of the Virtues.

Tarshishim—the angelic choir associated with Netzach, the seventh sephira of the Tree of Life. This choir is identified with the Virtues.

Tatrasiel YHVH—one of the most exalted princes of the Divine Presence.

Tebliel—one of the seven regents of the Earth.

Teoael—The angel who rules maritime expeditions and new businesses. He also predicts the future and belongs to the choir of the Thrones.

Teiazel—the ruling angel of writers, artists, and librarians.

Temeluch—the angel who protects small children from childbirth. He is also said to torment the souls of sinners upon their death.

Tephros—an entity that cures fever and who can also bring darkness and set fire to the ground. For that reason, he is said to be part angel and part demon.

Terathel—an angel of light who promotes freedom and the advancement of civilization. He belongs to the choir of the Dominions.

Terafiel—one of the Intelligences of the sphere of Venus.

Tezalel—an angel invoked to bring fidelity to marriage.

Theliel—an angel of love invoked to secure the affections of a person.

Theodonias—in Solomonic magic, this is one of God's names, used during rites of power.

Thoth—the god of wisdom among the Egyptians, also known as the greatest of the eons in Gnosticism. He is identified with Hermes and, in hermetic magic, he is the regent of the angels. He is often identified with Raphael. He is also associated with the Tarot cards, which are known as the *Book of Thoth*.

Tifereth—also Tiphereth, the sixth sephira of the Tree of Life. Its corresponding angel is Tiftheriel.

Tikarathin—one of God's secret names.

Tiriel—the Intelligence of Mercury, belonging to the choir of the Archangels.

Tzadkiel—see Sadkiel.

Tumael—one of the fallen angels.

Turel—another fallen angel.

Tutresiel—one of the great princes of the Divine Presence.

Tychagara—one of the seven great angels belonging to the choir of the Thrones who carries out the decrees of the superior choirs.

Tzafkiel—also Tzaphkiel, the ruling angel of Binah, the third sephira of the Tree of Life.

U

Ubaviel—one of the regents of Capricorn.

Umabel—one of the seventy-two angels of the Shemhamphora and one of the rulers of physics and astronomy.

Unael—one of the regents of the First Heaven.

Uriel—see chapter 9: The Four Great Archangels.

Urizen—according to William Blake, one of the ruling angels of England. The other is Orc. Urizen is said to rule logic and reason.

Urjan—another of Uriel's names.

Urzla—according to the Kabbalah, this is one of the glorious angels of the east, who is always willing to reveal God's mysteries to those who invoke him.

Usiel—according to the Kabbalah, this is one of the fallen angels, belonging to the fifth sphere of the Qliphoth or Infernal Tree. But the *Book of Raziel* describes him as one of the seven angels who stands before God's Throne and one of the nine who rules the four winds.

Uvall—one of the fallen angels, who belonged at one time to the choir of the Powers. He is now a great duke in the infernal hierarchy, with thirty-seven legions of demons under his command. He is invoked to win the love of a person.

Uvayah—one of Metraton's names.

Uzza—one of the ruling angels of Egypt. The other is Rahab. He is one of the fallen angels, identified with Semyaza.

Uzziel—identified with Usiel, his name signifies "God's power." He is one of the chief archangels in the rabbinical tradition, belonging to the choir of the Virtues and of the Cherubim. He is one of the princes of compassion associated with the Shekinah under the regency of Metraton.

V

Vacabiel—one of the regents of Pisces.

Valnum—one of the Intelligences of Saturn, residing in the First Heaven. He is also one of the regents of Monday.

Varcan—one of the regents of the sun.

Varchiel—also Verchiel, one of Leo's regents.

Varuna—one of the Suryas or Vedic luminaries, identified with the angels.

Vasariah—one of the seventy-two angels of the Shemhamphora.

Vashyah—one of the great angels who has power over the Heavenly Hosts.

Vasiariah—one of the ruling angels of lawyers, judges, and magistrates.

Vassago—one of the entities invoked in rituals of high magic, usually to discover women's secrets. He has a dual identity, and some authorities classify him as a fallen angel who specializes in revealing the future and finding lost things.

Vehuel—one of the seventy-two angels of the Shemhamphora, belonging to the choir of the Principalities.

Vehuhiah—an angel who rules the first rays of the rising sun. He is also one of the eight Seraphim who turns the prayers of the faithful into realities.

Vel—an angel residing in the Third Heaven and one of the regents of Wednesday.

Venibbeth—the angel of invisibility.

Verchiel—also known as Varchiel, one of the regents of Leo and the month of July. He is also one of the regents of the choir of the Powers.

Veualiah—the angel who invests kings with power and grants prosperity to their realms.

Vhnori—one of the regents of Sagittarius.

Vionatraba—one of the three spirits of the sun, who resides in the Fourth Heaven. He is one of the regents of Sunday.

Virtues—the fifth of the celestial choirs, according to Pseudo-Dionysius. Their principal mission is to create miracles on Earth. Their Prince Regent is Michael, but Raphael, Barbiel, Uzziel, and Peliel are also among their regents.

Voel—one of the regents of Virgo.

Vretil—often identified with Radweriel YHVH, this is the Divine Scribe who is the keeper of the sacred books and of God's wisdom. It is said that he is the wisest of all the angels. He is sometimes identified with Uriel, Dabriel, and Pravuil.

X

Xaphan—one of the rebellious angels who wanted to set fire to Heaven during the angelic wars. Before this treacherous plan was carried out, the rebellious hordes were defeated and thrown into the abyss by Michael and the Heavenly Hosts. With a touch of poetic justice, Xaphan is now in charge of the flames of Hell.

Y

Yabbashael—one of the regents of Earth.

Yahel—one of the regents of the moon, belonging to the choir of the Thrones.

Yahoel—also identified with Jehoel and Metraton, he was the preceptor of the patriarch Abraham.

Yahriel—one of the regents of the moon.

Yahsiyah—one of the names of Metraton.

Yehudiah—the beneficent angel of death, who descends to Earth with myriads of angels to gather the souls of the faithful when they die. He is one of the chief divine messengers.

Yehakel—one of the regents of Mercury.

Yerachmiel—one of the seven regents of Earth, identified with the seven planets.

Yeshamiel—one of the regents of Libra.

Yesod—the ninth sphere of the Tree of Life, identified with the moon. The angels associated with this sephira are the Cherubim.

Yofiel—one of the regents of Jupiter when it enters the sign of Sagittarius. He is also a great prince, with fifty-three legions of angels under his command.

Yomael—one of the princes of the Seventh Heaven.

Yurkemi—one of the ruling angels of hailstones.

Z

Zaafiel—one of the ruling angels of hurricanes and one of the angels of destruction sent by God to Earth to punish sinners.

Zabkiel—one of the regents of the choir of the Thrones.

Zacharael—one of the princes of the choir of the Dominions, who resides in the Second Heaven.

Zachiel—the supreme regent of the Sixth Heaven, identified with Sadkiel.

Zachriel—one of the angels who grants a good memory.

Zadkiel—identified with Sadkiel and Tzadkiel, he is the angel of benevolence, joviality, and compassion; a regent of Jupiter and Sagittarius; and Prince of the choir of the Dominions. He is said to grant the gift of a good memory, and he is also one of the nine regents of Heaven and one of the seven great archangels of the Divine Presence.

Zafiel—the angel of rain.

Zagiel—a fallen angel, formerly of the choir of the Archangels.

Zagzagel—one of the angels of wisdom. His name signifies "God's righteousness." It is said that this was the angel who appeared to Moses in the burning bush, but other authorities identify this angel with Michael. Zagzagel is one of the instructors of the younger angels, one of the Princes of the Divine Presence, and Prince Regent of the Fourth Heaven.

Zahun—the angel who rules over scandals.

Zakun—one of the angels of the Divine Presence. According to the legend, when Moses was on his deathbed, he wrote a prayer to God asking the Creator to extend his life. God sent Zakun and Lahash, another of his great angels, to intercept the prayer so that it would not reach Heaven, as the time had come for Moses to die. If the prayer were to reach God's Throne, it would have to be granted. Zakun descended from Heaven with Lahash and 184 myriads of angels to intercept this important missive, but Lahash refused to comply with God's orders at the last minute, perhaps feeling compassion for the Lawgiver. Zakun had to complete the mission on his own. As for Lahash, he was punished with sixty fire lashes for his disobedience and was immediately exiled from the Divine Presence.

Zaksakiel YHVH—one of the great princes of the Divine Presence.

Zaniel—one of the regents of Libra.

Zaphiel—also identified with Iofiel and Zophiel, this is one of the regents of the choir of the Cherubim and Prince of Saturn.

Zaphkiel—also identified as Zaphiel and Tzaphkiel, his name signifies "God's knowledge." He is the Prince Regent of the choir of the Thrones and one of the seven great archangels. He is also a regent of Saturn and the angel of Binah, the third sephira of the Tree of Life.

Zarall—one of the two Cherubim engraved on the Ark of the Covenant.

Zarobi—the angel of precipices.

Zathael—one of the twelve angels of vengeance, among which are Michael, Gabriel, Raphael, Uriel, and Nathanael. The angels of vengeance were the first to be emanated from God and are among the angels of the Divine Presence.

Zazail—an angel of the Lord, who is invoked during the exorcism of evil spirits.

Zazel—in Solomonic magic, this is one of the angels invoked in love rituals. He is said to be one of the spirits of Saturn, whose number is forty-nine.

Zasriel—one of the princes of the Divine Presence who represents the power of God.

Zebul—this angel rules the Sixth Heaven at night, while Sabath rules it during the day. This is also the name of the Second Heaven, according to Enoch, and the name of the Third, according to Ezekiel. The name signifies "temple" or "habitation."

Zebuliel—one of the principal regents of the Western side of the First Heaven, who accompanies the prayers of the faithful to the Second Heaven. It is said that he only rules when the moon appears.

Zechariel—one of the seven regents of Earth.

Zehanpuryuh—one of the great princes of the Divine Presence. He is also one of the princes of the Merkabah, with a higher rank than Metraton. He is also one of the chiefs of the Heavenly Hosts and, together with Michael, weighs the souls of the dead on the scales of Divine Justice. He is the guardian of the Seventh Hall of the Seventh Heaven.

Zephaniel—the regent of the tenth choir, according to the Kabbalah. This choir, known as Ishim, is identified with the souls of the saints or the Lord's Elect. The Pseudo-Dionysius classification does not include this choir.

Zephon—also known as Zefon, this is one of the principal regents of Paradise, belonging to the choir of the Cherubim.

Zerachiel—one of the angels of July and

the sign of Leo. He is also one of the Grigori who did not fall and who protects Heaven from the forces of evil.

Zikiel—the angel of lightning and of comets.

Zohariel YHVH—one of the secret names of God. This is also one of the highest-ranking princes of the Divine Presence. To the kabbalists, this angel is one of the principal objects of the Merkabah vision, associated with the Holy Shekinah.

Zophiel—in Solomonic magic, one of the angels invoked during rites of power. This is one of the angels who assists Michael in battle when the great archangel bears his standard. The other angel is Sadkiel. Zophiel's name signifies "God's spy."

Zotiel—this is one of the angels belonging to the choir of the Cherubim, sometimes identified with Johiel, a guardian of Paradise. His name signifies "little one of God."

Zuriel—a regent of the sign of Libra, who also cures stupidity. He is sometimes identified with Uriel as the ruler of September. Zuriel is the Prince Regent of the choir of the Principalities. His name signifies "my rock is God."

Bibliography

Abano, P. de, *The Heptameron*, London, 1965.

Adler, M., *The Angels and Us*, New York, 1982.

Agrippa, C. , *Three Books of Occult Philosophy*, Chicago, 1913.

Albertus Magnus, *The Secrets of Albertus Magnus*, London, 1933.

Almadel of Solomon (in the *Legemeton*), L.W. de Lawrence, ed., New York, 1916.

Ambelain, R., *The Practical Kabbalah*, London, 1958.

Apollonius of Tyana, *The Nuctemeron*, London, 1965.

Arbatel of Magic, New York, 1974.

Aristotle, *Metaphysics*, Michigan, 1966.

Aude Sapere, *The Chaldean Oracles of Zoroaster*, New York, 1963.

Augustine, Saint, *The Confessions of Saint Augustine*, New York, 1967.

———, *The City of God*, New York, 1957.

Ausable, N., ed., *A Treasury of Jewish Folklore*, New York, 1960.

Bamberger, B. J., *Fallen Angels*, Philadelphia, 1952.

Bardon. F., *The Key to the True Quabbalah*, Freiburg, 1957.

———. *The Practice of Magical Evocation*, Freiburg, 1991.

Barnstone, W., *The Other Bible,* New York, 1984.

Barrett, F., *The Magus*, London, 1959.

Bate, N. H., *The Sybilline Oracles*, London, 1937.

The Bible, St James Version, New York, 1957.

Blake, W., *Complete Writings*, London, 1957.

Blavatsky, H. P. , *The Secret Doctrine*, Pasadena, 1952.

Bloom, H., *Blake's Apocalypse*, New York, 1963.

Book of Enoch, transl. H. Odenberg, New York, 1928.

Book of Jubilees (The Little Genesis), transl., R. H. Charles, London, 1917.

Box, G.H., ed., *The Apocalypse of Abraham*, London, 1918.

———, *The Testament of Abraham*, London, 1927.

Briggs, C. V., *The Encyclopedia of Angels*, New York, 1997.

Buber, M., *Tales of Angels, Spirits and Demons*, New York, 1938.

Budge, E. A., Wallis, *Amulets and Talismans*, New York, 1961.

———, *Book of the Dead*, London, 1967.

———, *Egyptian Magic*, New York, 1971.

Bulfinch, T., *Mythology*, New York, 1972.

Bunson, M., *Angels A to Z*, New York, 1996.

Bunyan, J., *Complete Works*, Philadelphia, 1872.

Burham, S., *A Book of Angels*, New York, 1990.

Burrows, M., *The Dead Sea Scrolls*, New York,1956.

Butler, E. M., *Ritual Magic*, New York, 1959.

Cabell, J. B., *The Devil's Dear Own Son*, New York, 1959.

Caird, G. B., *Principalities and Powers*, Oxford, 1956.

Camfield, B., *A Theological Discourse of Angels*, London, 1934.

Charlesworth, J. H., *The Old Testament: Pseudoepigrapha*, New York, 1983.

Christian, P., ed., *The History and Practice of Magic*, New York, 1963.

Claremont, Lewis de, *The Ancient's Book of Magic*, New York, 1958.

Cohen, C., *Foundations of Religion*, London, 1930.

Connell, J. T., *Angel Power*, New York, 1995.

Connolly, D., *In Search of Angels*, New York, 1993.

Cordovero, M., *Orchard of Pomegranates*, London, 1945.

———, *The Palm Tree of Deborah*, London, 1960.

Crossan, J. D., *Jesus: A Revolutionary Biography*, San Francisco, 1994.

Danby, H., transl., *The Mishnah*, Oxford, 1933.

Daniels, J., *Clash of Angels*, New York, 1930.

Dante Alighieri, *The Divine Comedy*, New York, 1958.

Davenport, B., *Deals With the Devil*, New York, 1958.

David-Neel, A., *Magic and Mystery in Tibet*, New York, 1965.

Davidson, G., *A Dictionary of Angels*, Toronto, 1966.

Davies, A. P., *The Meaning of the Dead Sea Scrolls*, New York, 1956.

Davies, P., *The Mind of God*, New York, 1992.

Dimmitt C., and J. A. B van Buitenen, *Classical Hindu Mythology*, Philadelphia, 1978.

Dionysius the Aeropagite (Pseudo-Dionysius), *The Mystical Theologie and the Celestial Hierarchies*, Surrey, England, 1949.

Dorese, J., *The Secret Books of Egyptian Gnostics*, New York, 1960.

Duff, A., *The First and Second Books of Esdras*, London, 1931.

Dupont-Sommer, A., *The Dead Sea Scrolls*, Oxford, 1954.

Durant, W., *The Story of Philosophy*, New York, 1952.

Eisenmenger, J. A., *Traditions of the Jews*, London, 1926.

Eleazor of Worms, *Book of the Angel Raziel*, British Museum (published in English, 1701).

Ferrar, W., *The Assumption of Moses*, London, 1918.

Follansbee, E., *Heavenly History*, Chicago, 1927.

Fortune, D., *The Mystical Qabalah*, London, 1951.

Fosdick, H. E., *The Man From Nazareth*, New York, 1949.

Fox, M., and R. Sheldrake, *The Physics of Angels*, New York, 1996.

France, A., *The Revolt of the Angels*, London, 1925.

Frank, A., *The Kabalah*, New York, 1926.

Frazer, J. G., *The Golden Bough*, New York, 1951.

Fuller, J. F. C., *The Secret Wisdom of the Qabalah*, London, n.d.

Gaster, M., *The Sword of Moses*, New York, 1968.

Gaster, T., *The Dead Sea Scriptures*, New York, 1956.

Gaynor, F., *Dictionary of Mysticism*, New York, 1953.

Geffcken, J., ed., *The Sybilline Oracles*, London, 1972.

Gibb, H. A. R. and J. H. Kramers, eds., *A Shorter Encyclopedia of Islam*, New York, 1961.

Gilmore, G. D., *Angels, Angels, Everywhere*, New York, 1981.

Ginsburg, C. D., *The Essenes and the Kabbalah* (two essays), London, 1972.

Ginzberg, L., *The Legends of the Jews*, Philadelphia, 1954.

Gleadow, R., *Magic and Divination*, London, 1941.

Goldin, J., *The Living Talmud*, New York, 1957.

González-Wippler, M., *A Kabbalah for the Modern World*, St Paul, 1995.

———, *The Complete Book of Spells, Ceremonies & Magic*, St Paul, 1990.

———, ed., *The Sixth and Seventh Books of Moses*, New York, 1982.

Graham, B., *Angels: God's Secret Agents*, Texas, 1986.

Grant, R. M., *Gnosticism and Early Christianity*, New York, 1959.

Graves, R., *Hebrew Myths*, New York, 1964.

———, *The White Goddess*, New York, 1958.

Grillot, E. G., *Witchcraft, Magic and Alchemy*, Boston, 1931.

Grimoire of Honorius, London, 1952.

Grimorium Verum (The True Clavicle or Key of Solomon), transl., Plaingiere, M., London, 1926.

Grubb, N., *Revelations: Art of the Apocalypse*, New York, 1997.

Guignebert, C., *The Jewish World in the Time of Jesus*, New York, 1959.

Guillet, C., *The Forgotten Gospel*, New York, 1940.

Gurdjieff, G., *All and Everything and Beelzebub's Tales to his Grandson*, New York, 1964.

Gurney, O. R., *The Hittites*, London, 1952.

Hahn, E., *Breath of God*, New York, 1975.

Hammond, G., *A Discourse of Angels*, London, 1979.

Hartmann, F., *Magic, White and Black*, Chicago, 1910.

Harvey, H., *The Many Faces of Angels*, California, 1986.

Hastings, J., *Encyclopedia of Religion and Ethics*, New York, 1955.

Hermes Trismegistus, *The Divine Pymander*, London, 1978.

Heywood, T., *The Hierarchy of the Blessed Angels*, London, 1982.

Hurtak, *An Introduction to the Keys of Enoch*, California, 1975.

Huxley, A., *The Devils of London*, 1952.

———, *The Perennial Philosophy*, Ohio, 1968.

James, W., *The Varieties of Religious Experience*, New York, 1963.

Jameson, A. B., *Legends of the Madonna*, London, 1903.

Jacolliott, L., *Occult Science in India and Among the Ancients*, New York, 1973.

Jayne, W. A., *The Healing Gods of Ancient Civilizations,* New York, 1962.

Jeffrey, G. R., *Heaven: The Last Frontier*, New York, 1990.

Jellinek, A., *Beth ha-Midrasch*, Jerusalem, 1938.

Josephus, F., *The Works of Flavius Josephus*, Philadelphia, 1959.

Jung, L., *Fallen Angels in Jewish, Christian and Mohammedan Literature*, Philadelphia, 1926.

Kaufmann, W., transl., *Faust,* New York, 1961.

King, L. W., *Babylonian Magic and Sorcery*, London, 1896.

Knight, G., *A Practical Guide to Qabalistic Symbolism*, London, 1969.

Kramer, S. N., *From the Tablets of Sumer*, Colorado, 1956.

Langton, E., *Essentials of Demonology*, London, 1949.

Laurence, L. W. de, ed., *The Legemeton or Lesser Key of Solomon (Goetia)*, New York, 1916.

———, *The Greater Key of Solomon*, New York, 1942.

Leadbeater, C. W., *The Astral Plane*, India, 1963.

Levi, E., *The Occult Philosophy*, London, 1974.

———, *Transcendental Magic*, London, 1967.

Lewis, J. R., and E. D. Oliver, *Angels A to Z*, Michigan, 1996.

Lindsay, F. N., *Kerubim in Semitic Religion and Art*, New York, 1912.

Longfellow, H. W., *Poetical Works*, Boston, 1982.

Lost Books of the Bible and the Forgotten Books of Eden, New York, 1930.

MacKaye, P., *Uriel and Other Poems*, Boston,1912.

MacKenzie, D. A., *Egyptian Myth and Legend*, London, n.d.

———, *Myths of Babylonia and Assyria*, London, n.d.

Maimonides, M., *The Guide for the Perplexed*, New York, 1956.

———, *Mishna Torah*, New York, 1922.

A Manual of Exorcism, transl. E. Beyersdorf, New York, 1975.

Malchus, M., *The Secret Grimoire of Turiel*, London, 1960.

Mathers, S. L. M., *The Almadel of Solomon*, London, 1954.

———, *The Kabbalah Unveiled*, London, 1978.

Mead, G. R. S., *Fragments of a Faith Forgotten*, New York, 1960.

———, *Pistis Sophia*, London, 1921.

———, *Thrice-Greatest Hermes*, London, 1976.

Michelet, J., *Satanism and Witchcraft*, New York, 1939.

Milton, J., *Paradise Lost*, London, 1983.

Moolenburgh. H. C., *A Handbook of Angels*, London, 1984.

Moore, T., *The Loves of Angels*, London, 1956.

Muller, E., *History of Jewish Mysticism*, Oxford, 1946.

Myer, I., *The Qabbalah*, New York, 1967.

Nathan, R., *The Bishop's Wife*, London, 1928.

Neubauer, A., ed., *The Book of Tobit*, London, 1985.

Neusner, J., *A History of the Jews in Babylonia*, New York, 1965.

Nigg, W., *The Heretics*, New York, 1962.

Odeberg, H., ed., *The Hebrew Book of Enoch*, Cambridge, 1928.

Ouspensky, P., *In Search of the Miraculous*, London, 1967.

Papus (Gerald Encausse), *Sepher Yetzirah*, London, 1954.

———, *Absolute Key to Divine Science*, London, 1968.

Paracelsus, *Four Treatises*, Baltimore, 1948.

Parente, P. P., *The Angels*, New York, 1968.

Parfitt, W., *The Living Qabalah*, New York, 1988.

Pauline Art (part of the *Legemeton* or *Lesser Key of Solomon*).

Payne, R., *The Holy Fire*, New York, 1957.

de Plancy, C., *Dictionnnaire Infernal*, Paris, 1947.

Ravenwolf, Silver, *Angels: Companions in Magick*, Minn., 1996.

Redfield, B. G., ed., *Gods/ A Dictionary of the Deities of All Lands*, New York, 1951.

Regardie, *The Art of True Healing*, London, 1966.

———, *The Golden Dawn*, Minn., 1989.

Regamey, R. P., *What Is an Angel?*, New York, 1960.

Reider, J., *The Holy Scriptures*, Philadelpha, 1937.

Robbins, R. H., *The Encyclopedia of Witchcraft and Demonology*, New York, 1959.

Ronner, J., *Know Your Angels*, Tenn., 1983.

Runes, D., *The Wisdom of the Kabbalah*, New York, 1957.

Sale George, ed., *The Koran*, Philadelphia, 1912.

Serres, M., *Angels: A Modern Myth*, Paris, 1995.

Schaya, L., *The Universal Meaning of the Kabbalah*, New Jersey, 1971.

Scheible, J., ed., *The Sixth and Seventh Books of Moses*, Illinois, n.d.

Scholem, G., *Jewish Gnosticism*, New York, 1960.

———, *Major Trends in Jewish Mysticism*, New York, 1941.

———, *On the Kabbalah and Its Symbolism*, New York, 1965.

Schweitzer, A., *The Quest for the Historical Jesus*, London, 1925.

Scot, R., *Discoverie of Witchcraft*, Illinois, 1964.

Shah, I., *The Secret Lore of Magic*, New York, 1956.

Shaw, G. B., *Back to Methusaleh*, New York, 1921.

Simon, M., *Tractate Berakoth: The Babylonian Talmud*, London, 1990.

Smith, J., transl., *The Book of Mormon*, Salt Lake City, 1950.

Spence, L., *An Encyclopedia of Occultism*, New York, 1959.

Steiner, R., *The Mission of the Archangel Michael*, New York, 1961.

————, *The Work of the Angels in Man's Astral Body*, New York, 1960.

Summers, M., *The History of Witchcraft and Demonology*, New York, 1956.

Swedenborg, E., *Heaven and Its Wonders and Hell*, New York, 1956.

Talmud, London, 1961.

Taylor, T. L., *Messengers of Light*, California, 1990.

Taylor, T., *Iamblichus on the Mysteries of the Egyptians, Chaldeans and Assyrians*, New York, 1957.

Thompson, K., *Angels and Aliens*, New York, 1991.

Torah, The (Five Books of Moses), Philadelphia, 1962.

Trachtenberg, J., *Jewish Magic and Superstition*, New York, 1961.

Trithemius, J., *Book of Secret Things*, in Barrett's *The Magus*.

————, *Of the Heavenly Intelligences*, London, 1936.

Valentinus, B., *The Triumphal Chariot of Antimony*, London, 1962.

Van der Loos, E., *The Miracles of Jesus*, New York, 1965.

Waite, A. E., *The Book of Ceremonial Magic*, London, 1967.

————, *The Holy Kabbalah*, London, 1945.

Waldherr, K., *The Book of Goddesses*, Oregon, 1995.

Weiner, H., *9½ Mystics: The Kabbala Today*, New York, 1969.

Welsh, R. G., *Azrael and Other Poems*, New York, 1925.

Wendt, H., *In Search of Adam*, Boston, 1956.

West, R. H., *Milton and the Angels*, Georgia, 1955.

Westcott, W. W., *Sepher Yetzirah (Book of Formation)*, London, 1911.

Yadin, Y., ed., *War Between the Sons of Light and the Sons of Darkness*, Jerusalem, 1956.

Young, M., *Angel in the Forest*, New York, 1945.

The Zohar, G. Scholem, ed., New York, 1949.

Index

REACH FOR THE MOON

Llewellyn publishes hundreds of books on your favorite subjects!
To get these exciting books, including the ones on the following pages,
check your local bookstore or order them directly from Llewellyn.

Order by Phone
- Call toll-free within the U.S. and Canada, 1-800-THE MOON
- In Minnesota, call (651) 291-1970
- We accept VISA, MasterCard, and American Express

Order by Mail
- Send the full price of your order (MN residents add 7% sales tax) in U.S. funds, plus postage & handling to:

  Llewellyn Worldwide
  P.O. Box 64383, Dept. K293-3
  St. Paul, MN 55164–0383, U.S.A.

Postage & Handling
(For the U.S., Canada, and Mexico)
- $4.00 for orders $15.00 and under
- $5.00 for orders over $15.00
- No charge for orders over $100.00

We ship UPS in the continental United States. We ship standard mail to P.O. boxes. Orders shipped to Alaska, Hawaii, the Virgin Islands, and Puerto Rico are sent first-class mail. Orders shipped to Canada and Mexico are sent surface mail.

International orders: Airmail—add freight equal to price of each book to the total price of order, plus $5.00 for each nonbook item (audio tapes, etc.).

Surface mail—Add $1.00 per item.

Allow 2 weeks for delivery on all orders.
Postage and handling rates subject to change.

Discounts
We offer a 20% discount to group leaders or agents. You must order a minimum of 5 copies of the same book to get our special quantity price.

Free Catalog
Get a free copy of our color catalog, *New Worlds of Mind and Spirit*. Subscribe for just $10.00 in the United States and Canada ($30.00 overseas, airmail). Many bookstores carry *New Worlds*—ask for it!

Visit our website at www.llewellyn.com for more information.

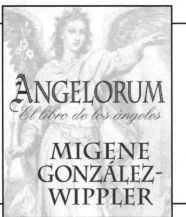

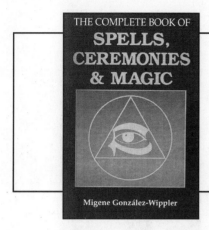

The Complete Book of Spells, Ceremonies & Magic
MIGENE GONZÁLEZ-WIPPLER

This book is far more than a historical survey of magical techniques throughout the world. It is the most complete book of spells, ceremonies, and magic ever assembled. It is the spiritual record of humanity.

Topics in this book include magical spells and rituals from virtually every continent and every people. The spells described are for love, wealth, success, protection, and health. Also examined are the theories and history of magic, including its evolution, the gods, the elements, the Kabbalah, the astral plane, ceremonial magic, famous books of magic, and famous magicians. You will learn about talismanic magic, exorcisms, and how to use the I Ching, how to interpret dreams, how to construct and interpret a horoscope, how to read Tarot cards, how to read palms, how to do numerology, and much more. Included are explicit instructions for love spells and talismans; spells for riches and money; weight-loss spells; magic for healing; psychic self-defense; spells for luck in gambling; and much more.

No magical library is complete without this classic text of magical history, theory, and practical technique. The author is known for her excellent books on magic. Many consider this her best. Includes over 150 rare photos and illustrations.

0-87542-286-1
6 x 9, 400 pp., illus. $14.95

What Happens After Death
Scientific & Personal Evidence for Survival

MIGENE GONZÁLEZ-WIPPLER

What does science tell us about life after death? How do the different religions explain the mystery? What is the answer given by the strange mystical science known as Spiritism? These and other questions about the life beyond are explored in *What Happens After Death*.

The first part of the book is an objective study of the research about life after death. The second part is a personal narrative by a spirit guide named Kirkudian about his various incarnations. While the two sections could be considered two separate books, they simply express the same concepts in uniquely different ways.

Experience for yourself one soul's journey through the afterlife, and discover the ultimate truth: that every soul is created in union with all other souls, and that we are all manifestations of one purpose.

1-56718-327-1
5³⁄₁₆ x 8, 256 pp. $7.95